At the Margins of the Economy

Women's Self-Employment in Finland, 1960–1990

ANNE KOVALAINEN
Economic Sociology
Turku School of Economics and Business Administration

Avebury

Aldershot • Brookfield USA • Hong Kong • Singapore • Sydney

First published by the Turku School of Economics and Business Administration 1993

Published by
Avebury
Ashgate Publishing Limited
Gower House
Croft Road
Aldershot
Hants GU11 3HR
England

Ashgate Publishing Company
Old Post Road
Brookfield
Vermont 05036
USA

British Library Cataloguing in Publication Data

Kovalainen, Anne
    At the Margins of the Economy: Women's
    Self-Employment in Finland, 1960–1990
    I. Title
    305.43094897

ISBN 1 85972 213 X

Library of Congress Catalog Card Number: 95-80351

Printed and bound by Athenaeum Press, Ltd.,
Gateshead, Tyne & Wear.

Contents

List of tables

ix

Preface and acknowledgements

Finnish society is in the process – due to a drastically worsened economic situation – of going through a number of major changes. Self-employment and entrepreneurship have been brought into sharp focus in the search for cures for the current recession and high unemployment. In this, the Finnish example resembles the British. However, very little is known about the relationship between unemployment and self-employment. In the light of the studies made, self-employment does not seem to be the best long-time cure for the present situation in Finland, at least not without the provision of strong state-support.

The interest that has arisen among the policy-makers and researchers in self-employment as a solution to unemployment reminds me of the situation a few years ago when I started my present study. The high hopes held for self-employment, as a solution for problems of working life such as the 'glass ceiling' phenomenon amongst career women were, for a long time, the leading ideas in research literature on women's self-employment. Gradually, the multifaceted picture of women's self-employment and their narrow position in the economy has been revealed. The study at hand shows that women's self-employment, measured in terms of their number, development over the years and scope of business activities does not broaden the scope of women's position in the economy. On the contrary, women seem to stay at the margins of the economy in terms of self-employment and entrepreneurship. Thus, my definition of 'marginal' stems from the stability and rigidity of economic structures, though in their own lives self-employed women are not at the margins.

It also seems that self-employment is far from being an easy option to women, as an alternative for paid employment. It remains for the future analyses to show whether self-employment fostered by the present social changes and restructuring in the economy will become an easy solution to the unemployment.

There are a number of people I would like to thank for discussion, comment and intellectual stimulus at various stages of my work. First of all, I extend warm thanks to Professor Timo Toivonen, who once suggested the subject of women in self-employment to me, while himself working on a study in self-employment. I am grateful to him for giving me an opportunity to start my research career and for his useful comments as a reviewer of this manuscript.

I also want to warmly thank Dr. Harriet Silius, who acted as the other reviewer of my manuscript, for her constructive and insightful comments which have provided ideas for further study. At the final stage of my work, I gratefully acknowledge the encouraging comments of Professor Liisa Rantalaiho. I would also like to thank Professor Sheila Allen for inviting me to the University of Bradford as a visiting research fellow.

Mike McDaid commented the language of the early versions of chapters 1, 2 and 3. Alex Frost has taken great trouble in checking the language of the whole manuscript, revising and adding fluency to my English text, and keeping the sometimes tight and demanding timeschedules. Petteri Jarva has acted as a skillful research assistant at the final preparation of the manuscript. My colleagues in Economic Sociology at Turku School of Economics and Business Administration, and colleagues in Sociology at the University of Bradford have been on hand for many rewarding discussions.

Financial support from the following foundations is gratefully acknowledged: the Finnish Cultural Foundation, the Fund of Varsinais-Suomi, the Foundation of Economic Education, the Foundation of Oskar Öflund, the Foundations of Turun kauppakorkeakoulu.

Last, but not least, I thank my parents, my sister and my nearest and dearest for being there for me, and for all the joy they have brought into my life.

London, 16.11.1993

Anne Kovalainen

Part I

Part I

1 Introduction

1.1. The starting point of the research

Of the many employment changes which took place in industrial societies during the 1970s and 1980s, perhaps the most noteworthy have concerned changes in unemployment levels and the composition of the work-force. Many countries have witnessed shifts in working patterns from full-time to part-time employment, from manufacturing to services and from stable, secure work to casual, precarious work. Furthermore, so-called traditional forms of labour market structuration, or more precisely standard patterns of employment, have given way to more or less atypical forms of employment, including self-employment. Even if the nature and extent of these changes are country-specific, some common traits are to be seen. One of these is the rise in atypical forms of women's employment in many OECD countries. Atypical forms of employment are usually defined as self-employment, part-time work and period-time work. Of these three forms of atypical employment, women's self-employment differs most from the typical form of employment. In Finland part-time employment has so far not developed into such an important form of employment as it has in several other countries (Sweden, UK, US), where the part-time labour force is a feminised one.

Recognition of women's growing role in the labour market, and of the changing patterns of employment and unemployment, has prompted research both on women's participation in the labour market and on different forms of employment since the 1960s. It has become apparent that in most industrialised countries the patterns of women's employment and unemployment have been different from those of men.[1] An extensive research literature exists concerning the different forms of female labour force participation and, linked to this, on processes of de-industrialisation, restructuring of the economies, and the

---

1. Even though, beginning in the early 1960s in most OECD countries, women entered the paid labour force in increasing numbers and their attachment to employment became more permanent by nature.

3

decline of manufacturing employment in the developed industrialised countries, as well as the rise of the service sector as a part of these processes.

Despite the growing amount on empirical research of women's work in general, less attention is given to those women who fall into the category of the self-employed than to women who are classified as employees. The main sociological interest – not only in the Finnish research context[2] but more or less in general – has been in employees and their work. For a long time now it has been common to see self-employment as a contradictory and diminishing part of the petit bourgeoisie's economic activity, rather than a part of an extended or atypical form of employment (Nätti 1990).

The idea of overcoming gender-based forms of subordination within the labour market with the help of small business ownership or self-employment received more attention during the 1980s, which was a decade of economic recovery and growth of self-employment in many countries. According to the statistics, increasing numbers of women are running their own businesses in most OECD countries, and this also seems to be an important source of dynamism in local economies and the local labour market. What is the role of self-employed women in the development of the economy, or should the question be raised as to whether self-employed women have any role at all in the development of the economy? Are any gendered patterns visible, or is it really the case, as the few studies that have been made on women entrepreneurs suggest, that self-employment offers greater possibilities than waged work does to women who wish either to overcome subordination in the labour market, or to carry on with their work careers in a more independent way? (See Webb 1982; Goffee – Scase 1985)

The idea of women's self-employment as a route to escape from the yoke of paid work rests upon the assumption that self-employment naturally provides benefits superior to those found within waged forms of work. This idea has much to do with the nature of the research undertaken; as James Curran and Roger Burrows argue, the existing research on female small-scale entrepreneurs has generally been very limited and based solely on non-random samples (Curran – Burrows 1986, 172). However, so far the evidence supporting this idea has been more or less ambiguous (Goffee – Scase 1985; Dale 1986; Kovalainen 1992).

This study concerns self-employed women and the gendered nature of self-employment. More specifically, my intention is to examine the development of women's self-employment in the Finnish economy, and in relation to the general economic development that has taken place in Finland from the 1960s up until the end of the 1980s. How does the situation of women entrepreneurs

---

2. For a more detailed discussion of this point see Julkunen 1985.

relate to general developments which have taken place in the economy, and specifically to developments in women's paid work? My interests are in the conceptual construction of self-employment, how women's self-employment is related to that concept and, furthermore, in the industrial development of women's self-employment. In addition, my intention is to explore whether women's self-employment is proportionately balanced in the context of women's employment as a whole.

Studies of self-employment have spread across the different disciplines, and this is partly the reason for the under-development of the social analysis of entrepreneurs and of the self-employed.[3] Equally, *the equation of small-scale enterprise with 'economic man'* has been unchallenged until comparatively recently (Curran – Burrows 1986, 164, 170). In the discussion on self-employment in chapter 4, I examine the problems inherent in these two approaches. Even if women have been involved with small-scale enterprises as assisting family members, either they have not been the focus of research, or the focus has been mainly on the comparison between men and women, and their businesses, so that the development of women's self-employment in relation to women's labour market position and role in the economy in general has been ignored.

What does this latter relationship between women's self-employment and their labour market position tell us? Above all, it raises two questions. Should gender be examined more concretely, on all its various levels, or should the focus of study be the conceptual level? Either way, what can be learned from an empirical examination of the gender system? First, the relationship between women's self-employment and their labour market position makes gender the focus of research. However, gender, or to be more specific, the gender system, does not appear as an atomistic element in society; rather it has been defined as a general and basic asymmetrical structure, which defines both genders, and organises relations within the division of labour, power, culture and social interactions (Rantalaiho 1988, 1986b). This definition of the gender system has certain implications for research: it does not include the idea of a universal oppression of women by men, nor does it emphasise the stable nature of this relationship. The starting point for the concept here is that *while gender is a central element in the structuration of society, the concrete relationship between the genders varies both historically and culturally* (Julkunen – Rantalaiho 1989, 19; Salmi 1991).[4]

---

3. By this I mean that the research on self-employment done in various disciplines (sociology, economics, business economics) seems not to have a common discourse ground.

4. More detailed discussion in chapters 3 and 4.

At the final time of writing of this study, the Finnish economy is in middle of a period of deep recession, as yet largely unanalysed.[5] The recession of the 1990s seems to include several features of transition in the structure of the economy that have not previously emerged in Finland, such as changes in our financial institutions, the functioning of the capital markets, shifts away from the welfare state model towards the privatisation of services, and changes in employment. Even if the term recession is far from clear, while carrying connotations which contextualise all events in political and social life, it perhaps more precisely relates to changes in the economy. Furthermore, the recession has caused a sharp rise in the unemployment, now close to 20 per cent of the working population. While the impact of the recession has been largely seen to date in terms of male unemployment (see e.g. Allen 1989b), some studies of women's experience of redundancy and unemployment have been undertaken (see Martin and Roberts 1984 in the UK, Kolehmainen 1991 in Finland).

While the gender divisions are relevant to our understanding of the current recession, the recent rapid rise of unemployment and changes in the patterns of unemployment also open up new perspectives to self-employment from a gender perspective. Restructuring in Finland from a gender perspective has meant changes first of all in the employment of health and social services. However, they are not yet visible in the statistical content used in this study. The current recession and high levels of unemployment can be expected to set off similar patriarchal pressures on women's employment as has occurred in British society, described by Walby (1986). In fact, in public discussion these pressures have already emerged.

1.2. Background for the study

Until the 1970s, the principal all-pervasive trend within the industrialised countries was for a decline in the small business sector, not only in terms of the size of the self-employed sector as a proportion of the total economically active population, but also in respect of the share of total production accounted for by small and medium-sized companies (e.g. Bolton Report 1971; Boissevain 1981; Toivonen 1987). In the main, this trend has been explained by reference to changes in the industrial structure: employment in the agricultural sector with its traditionally large self-employed population has diminished markedly in all industrial countries, but a similar phenomenon has taken place in the industrial

---

5. Except for a recent research report, "Shaping Structural Change in Finland" by Ministry of Social Affairs and Health, 1993.

6

and service sectors as well.

A clear change in the relative proportion of the self-employed to the total economically active population can be seen in the 1970s; in which the decline was halted, or even reversed, in most countries (table 1.1.A in appendix). Changes in the relative proportions of the employed and the self-employed do not necessarily correspond to any real growth in the relative size of the self-employed, since the number of employed persons has also grown in most countries, which makes the ratio rather stable (OECD 1986a, 44). *Thus, even on a conservative estimate it seems that the size of the self-employed population has grown in most OECD countries.*[6] OECD country-specific research reports show that this trend took place mainly during the 1970s and 1980s (Curran 1986 a, 1986b; Creigh et al. 1986, Bögenhold 1988).

The onset of the decline in the development of self-employment within the Finnish economy has been periodised differently in different studies. According to Kettunen's study, for example, the number of *small businesses* in Finland was already in decline by the 1930s. Moreover, this decline actually quickened in the 1960s (Kettunen 1980, 12-15). However, Alestalo (1985, 150-151) and Kerkelä (1982, 156-158), among others, note that the decline did not start until the 1950s. Whether the decline did set in during the 1930s and continue through the 1960s, or whether it started two decades later, is of minor importance here. At the beginning of the 1980s it even increased during some years (Toivonen 1984). Of greater significance is the fact that this trend has been similar in most industrial countries since the end of the 1970s.[7]

One of the general grounds usually given for the decline in the number of small businesses is that large-scale producers enjoy a competitive advantage over their smaller rivals through the realisation of economies of scale. Advantages are especially visible in those industries where the R&D and investment costs are usually high. In addition to economic factors, other reasons for the decline of small businesses have been given.[8] One of the most important concerns the policy of state support for industry which, in the 1960s

---

6. One important, although hidden aspect of this growth is the number of self-employed people who work in the 'grey' or 'black sector' of the economy. Estimates of the rise of this sector vary considerably, e.g. in Great Britain the size of the black sector is estimated to be 5 to 8 per cent of the GNP (Finnegan 1985, 160). I will come back to this question in the section dealing with the definition of self-employment in chapter 1.5.

7. See table 1.1.A in the appendix; also Toivonen 1984, table 1.

8. It has been noted that generational changes in the ownership of a business affect its long term prospects. The available evidence suggests that as a new generation takes over the running of a business from the founding generation, the level of resources devoted to its development tends to decline. (Boswell 1973, 130). A clear connection between generational change and company bankruptcy has also been established.

and 1970s was directed towards large-scale production in many countries, so that the small business sector was effectively left without any state support at all. This is shown to have happened in Sweden and in Germany, (see Curran 1982, 16, and Goffee – Scase 1987a), as well as, to a minor extent, in the UK, (see e.g. Rothwell 1986). These policy initiatives were based upon a general assumption that whereas large scale industrial production was important for a nation's long term economic development, small scale production was unimportant to such development, and would inevitably diminish.[9]

Structural changes in demand and supply factors within the Finnish economy have partly shifted the relative advance of employment to the small business sector (e.g. Bade 1987). According to Hannu Tervo (1985, 238), large companies have reacted strongly to new economic trends by reducing the size of their work forces, while the small business sector has remained more stable in this respect, even though employment and its development cannot be seen directly by measuring production.[10] One reason for the relatively stable development of employment in the small business sector in Finland may reside in the nature of the country's regional policy, which has supported labour-intensive production. In Finland labour-intensive production has mainly been industrial production, much of which takes place in the developing areas of the country. The industrial structure has become more diversified in these areas during the 1960s and the 1970s, partly as a result of supportive regional and state policies (Tervo 1985, 241).

Given the decline in the number of small businesses from the post-war period until the 1970s, discussions of the recent reversal of this trend (the re-emergence of self-employment, which has been noticeable – despite minor country specific variations – in most European countries during the 1980s) have provoked much controversy (Granovetter 1984). In the UK the trend was fairly stable after 1975, with the strongest increase occurring between 1983 and 1985, during which period the registration of new companies rose by some 43 per cent. Women's self-employment in the UK rose strongly in the 1980s, even though 75 per cent of all self-employed are men (1985) (Shutt – Whittington 1987, 176; Creigh et al. 1986). The rise in self-employment has been concentrated in a few particular industries in most countries, especially in the

---

9. E.g. Schumpeter (1934) and Galbraith (1957) supported this view which for a very long period of time remained very influential in the field of economics. It could be said, rather 'tongue in cheek' that the idea of the invisible hand acting in the market made it impossible for middlemen to operate.

10. Growth in production does not always presuppose growth in employment, and decline in production does not necessarily mean that employment declines to the maximum extent possible. This results naturally from the employee's legal status. One way of minimising the employee costs is to subcontract (for more, see e.g. Berger 1981).

service industries, and in construction (Creigh et al. 1986).

What factors, then, have led to the rise of the small business sector in different countries? For at least the last five to seven years, the small and medium-sized business sector has been strongly in the spotlights of both research interest and political discussion. Even if such attention does not encourage the rise of this sector, the fact is that the importance of small and medium-sized businesses has been recognised. Economic and employment policies favourable to this sector have been promoted, as the negative unplanned consequences of previous policies directed towards large scale industry have become apparent. According to Frank Bechhofer and Brian Elliott, in contrast to the earlier situation of political disunity, support for the small business sector towards the end of 1970s and at the beginning of 1980s has gained political acceptance (Bechhofer – Elliott 1981, 189).

So far I have discussed research concerning small businesses rather than actual self-employment. The general trends are to some extent difficult to define: different statistics give different kinds of figures. The owner of the company is classified as employed by his/her own company, and thus belongs to the waged workers, even if he or she is the only worker and sole shareholder in the company, and otherwise fulfils the characteristics of the entrepreneur. This is probably the largest group responsible for lowering the numbers of self-employed in most OECD countries (OECD 1986a, 43-44; Haber et al. 1987, 18). The differences between the definitions of self-employment and small business ownership are discussed in more detail in the next chapter.

As noted above, the amount of research on small businesses and self-employment has grown, both in Finland and elsewhere. This research has, however, left some important aspects of the phenomenal growth of the sector unexamined. Examples of such under-researched areas include small business bankruptcies, 'success factors' underpinning successful business concepts, and alternative forms of business organisation. Another of these areas concerns the empirical and theoretical aspects of women's self-employment. As mentioned earlier, the growth in the size of self-employment has been based on the growth in women's self-employment in many countries. Finland, though, is an exception from this. In Finland, almost 30 per cent of all the self-employed outside agriculture were women at the end of 1980s. Given that the growth in the theoretical importance of women's studies has raised some very important objections to the stable, traditional ways of explaining social and economic phenomena, it is interesting to explore the extent to which traditional ways of explaining women's self-employment have also been brought into question by the rise of these new perspectives.

9

Interest in female self-employment has risen mainly as a result of the rise observed in their numbers. Similarly, research on women's self-employment has emphasised empirical trends; however, more often than not the data have been limited to small, non-random samples. As a consequence of this limitation a somewhat distorted picture of women's self-employment has been created. Only minor use has been made of relevant statistical material in such studies, even though statistical series reveal the extent of the remarkable acceleration in the growth of women's self-employment, to the extent that the rise in women's self-employment actually exceeds the rise in women's waged work in some OECD countries (OECD 1986b). The participation of women in self-employment has increased in Western Europe as well as in the United States. The OECD reports that between 1969 and 1986 the proportion of self-employed women in non-farm employment increased from 24.1 per cent to 28.4 per cent in its sixteen member countries taken together.[11]

Furthermore, there has been a clear change in women's general labour market behaviour in OECD countries, and it may be assumed that this is partly due to the rise of women's self-employment (e.g. Webb 1982; Martin – Roberts 1984 on the UK; Aarnio – Eriksson 1987, on Finland). This rise of women's labour market participation has not been unilinear, although it has had its own developmental line following the development of the welfare state in Nordic countries.[12]

It may be noted that in explanations of women's labour force participation and participation in other economic activities[13], women's roles are usually hidden under the concept of the official economy. Thus, those factors which have an influence on women's participation in economic activities cannot be fully explained by recourse to the terminology used in labour market studies or

---

11. This increase was not uniform across individual countries, however. In the Mediterranean countries, notably Italy, self-employment among women appears to have declined during the period (OECD 1986b). Unfortunately the OECD statistics do not necessarily report 'real' figures for women's share of self-employed in general labour force statistics (e.g. Allen 1989b).

12. I use the terms 'Scandinavian countries' and 'Nordic countries' to include Denmark, Iceland, Norway, Sweden, and Finland, even though 'Scandinavian countries' often refers only to Norway, Sweden and Denmark, which form the Scandinavian cape.

13. By economic activities in this context I mean formal definitions of such different activities as waged work, self-employment etc., not housework. The domestic labour and work done at home is usually excluded from the framework when analysing e.g. the divisions of labour force. This means that 'the production' and 'the economy' are treated as synonymous. However, housework never has linked up completely to the labour producing value in the context of the market. As I see it, the complete understanding of female labour requires a categorisation which encompasses women's dual roles, in domestic and in paid labour.

economic studies. In short, these studies need to be supplemented by a more gender sensitive sociological approach. Information about familial status and structure, demographic factors or general economic developments, all effect a woman's labour force participation and the labour market choices open to her.[14] In Finland, for example, many social policy initiatives have encouraged women to enter into waged employment (e.g. separate taxation of spouses, social security based on waged work, the extension of the children's day-care system, etc.).

The extension of women's waged work has been seen as a historical project, aimed at breaking down gender-based segregation, even though entry into the labour market has taken place principally on the basis of segregated markets (Julkunen 1985, 57-58; Siltanen 1986). In order to understand the gender specific activities that women perform in the economy, and the historical development and condition of that activity, we cannot completely separate the examination of women's self-employment from an analysis of general developments in waged work.

To a large extent the development of women's self-employment has taken place in the shadow of a rapid growth both in women's waged work and in the public sector taken as a whole. Basically, the development of women's self-employment has followed the main lines of the development of self-employment in general. At the more detailed level of study, however, a greater degree of change and variation can be found both in the industrial location and development within industries.

1.3. On the concepts of self-employment and entrepreneurship

The meaning and measurement of self-employment is itself something of an enigma, as readers of this study will discover. Definitions of the terms *'self-employment'*, *'small business'* and *'entrepreneurship'* are not only difficult to agree upon; they also tend to change as attempts are made to use them in concrete situations. As Angela Dale notes, although both *'self-employed own-account workers'* and *'the self-employed with employees'* may be described as *'small business owners'*, there is a notable distinction between these two groups (Dale 1991, 35). This distinction is reflected not only in their specific work situations, or the size of the businesses, but in their personal

---

14. As Swedberg has noted: "The optical illusion of a market system, which works by itself and which is understandable exclusively in monetary terms, is based on the necessary assumption that women's work - in the home as well as in the workplace - remains 'invisible' or at least poorly understood." (Swedberg 1987, 66).

11

characteristics as well (Curran – Burrows 1988).

Three different dimensions distinguish the self-employed from employees. These may be classified as either sociological, legal or statistical. The sociological characteristics are: ownership of the means of production, autonomy at work and, for employers, expropriation of the labour power of others (Bechhofer – Elliott, 1974; Goldthorpe et al., 1987; Wright 1985). The legal definitions of self-employment concern mostly the facts of ownership and control over work (Hakim 1988, 424).

No unambiguous definition for the self-employed exists in Finnish statistics. This is by no means characteristic only of Finnish statistics; the same difficulty is apparent in other countries. In the classification standards of the Central Statistical Office of Finland, the concept of self-employed is treated with reference to socio-economic status, occupation, industries, and income statistics. These classifications do differ to some extent from each other and, in addition to the information gathering methods, these factors cause the differences in the numbers of self-employed people. Statistical series are generally premised upon an acceptance of either a self-definition of employment status, or information on taxation or national insurance in some countries (see e.g. Dale 1991).

The above-mentioned criteria do not completely cover the whole of the *self-employed*. If we look at the definitions used in some of the key sociological – and economic – literature, it is noticeable that the *self-employed own-account worker* and the *small business owner* are widely assumed to occupy a sufficiently distinctive class position as to be allocated a separate class location, distinct from employees, the professional self-employed or large business owners (Goldthorpe et al. 1987; for a more detailed discussion see Dale 1991).[15] Notable differences in methods of counting the self-employed in different countries make international comparisons somewhat difficult.

The sociological literature in this area seems to establish at least one major distinction, that is between the 'petit bourgeoisie' and higher occupational level self-employed professionals (see Dale 1991). However, it does not treat the latter as a separate class grouping, but places them in the same group with other higher level employees. It also seems that most of the sociological literature on entrepreneurship is concerned with the 'petit bourgeoisie' or with small manufacturing entrepreneurs and not with self-employed people in, for example, the service sector. Yet small manufacturing businesses form only a minority of all small enterprises. All in all, as Roger Burrows and James

---

15. As Dale notes, both Goldthorpe and Wright identify small proprietors, self-employed artisans and 'own-account workers' as groups distinct from the professional self-employed, in terms of their class position (Dale 1991, 37). See also Curran - Stanworth 1986.

Curran (1989) note, it seems still necessary for the topic of small business to become a more central part of the wider sociology of economic life.

In contrast to the majority of sociological definitions of *entrepreneurs,* no reference is made to the questions of ownership, control and autonomy of work when the concept of the entrepreneur is defined for statistical purposes. Social surveys usually reflect legal definitions of entrepreneurs; with 'workers' being defined according to criteria of supervision, discipline (control), and payment. In other words, if the manager is employed by a company, s/he is classified as an employee until 1987, when the classification was changed to employer. However, the legal definitions do not always correspond to statistical criteria (Dale 1991). There are at least two sets of workers who are generally identified as self-employed in accordance with standard statistical criteria, but who nevertheless do not meet recognised legal definitions of self-employment, or who fail to fulfil criteria set by sociological definitions of the petit bourgeoisie (see e.g. Hakim 1984; Dale 1986). These two groups of workers, or self-employed persons are *'home-based workers'* and *'labour-only subcontractors'*. The legal distiction between own-account workers (self-employed with no employees) and employees can be derived from the employment legislation which defines and sets limits to the term 'employed'. Home-based workers do not fulfil the criteria of supervision and control, which is a crucial element in the definition of an employed person. Qualitative studies on homeworkers (Allen and Wolkowitz 1987 in UK; and Salmi 1991 in Finland) show that many workers have neither autonomy nor ownership of the means of their production.

A clear trend in many countries (see Minna Salmi of the Finnish data 1991; Sheila Allen and Carol Wolkowitz 1987, and Jane Humphries and Jill Rubery 1988 of the British data) is the increased number of women working at home. Minna Salmi notes that at least in Finland, there appear to be various ways of working at home: white-collar and service work, both traditional and modern, seem to have made substantial progress in 'homeworking'. What factors lie behind the expansion in homeworking, particularly by women who are not genuinely self-employed? The data concerning the poor remuneration of homeworkers, or the savings in the labour costs that can be made by their employment, is freagmentary, and does not necessarily tell the whole truth (Salmi 1991). One interesting point in the definition of self-employment is, however, that homework is not only a strategy for firms in declining industries, but is also used to an increasing degree by expanding new small firms (e.g. Hakim 1984). For women who choose, or are forced to choose, working at home, the terms of taking care of family life and work seem to be almost the same as for those self-employed women who are own-account workers and have their business at home (see Salmi 1991; Allen – Wolkowitz 1987).

Evidence suggests that a considerable number of people recorded as self-employed in official statistics should really be considered as employees when sociological criteria such as ownership of the means of production, autonomy, etc., are taken into consideration (Dale 1986, 1991; Hakim 1988).[16] Some researchers argue that this group has grown during the last few years, as larger companies have made increasing use of homeworkers, temporary contract workers and subcontractors (Casey – Creigh 1988).[17]

But as Angela Dale notes, in the vast majority of cases all three bases for definition (sociological, legal and statistical) obviously coincide and, as with all definition problems, the definition used in the research should reflect the underlying purpose of a study. Therefore there can be no single 'correct' definition of 'self-employment' (see also Dale 1991, 43). Thus, although I will return to the question of definition later in chapter 4., unless otherwise stated, I use the terms entrepreneur and self-employed being as roughly synonymous. Furthermore, I will use terms 'own-account worker' meaning a self-employed person without employees, and 'employer' referring to self-employed with employees, despite the fact that most self-employed workers do not meet the classical criteria of entrepreneurship defined by early economics, and in sociology: that is, individuals with a unique mission of breaking new ground in the production and/or distribution of goods and services. When the self-employed, for a variety of reasons, have chosen to work for themselves, they have also taken some degree of autonomy, control and risk over their work which is not held by the majority of waged workers. Official statistics show that the instance of self-employed people who employ no others directly is very common, especially in services. And of these people a remarkable number are women.

If we compare the number of self-employed in Finnish statistics, the numbers vary depending on their source (table 1.1.). As the table shows, there are more employed and self-employed according to the Labour Force Survey than there are according to other statistics. In the case of the Labour Force Survey, the results are affected by the short research period (data gathered during one week every month), and by random errors and loss. According to the Statistical Office, the largest loss is in the Household Surveys (25 per cent),

---

16. Still, we cannot accept the viewpoint that self-employment is basically merely an alternative means of earning a living by the sale of one's own labour. This viewpoint is applied by several economists (e.g. Aronson 1991).

17. The immigrant workers in some OECD countries, as in the United Kingdom, create a hidden workforce which falls into the grey area between self-employment and employee status. They work mostly for the clothing industry and in personal services such as cleaning and household work (for more, see Mitter 1986).

Table 1.1. The number of self-employed people in Finland reported by various statistics 1980 and 1981

Number of self-employed	Population Census (1980)	Labour Force Survey (1980)	Household Survey (1981)	Income Distribution Statistics (1980)
All	318 000	379 000	360 000	352 000
Self-employed of these	213 000	311 000	237 000	230 000
Self-employed in agriculture	125 000	190 000	146 000	142 000
Non-farm self-employed	88 000	121 000	91 000	88 000
Assisting family members of these	105 000	68 000	122 000	122 000
Assisting family members in agriculture	93 000	56 000	*	105 000
Other assisting family members	12 000	12 000	*	17 000

* included in the figure above

the next largest loss is in Income Distribution Statistics (15 per cent), followed by Labour Force Surveys (5-7 per cent). The Population Census has the largest cover; only above 1 per cent of all the economically active are outside the census. The controversial nature of self-employment is visible in statistics: if we compare the figures given in the Industrial Statistics and Company Statistics, we get rather a different picture.[18] The figures in table 1.1. are from the 1980s. However, the registration of self-employment has not been radically changed since that time.

As we see, the highest totals of self-employed are reported in Labour Force Surveys, whereas the Population Censuses report the lowest figures for self-employment.[19] The reverse takes place in the number of assisting family members, which seems to be best reported by the Household Survey, Income Distribution Statistics and Population Census. The smallest number of assisting family members reported is in the Labour Force Survey. As far as personnel

18. The basic unit in the industrial statistics is the place of business. From 1954 onwards, the statistics register only those business units which employ at least 5 persons. The Company Register includes all manufacturing businesses, even the smallest ones.

19. See also Yrittäjätyöryhmän raportti (1986).

are concerned, The Register of Enterprises and Establishments covers 99 per cent of non-agricultural industries. The Register of Enterprises and Establishments includes enterprises subject to turnover tax from the year 1972, and since 1989 all other enterprises subject to taxation under the Business Tax Act.

1.4. Some general features of the waged workforce and the self-employed

There was a total of 331 000 corporate enterprises and personal businesses in Finland in 1990. Of these, 129 000 were registered employers and enterprises subject to turnover tax, 112 000 were agricultural farms, 89 000 were classed as other enterprises, plus 170 unincorporated local government enterprises. (CSOF 1992a) Small enterprises, with a work-force of less than 100, have statistically grown in importance over the last few years. Not only has the number of employed grown in the late 1980s, but their share of the total turnover has grown as well.

In the 1990s, companies with more than 500 personnel account for more than 50 per cent of all employed in Finland, even though these companies constitute just 0.4 per cent of all companies registered in Finland. Against this, companies and businesses employing less than 5 persons currently constitute more than 70 per cent of all businesses in Finland. Table 1.2. indicates the size, distribution and number of employees in companies in Finland in 1990 (CSOF 1992a).

According to annual census information from the Company Registration Office, a change in the volume of business start-ups took place in 1977, involving a sharp upward trend in the number of new company registrations that continued up until 1990. On closer inspection, the figures for this net rise in business start-ups follows a common pattern, thus implying an absolute increase in the total number of registered companies. The number of new companies registered actually doubled between 1977 and 1984, and this rising trend continued until 1990 (Figure 1.2.A.). What is interesting here is that the number of new registered companies rose in all categories, with the highest rise in registered business names.

However, for statistical reasons, not all information about entrepreneurs and their companies is available from the Company Registration Office, since only employers with at least two employees and a stable location, or who start an open or a public limited company, have to register with the office. This means that census data provides the best way to obtain information of a structural

Table 1.2. Companies registered for turnover in Finland, 1990, size and relative share distribution

Number of employees	Number of companies	%	Number of employees	%
0-4	97 475	75.5	160 150	11.6
5-9	15 342	11.9	98 385	7.1
10-19	8 165	6.3	108 792	7.9
20-49	5 140	4.0	151 793	11.2
50-99	1 463	1.1	100 771	7.3
100-199	724	0.6	98 580	7.2
200-499	450	0.4	138 843	10.0
500-999	138	0.1	95 208	6.9
1000-	138	0.1	424 777	30.8
Total	129 035	100.0	1 377 299	100.0

Source: CSOF 1992a

Table 1.3. Non-farm self-employment as percentage of EAP, 1960-1990 (%)

Year	1960	1970	1975	1980	1985	1990
Employers	1.7	2.1	1.4	1.7	1.9	..
Own-account workers	3.8	3.4	3.2	2.8	3.2	..
Total	5.5	5.5	4.6	4.5	5.1	6.5

Source: CSOF 1988a

nature about entrepreneurs.

The development of self-employment seems to follow general economic cycles, and the trend was clearly one of decline during the period 1970 to 1975. Table 1.3. shows the distribution of all self-employed people as a percentage of the economically active population, and in classes of employers and own-account workers during 1960–1990. A detailed industry by industry analysis of trends during the last few years reveals a rise in the number of self-employed in certain industries during the 1980s. In fact, the total number of self-employed outside agriculture has grown by almost 30.000 between 1980 and 1985. The rise did continue at the end of the 1980s, as well. The year 1988 seems to be a turning point in the sense that the net rise in the number of companies was over 4 per cent compared to the earlier year, 1987.

Table 1.4. presents the proportions of the economically active population employed outside agriculture divided into three groups: the employees, the self-

Table 1.4. Non-farm employment, by class of worker and gender, 1985

Class of worker	Female	%	Male	%	Total	%
Employees	998 953	49.1	1 036 103	50.9	2 035 056	100
Self-employed	34 556	29.6	82 184	70.4	116 740	100
Employers	10 095	23.8	32 317	76.2	42 412	100
Own-account workers	24 461	32.9	49 867	67.1	74 328	100
Total employed	1 033 509	48.1	1 118 287	51.9	2 151 796	100

Source: CSOF 1988a

employed and the employers. Self-employed women constituted almost 30 per cent of all self-employed in 1985. The greater part of women's self-employment is accounted for by own-account working, and nearly one third of all own-account workers (32.9 per cent) are women.

In numbers, this means that c. 34 500 women were engaged in non-farm self-employment in 1985. In addition, there was a sharp and relatively consistent difference in the percentages of men and women who were self-employed. Men still constitute a majority of the non-farm self-employed. As noted earlier, women have been entering self-employment in slightly growing numbers.

Even if the results of this analysis of the gendered industrial division of labour in Finland provides few surprises, an analysis of this kind is essential to establish a *general picture of structural change in self-employment patterns between the various industrial sectors as well as change within individual industries*. My intention here is not to concentrate on the births or deaths of businesses, nor on economic questions related to business start-ups. Even if such questions are of great interest in their own right they cannot be dealt with in the present study. There have been major changes in the size composition of businesses within different industries. Changes have also occurred in the relative importance of different industries within the economy as a whole. As far as the development of the service sector is concerned, the clearest difference between Finland and other OECD countries is the relatively low share of total national production and employment accounted for by service sector industries in Finland, compared to the OECD average (OECD 1986a, 1987a).

The general direction of change in Finland's post-war industrial and employment structure is well-documented. The size of the economically active population engaged in agriculture has declined steadily, while in the 1980s in

Table 1.5.   **The industrial structure of the EAP in the three main industrial sectors, 1960 - 1985 (%)**

Year	1960	1970	1975	1980	1985
Agriculture	36	20	15	13	11
women	32	16	12	11	8
men	38	24	17	14	13
Manufacturing	31	36	37	35	32
women	22	24	25	23	20
men	38	45	47	45	45
Services	33	44	48	52	57
women	46	60	63	66	72
men	24	31	36	41	42

Sources: CSOF industrial statistics 1960-1985; Toivonen 1988, 68.

particular, the proportion of the population economically active in various service sector activities, especially services falling within ISIC industrial class 9 (community, social and personal services), has grown markedly.

The employment share of the broad category "various services" has grown over 10 percentage units since the 1970s so that it accounts for almost 30 per cent of all Finnish employees. The number of economically active people employed in manufacturing industry increased rapidly from the 1960s until 1975, but declined slowly thereafter, so that by 1989 only 23 per cent of all economically active people were employed in manufacturing industry, compared with 37 per cent in 1975 (table 1.5.).[20] Reija Lilja and Tuire Santamäki's study of structural change in employment sheds interesting light upon the overall impact of these industrial trends since the 1970s. Their findings show that structural change has resulted in a decline in manufacturing work, an increase in clerical occupations, and a regional concentration of the workforce in the southern county of Uusimaa (Lilja – Santamäki 1988).

At the present time, the main class of services constitutes the most highly innovative and entrepreneurial industry, while the lowest levels of entrepreneurship are to be found in manufacturing. However, inside manufacturing industry the number of entrepreneurs varies considerably. This variation is interesting, since most of the research on entrepreneurship has been concentrated on *manufacturing industries*, so that, by and large, service sector entrepreneurship has not been extensively studied, except for a few very recent

---

20. These two figures are not directly comparable since they have been drawn from different statistics.

studies (see Toivonen 1989). The emphasis on manufacturing industries, despite their minority status in terms of employment, for example, has been noted in British research context as well (Burrows – Curran 1989). However, as Toivonen notes, official statistics suggest that the differences between industries are diminishing: in 'new' industries in particular, the number of entrepreneurs is rising independently of the industry in question, whereas in 'old' industries it is declining (Toivonen 1984, 195). Both on the basis of the number of entrepreneurs and the composition of the labour force, the whole economy may be divided into two large sectors: a diminishing sector (the old sector) in which agriculture, mining, manufacturing and construction are to be included; and a growing sector comprising different services.

An examination of historical record reveals a proportionate decline (since 1930) in the number of entrepreneurs when set against the total employed population, although the sharpest decline took place in the size of the agricultural population (Toivonen 1988, 92). This general decline in entrepreneurship was already visible in the 1930s in the form of a decline of small enterprises (Kettunen 1980, 12-15). Toivonen has shown that the number of entrepreneurs outside agriculture declined continuously until the 1980s, after which numbers began to rise again (Toivonen 1988). As Toivonen stresses, the most important factor influencing this process of decline has been structural in nature. On the one hand, the decline has followed changes in industrial structure, while on the other, the number of entrepreneurs within different industries has grown recently.

1.5. General notes on women's labour force participation and self-employment [21]

Statistics covering OECD countries show few clear trend changes in women's labour force participation. First, between 1979 and 1985 women's labour force participation grew faster than men's, the only exception to this trend being the UK (OECD 1987a). Secondly, growth has been strong not only in the service sector but also in manufacturing industry, especially in high-tech industries such as chemistry, plastics and electronics (OECD 1987a, 23-25). Thirdly, there is a clear trend in the rise of women's self-employment in some OECD countries (see figure 1.1.A.).

---

21. Both the specificity of women's labour market situation and situation in the field of self-employment, and also the notions that such specificities would be only understood by exclusive reference to women's family situation caused me to separate chapters 1.4. and 1.5.

In Finland, as in many other industrialised countries, the growth in general labour force participation has been based on an expansion of women's labour force participation, mainly in the service sector of the economy. In the United States, where the growth in women's labour force participation has taken place somewhat later than, for example, in the Scandinavian countries, it is estimated that the expansion of the services has affected not only the level of women's participation in different sectors of the economy but also the number of self-employed women. The number of own-account self-employed women grew almost 53 per cent between 1970 and 1979 (SBA 1980), and a 'new' group of women, i.e. young women with small children, has entered into waged work and self-employment. Nevertheless the American occupational structure, like its counterparts in other industrial societies, remains highly segregated by gender, and recent analyses have documented that this occupational segregation shows little sign of lessening (e.g. Roos 1985).

During the Second World War large numbers of women in almost all industrialised countries (Finland being one of a small number of exceptions) moved outside the home and into the labour market - especially into manufacturing industry - only to return to the home again after the war (OECD 1988b; Bergmann 1986, 21). Beginning in the early 1960s, in most countries two important changes occurred in the way women work. First, in addition to entering the paid labour force in increasing numbers, women's attachment to employment also became much more permanent. As a consequence of this, participation rates rose for all types of women. This meant the blurring of the differences which previously existed due to marital status, age, or number of children (Hagen – Jenson 1988). Secondly, working women entered the public consciousness and became a subject of political debate and action. Women became a more permanent and normal part of the labour force.

The growth in women's labour force participation was partly due to the growth in the service sector and manufacturing devoted to the mass production of consumer durables, and partly because of war-time labour shortages. Moreover, growing public sector services also required an increase in the size of the labour force. The models for such labour force participation, as well as its timing, are country specific.[22] In Finland, women's labour force participation was already growing during the early years of industrialisation, when the model of industrial production spread, shifting part of production outside the home, whereas in many countries the growth in women's labour force participation did not occur until the 1960s and 1970s. The above-

---

22. However, it has been suggested that in some cases the success of businesses in manoeuvring a way through economic restructuring may very well depend upon the employment of women (Hagen – Jenson 1988).

mentioned model remained unchanged in Finland until the 1960s (Jallinoja 1985, 225), by which time women represented approximately 39 per cent of the total labour force, and most women worked in manufacturing industries. The growth of services increased women's share of service sector occupations, while at the same time their share of manufacturing occupations clearly decreased.

Apart from economic and demographic changes, general changes in the family structure (e.g. a decrease in the birth rate and the time women devote to the care of children) also influenced women's labour force participation. Furthermore, a number of country specific social policy measures helped to differentiate the development of women's labour force participation. In the UK and the US, for example, *part-time work* became increasingly common after the second World War, and has remained a model for waged work ever since (e.g. Martin – Roberts 1984).

Growth in the labour force in most OECD countries has been based upon growth in women's labour force participation. In addition, a number of developments during the 1980s increased the supply of part-time work in OECD countries. In some countries the net growth in the supply of jobs has taken place mainly in part-time employment in the service sector (OECD 1988a). In EC-countries, female part-time employment has increased from 27.7 per cent of total part-time employment in 1983 to 30.2 per cent in 1987. Several reasons may be cited for the growth in part-time work including labour market conditions, changes in industrial and enterprise structures, the role of the public sector, minor labour expenses, and labour supply patterns (Meulders – Plasman 1989, 17).

According to population censuses, women's waged work in Finland was relatively common for young unmarried women in the 1950s and 1960s, although waged work became increasingly common among 35-44-year-old married women from the 1960s onwards. This shift in working patterns was supported by an ideological change in women's role within society. These latter changes were connected in turn to various societal changes dating from the 1960s and 1970s, which placed a greater emphasis upon individualism and, in the process, influenced the reform of state family policy, the supply of communal day-care and publicly financed social welfare and family support (Jallinoja 1984, 77, 80-81). This social policy development also emphasised equality and individuality in the economic realm. These ideas may be seen as part of the background to legislative improvements which made it easier for women to participate in the labour market in the 1970s (see also Anttonen 1989).

In addition to the indirect effects of general societal changes since the 1960s, the rapid broadening of labour markets has also increased the demand for labour, which has in turn had an influence upon women's labour force participation patterns. The pattern of labour force participation for women and men in Finland has been very similar: an increase in the participation rate until women enter their thirties or forties is followed by a tailing off thereafter to produce a single peak. However, women have lower participation rates than men of the same age. 'A double peak' is the most common pattern for female labour force participation in other industrialised countries.

Indeed, Finland is the sole example of a single peak OECD-country (Gustafsson – Lantz 1985, 47-48; Roos 1985). In Ireland, Israel and the Netherlands, the employment career patterns of women are characterised by early peaks followed by sharp declines in levels of labour market participation. Moreover, average female rates of participation in these countries are low by international comparison, with the highest rates found prior to both marriage and the immediate childbearing years. Roos has extrapolated from the historical experience of the United States that these three types of female participation could be placed on a continuum, with countries initially exhibiting an early peak, then shifting to a double peak pattern, and finally to a single peak pattern (Roos 1985, 43).

The most prominent feature of women's participation in the labour market is an increase in the prevailing levels of occupational gender segregation. In 1984 almost half of the employed population in Finland (48 per cent of men, 34 per cent of women) were in wholly segregated occupations; that is in occupations where one gender accounted for 91-100 per cent of the workforce. Women work in fewer occupations than men, and when men's and women's labour market positions are compared, it is clear that the position occupied by women is generally the minor one. Lower wage levels, despite task similarities, a lower hierarchical status, and more restricted mobility in career or work are evidence of the fact that women are in a secondary sector of the labour market. Occupational segregation is a universal, and also characteristic, consequence of the way work and home responsibilities are organised in industrial countries. This segregation is not only restricted into matters of work and home life, but also into matters of, for instance, education.[23]

It could be argued that the phenomenon of segregation – as well as gender equality – is clearly revealed in numerous statistics and surveys, as if it was an objective truth. However, as Rosemary Crompton and Gareth Jones have remarked, a problem of measurement and classification remains to be overcome: in practice men and women in the same occupations may have very

---

23. However, the educational *level* of women in Finland is higher than the educational level of men.

different opportunities for occupational mobility and advancement (Crompton – Jones 1984). This means that the end is not defined by the means of work or occupation, but instead by gender; a fact obscured in the statistics. Päivi Korvajärvi and Liisa Rantalaiho note that even if the cultural definition of occupations and work changes from one country to another, there is one common factor - and that is that gender roles and work roles are defined simultaneously (Rantalaiho 1986c).

2 The research setting

2.1. The aims and objectives of the study

The starting point for this study is the lack of research on women in the economy, both as entrepreneurs and as self-employed persons. The concept of gender can be seen as one of the main factors in the division of labour: the segregation of work into men's and women's jobs has not come about automatically, nor has it been a natural consequence of the "free play of market forces" in the labour market or in the economy, but rather, as noted in the introduction, it must be seen as more or less a consequence of a logical process of segmentation based on gender (Anttalainen 1986; Murgatroyd 1986). The gendering processes are present also in self-employment, not only in paid labour. Furthermore, the direction of my study has been influenced by theoretical and methodological debates within women's studies and feminist research.

The objectives of my study may be thought of as having two distinct but closely linked dimensions. *First, the study sets out to analyse and create a conceptual picture of the female entrepreneur, and to sketch a picture of self-employed women as given in research reports. Secondly, with the help of a theoretical discussion and empirical material based upon Finnish data, I seek to establish a general sketch of the development of women's entrepreneurship from the 1960s up until the 1990s.*

Women's entrepreneurship is treated here as being 'the other side of the coin' of an economy, based upon waged work. Still, women's non-farm self-employment is not merely a mirror image of the women's labour force. I will look at some aspects of the connections between the recent development in women's self-employment and waged work. Because only a little research has been conducted on women's self-employment and its development, completing the above research tasks also requires that some main lines of the development of self-employment are related to general aspects of the development of the economy as a whole; to changes in the number of entrepreneurs in general; and

25

to the development that has taken place in women's waged work.

Research on women's self-employment may be divided roughly into two parts: the majority of the research is concentrated around *the motives of women entrepreneurs and what differentiates them from male entrepreneurs.* Usually the starting point for this type of research is that the category 'male', and the results of research conducted around this category, create the norms for research on women. Such male-centred studies have mostly dealt with women's self-employment from a psychological and historical perspective, which means that - in addition to motives - the focus for the research has been on different psychological qualities, socio-demographic variables, and different role models. This part of the discipline is virtually untouched by gender issues, even though it is open to the same "additive approach" of simply adding the study of women onto the existing body of knowledge about men.

However, these pieces of research have usually failed to bring out the significance of entrepreneurship as a factor structuring women's lives. Another form of research that has received a great deal of attention has been *the 'from rags to riches' type of descriptive monograph, which focuses on the small number of exceptional women who have made it to the top.* This 'hidden' presumption in the literature of the exceptionality of the self-employed woman is to be found in many research settings (for a more detailed discussion of this point see Kovalainen 1988, 1989c). Owing to the definition of gender adopted in my research, gender comparison as such has a less important role than might otherwise be expected. I will return to the issue of defining gender later in chapter 3.

The growth in entrepreneurship apparent in almost all industrialised countries has led to an increase in research on its general economic prerequisites, as well as on changes in the numbers of entrepreneurs in different sectors of the economy. Moreover, most countries display similar forms of both women's entry into the labour market and of their striving for economic independence. In 1989, women made up 47,1 per cent of the Finnish labour force. This may be compared with women's 43,8 per cent share of the labour force in the USA (OECD 1988a). Independent of country specific features or of how fast economic development has proceeded, women have occupied a position in the labour market inferior to that of men; the discussion of segregated labour markets begun in the introduction points both to a vertical and a horizontal division of labour by gender.

Women are not only more likely to be concentrated at the lower levels of waged work hierarchies; they are also usually lower paid than men who carry out similar work tasks. The division of work into a formal and an informal economy is not central in this respect, since the gender-based division of work

26

exists in the home as well as in paid employment: in the 1980s women carried out 64 per cent of all housework in Finland, compared with 67 per cent in the USA. As Raija Julkunen (1985) and later Minna Salmi (1991) have argued, not even time is gender-neutral; time use is constructed differently for women than for men (see also Karen Davies 1989).

The two research questions mentioned earlier can now be further elaborated: *the study sets out to analyse the general picture and conditions under which a self-employed woman is defined and to look at, how this description, given the help of various disciplines, corresponds to the sketch of self-employed women and their place in the economy.* Listing the contents may give an impression of the mechanical division between disciplines. However, I see this division of chapters according to disciplines more as a heuristic tool in an exploration of the various facets of self-employment, than as a strict barrier of thought.

Sketching out the picture of self-employed women in the economy and the development of self-employed women during years, is another task of this study. This means mainly an analysis of the industrial division, and data gathered from population censuses. The use of industrial division has advantages and disadvantages: the greatest advantage is that it is directly connected into the development of the economy, whereas the usage of other statistical material, such as occupational data, does not allow that sort of examination. On the other hand, I have used company statistics whenever possible. Unfortunately the owner is not identifiable in the company statistics, so the use of industrial statistics has helped in giving a general idea of the development in the industry in question. In addition to statistical material I use interview and questionnaire data gathered from self-employed women within various industries in order to highlight some of the problems which these women face in the entrepreneurial life (see appendix for further information on the interview material).

2.2. The nature of the study and the empirical data material used

The virgin nature of the research field was apparent from the theoretical discussion: in the greater part of the field dealing with entrepreneurship and self-employment, gender has not been seen as a relevant concept that has to be taken into consideration. If gender is present, it is treated more or less as a single variable, not as a socio-cultural or analytic category. What I mean by the concept of gender as an analytic category will be discussed in chapter 3. Since the debate surrounding theories of self-employment rarely takes gender seriously, and since participants in this debate often emphasise the facts about women's suitability for self-employment, my emphasis has been directed more towards theoretical approaches which explain the division of labour by reference to gender. Taken together, these latter gender-sensitive approaches offer better tools for the analysis of women's self-employment. Furthermore, studies of women's work and everyday life, and the theoretical debate connected to these studies, provide another important source of inspiration for my own research.

The main tasks in this study are analytical and descriptive. After completing my analysis of self-employment as a theoretical construction, and the sketch of self-employed women on the basis of an extensive review of the research literature, I will describe the development of self-employed women in Finland. The statistical material is introduced by descriptive distributions and tables. This kind of use of statistical material is important for several reasons: in Minna Salmi's words, self-employed women are – in a similar way to homeworkers in her study – first of all "an invisible group which is made visible"; secondly, "there has not been any information on them earlier", and thirdly; "international comparisons are not possible without the descriptive basic information" (Salmi 1991, 40-45).[1]

In order to discover connections between women's labour force participation and self-employment, I have used the shift-share analysis to examine whether the observed 'new' rise in women's self-employment is due to structural changes in the economy, or internal changes within the industry; and also to explore whether the rise in women's self-employment is connected to general changes in employment. The use of this method is, by nature, both explanatory and explorative.

The time period for the study has been limited to the period 1960-1990 for the following reasons. First, the 1960s are considered a transition period in economic, cultural and societal development: economic growth in terms of export and internal wholesale and retail trade had begun after the policy of economic control in the 1950s was relaxed (Lastikka 1984, 30). Even though the share of the economically active population in agriculture was still relatively high (36 per cent), changes in economic structure, such as the growth of the public sector, the service sector and industrial production, had already begun.

According to Alestalo, Finland could not be classified as an industrial society until the 1960s and 1970s (Alestalo 1985). Comparisons have been made between the years 1960-1985 (and 1960-1990) since it was possible to transform the data into a comparable form. However, the population survey for

---

1. To my surprise I found that Salmi has almost identical justifications for the use of descriptive analysis in her dissertation, so I borrowed her words to justify my own means. The translation is mine.

28

1990 was not fully available for analysis, so information of development fro that year is restricted. This is unfortunate and does to some extent diminish the analytical scope of the development which has taken place since 1985. It was really *after* 1985 that the changes in e.g. company registration took place, and the number of self-employed rose. Thus the comparison of earlier population surveys with the population survey of 1990 is left to future studies.

Agricultural entrepreneurship has been treated to only limited analysis in this study, since agriculture is by nature different from other forms of entrepreneurship, even though it nowadays includes many relevant subordinate sectors. These sectors also bring agricultural self-employment closer to other forms of self-employment in the problems they share. Most women who are economically active in agriculture are classified as assisting family members in the statistics.

In addition to the analysis of the conceptual construction of self-employment and entrepreneurship, I have also explored the structural development of women's self-employment. Population surveys have been the main source material for the longitudinal study of women's self-employment in Finland. Information on self-employment can be found in a number of sources, and the problem of discovering the real number of self-employed is a vexing one: various statistics give different numbers depending on the classification, the time period for data gathering, and the loss (table 1.1. in chapter 1.3.). Population surveys supply the best coverage of the labour force compared to labour force surveys and household surveys. Furthermore, the identification of the self-employed person (gender) and status (self-employed own account worker/employer), both crucial in this study, were to be found only in population surveys. For instance, company statistics, which are much used in small business studies, do not identify self-employed individuals.

In addition to population census data, I used the annual statistics of the Finnish Labour Force Surveys, which provide information about labour force participation, employment, unemployment and labour input. Statistics from the Company register, industrial statistics and time series for Finnish national accounts provided additional material in sketching the main industrial development.

The question as to whether the statistics 'reveal the truth' or 'hide part of the truth', is also relevant in this study. As I see it, the statistics reflect the thinking and ideas of their own time, and later research always poses new questions and thus also problematises old divisions (see also Vattula 1989). Statistical data is thus not produced nor utilised in a social vacuum, which would be free of interests. Statistics should be seen as a social product. One of the problematic divisions in the statistics I have used in my study is the question of assisting family members. Should women who are classified in the statistics as assisting family members be counted as self-employed or should they remain a category of their own?

I have solved this problem by discussing the group of assisting family members separately. First, the group of assisting family members could be regarded as the most invisible group in female self-employment. Even if those women in the position of being assisting family members lack the autonomy and independence which are usually related to the concept of self-employment, these women can, however, be of a crucial importance for the family business. As I will discuss later in my study, the existence of the group 'assisting family members' also clearly reflects the patriarchal nature of gender contracts in family businesses.[2] Secondly, the gender division in the group of assisting family members has remained more or less unchanged, whereas changes in actual self-employment have been greater. Thirdly, the logic of a family business is clearly tied into contract between spouses and the marital contract, which makes it different from non-family businesses.

Since gendered structures of economy do not necessarily reveal the gendering processes, or the everyday life experiences and diversities in the lives of self-employed women, I also interviewed women classed as self-employed, to explore the gendering processes in practice. This interview sample consisted of 19 entrepreneurs who were either own-account workers or employers, all running businesses in the south-western part of Finland, either in large or smaller, neighbouring towns. I conducted the interviews mainly during one entrepreneurial course attended by women. The interviews followed a semi-structured format, and in addition, all the women filled out a questionnaire, giving additional information which might have not come up in the interview. The information gained from respondents included their general background and personal characteristics, reasons for choosing self-employment, career, aspects of their work they liked and disliked, and various other questions related to their business and family and associated problems. I discuss in my study some of the key issues raised by the questionnaire responses and interviews.

Since I was a 'knowledgeable stranger' to these women - someone they would be unlikely to see very often again - the interviews were simultaneously awkward and interesting. I believe my situation – teaching them during the entrepreneurial course, especially on issues relating to women and self-employment – and my interest in their entrepreneurial situations, increased my credibility, since none of them refused to be interviewed. In addition, even

---

2. In addition to that, it reflects the gendered nature of statistical categories (see Kinnunen 1989).

though I did the 'instrument-based interview' (i.e. I tried to collect the same types of data from different people, and follow the structure of my questionnaire) many of the interviewed women did reveal more of their personal lives than would have been necessary 'for the research purposes'.[3] Brief descriptions of all the interviewed women and their business activities, and the interview scheme, are in the appendix.

2.3. The structure of the study

This study consists of four parts which together include nine chapters. Part I consists of chapters 1 and 2. In this first part I have discussed some central themes and background associated with my study, and presented the research area. This was done in order to clarify the aims and objectives, and set the research questions for my study in this chapter. The research perspective and the nature of the study are developed and further explained in part two, where I develop the theoretical frame of reference and analyse various aspects in relation to women's self-employment and how it has been explained.

Part II consists of chapters 3, 4 and 5. In this part I present initially the development in the concept of gender and its relation to feminist research (chapter 3), and secondly analyse the conceptual and theoretical discussion of self-employment and entrepreneurship (chapter 4). As I see it, it is necessary to describe the conventional or 'malestream' perspective, in order to give a full picture of the gendered conceptual discussion of which the studies of self-employment and entrepreneurship largely consist. Chapter 4 is specifically concerned with various theoretical aspects of self-employment, and how they relate to the way women's self-employment is defined. I discuss various ways of explaining women's economic activities in research in general, and finally relate these different conceptual ideas of self-employment, entrepreneurship and women's work into gender perspective. Finally, I consider the settings for women's self-employment and the general reasons for self-employment, and its possible growth at the societal level (chapter 5). This is done to clarify the approach in part III, which deals with general features of women's self-employment in Finland and their development over a period of time.

Part III consists of two large chapters, 6 and 7 which deal with the empirical material of the study. In this part of the study I examine women's self-employment in Finland, general features of women's self-employment, and the

---

3. The instrument-based interview is contrasted with 'interviewee-oriented interview', where the focus is on person and the 'intimacy' of open-ended, in-depth interviews is required (Reinharz 1992).

possible reasons for the change in the number of self-employed women, as well as exploring overall longitudinal development from the 1960s to the 1990s. I present the interview material together with statistical data, and relate women's self-employment to women's waged employment, to see if there is any kind of structural change from waged work forms into self-employment. Chapter 6 sketches out general features of women's self-employment in Finland, and sets parameters for its more detailed inspection. The development and distribution of women's self-employment according to industrial division, as well as the most important economic sectors for women's self-employment, are discussed in chapter 7.

Finally, in part IV, I collect the main results, summarise the theoretical and empirical threads together, and discuss the main theorectical conclusions of my study shortly in chapter 8.

Part II

3 Gender – Why and how?
   Methodological standpoint
   for the study

3.1. Why study gender? Methodological point of departure

Even though the basic philosophical premises are not common for all women´s studies, gender studies and feminist research, clearly distinct traditions of inquiry by which to categorise individual studies can be traced.[1] A common feature of different studies concerns the way they approach the theoretical substance of gender and the way they problematize it. Indeed, it may be said that challenges to mainstream social science have raised a variety of approaches to knowledge. Much of this theorising takes place at the theoretical and conceptual level of the social sciences, despite the fact that mainstream social science has been criticised for being empirically blind in respect of gender and "those aspects of society that gender affects" (Walby 1990, 16). However, this critique of mainstream social science has not assumed that research methods and the way knowledge is put together are themselves scientifically neutral.[2]

In the following, I will briefly discuss the development of the concept of gender, and give a short overview of its possible methodological consequences. My aim is to show the connections between different arguments, justify the use of gender as an analytical category, and develop a conceptual framework for the sociological theorizing on women's self-employment.

---

1. I mean here mainly the differences in the epistemological approaches which lie beneath various studies and theories. In her recent Ph.D. thesis, Margareta Hallberg has clarified the distinction between threefold distinction in terms of links to the women's movement, legitimising strategies, epistemological position and view of science (Hallberg 1992).

2. I am aware that it is somewhat misleading to use the term "mainstream social science". In this context I consider it, however, justified.

35

3.1.1. The development of the definition of gender

A number of different kinds of ways exist to classify – or make distinctions between – various types of gender or feminist research. Perhaps the most widely used classification in the Finnish context has been between liberal, radical and Marxist feminist research, whereas in the British context the division, and the debate, have mostly been between radical feminist and Marxist feminist research traditions; and in the USA between radical feminism and liberal feminism. Furthermore, an attempt has been made, mainly in American discussions, to synthesize Marxist feminist and radical feminist analyses in dual-systems theory (see e.g. Walby 1990; also Saarinen 1992).

In the Finnish context, Aino Saarinen (1986) has developed a classificatory schema based upon four groups which reflect the developmental phases in Finnish research on gender, and the relationship of feminist research to mainstream theories. This schema is close to classifications presented by Gerda Lerner, and several others. The first phase of Finnish research on gender was termed '*compensatory research*' and focused first of all on individual, exceptional women; The second phase was referred to as '*contribution research*' and focused on women mainly as an assisting group. During both these phases gender was treated as one variable among many and the theoretical basis of the research was left untouched. The third phase, termed '*transitional research*', focused on women as an autonomous group. And finally, a fourth phase of '*integrative research*', focused upon society as a gender system.

The first two phases are classified as being integrated into mainstream social science, whereas the third and the fourth phases, were clearly separate from it. The last phase has also been called an '*intervention project*', which refers to the intervention of feminist research settings and frameworks into mainstream social science conceptualisations. Saarinen's classification sets up clear boundaries between different phases and ties together the development of feminist research, the women's movement and the development of social science theory within a feminist and gender perspective.

Although the classifications in a sense give a too static picture of the reality, Saarinen's classification has proved useful for later discussions in the Finnish context and, clearly, divisions existed in the Finnish research context as well. Harriet Silius (1992) has presented a classification based upon the following thematic groups: '*sex role research*', '*social vs. biological sex*' research, and '*sex as relation and process*' research. This division is perhaps more illustrative than the division of feminist research into liberal, radical and Marxist categories, in the Finnish context at least, since the political women's movement has not played such an important role as it has done, for example, in the USA and Great Britain. Recently, with respect to Finland, Aino Saarinen has presented a more complicated and nuanced categorisation than her earlier one by relating the discussion to post-modernism (Saarinen 1992).[3] Even if it may sound a naive truism, feminist research has clearly established different theoretical ways of analysing both the construction of the concept of gender and, with the help of that concept, a number of different social phenomena. The various ways of conceptualising gender also reflect the time perspective associated with the development of each theoretical orientation.[4]

The second developmental phase in research on gender in the social sciences involved seeing gender as a form of learned role models which characterise individuals.[5] These shared roles or attributes then become a uniting label for a given group. Although the focus in this analysis of sex differences was partly integrated within the social science agenda prior to the 1960s, actual research was restricted to a few empirical studies. The study of 'sex roles' became a subject for serious research only in the late 1960s and 1970s. To a large extent the clearcut division into male and female roles stimulated criticism by feminist social scientists towards mainstream research settings in the 1970s and even 1980s. The grounds for this criticism were numerous. One such criticism was that in this approach it was assumed that men and women were part of homogeneous groups and, as a result, no account was taken of diversity within a group. Furthermore, objections were raised to the restrictive nature of the role theories. For example, a later line of criticism concerned the lack of an analysis of power relations between the two groups and the static picture of their roles and role maintenance presented in the theories (Hirdman 1990; see also Silius 1992).

One example of such an approach that is also directly related to the

---

3. Here I deliberately emphasise the Finnish context, even though from the very beginning Finnish research has been international in terms of ideas and contacts both to American and European traditions. However, it was not until the 1980s – with the rise of women's studies milieux and the establishment of a Finnish journal for feminist and women studies, Naistutkimus - Kvinnoforskning – that the number of publications and articles started to rise.

4. In fact, even in 1985, when I wrote my master's thesis, the comparison of similarities and differences between men and women within a very 'malestream' framework was still the usual way of doing research (Kovalainen 1988). Comparisons of men and women reflected the prevailing idea of the concept of gender, which assumed that there was a set of roles and characteristics that both genders shared. It has been stated that from the late 1960s to the mid-1980s, feminist theory exhibited a recurrent pattern: its analyses tended "to reflect the viewpoints of white, middle-class women of North America and Western Europe" (Nicholson 1990, 1).

5. Examining gender mainly as a single variable could be labelled as the first developmental phase.

37

discussion in this study, concerns studies of sex differences undertaken during the early 1970s in respect of the "motive to achieve". In what is now a classic study, Matina Horner (1970) reported the finding that women did not respond in the same way as men did on achievement-motivation tests. All in all, *this type of attribution theory has looked primarily at people's subjective interpretations of the reasons for success rather than at the conditions that reinforce gender-related perceptions. It is through this latter process that cultural myths play an important role* (Fuchs Epstein 1988). I will discuss this more in the context of the roles assumed by self-employed women in chapter 4.4.

The focus on roles and role models in research on gender is closely related to the concept of socialisation: the development of sex roles focuses on processes by which the genders assume to have different personality characteristics, skills and preferences. The question of whether women, or men, actually become the people the stereotypes predict remains open: following Cynthia Fuchs Epstein, the question may be posed by asking "how much a girl's occupational choice is affected by her being given a dress or overalls to wear, or a doll or truck to play with?" (Fuchs Epstein 1988, 139).

Knowledge about the relationship between so-called socialising experiences and later behaviour is still limited. However, it can be stated that the impact of socialisation is not dependent on any single act or set of acts or influences (doll/truck) but on their consistency and the absence of other socialising experiences, particularly later in life. According to Fuchs Epstein, the impact of socialisation depends on the way society defines the links between early experiences and later social roles. For example, boys who become doctors are disproportionately likely to have had fathers who were doctors (Fuchs Epstein 1988).

How are socialisation processes established and how are they changed? The role model does not provide any answer to this question, since it does not take into account changes between structures (e.g. societal roles) and actors (women's intentional behaviour). This has lead to the third definition of gender, namely that gender roles, or models of behaviour, are attached more closely to culture, than to the individual, even though such models seem to act on a specifically individual level (Rantalaiho 1988, 37). Thus, it may be argued that differences between cultures explain, for instance, differences in the behaviour of self-employed women in different countries. Common to these three above-mentioned definitions of gender is that *gender is assumed to be separate from the historical context in which it is developed. Gender is treated as a separate variable, and e.g. society is not seen gendered. Theories as such are treated as gender neutral.*

In the context of research on self-employed women, this means that women can be compared with men and that men´s and women´s personality traits can be compared, in terms of various theories. However, this definition of gender fails to question the theoretical underlying framework and its suitability (Acker et al. 1983). A discipline of this kind is virtually untouched by gender issues, even though the "additive approach" (which simply adds the study of women onto the existing body of knowledge about men) exists in much of the entrepreneurial research that deals with women.[6] However, studies employing an additive approach have usually failed to bring out the significance of entrepreneurship in the structuring of women's lives (see Kovalainen 1990).

As gender gained increasing emphasis as a theoretical construction and not only as a variable, attention focused more on the analytical problems, theoretical constructions and social structures of the social sciences. The analysis of gender and gendered structures entered a stage in which the premises of various theories were subjected to the critical analysis. In its widest meaning, *gender can be defined as social, cultural and ideological relationship*, and men and women as parts of this relationship. Thus gender is no longer taken as one neutral variable among others, or as a separate factor which lies loosely outside of theories. This definition means that *gender is structured inside social, cultural and ideological structures; it is an asymmetrical relationship and recreated continuously in the above mentioned structures* (Rantalaiho 1988).[7] Moreover, the idea of the biological basis of gender is restructured: The seemingly given biological nature of sex has been revealed to be a socially constructed and culturally changing phenomenon in many ways (Flax 1987; Rantalaiho 1988; Silius 1992). The definition of gender I use in this study derives from these ideas: I utilise the concept of gender as a *social* category. This means that my point of departure is that of gender being socially constructed category according to which hierarchies and dualities in society are created, and that different social conditions hold for both genders.

The social construction of gender, and its usage as an analytical category, means that the concept of gender is different from its 'everyday' meaning. According to this way of theorising the gender relationship, both men and women are created via gender relations (Flax 1987), but equality, for example, is found to be absent from gender relations once the power dimension is taken into account.

One essential aspect of the definition of gender has been that of the changing

---

6. As Maynard has argued, literature of this nature tends to be of the *'women and...'* variety, and it has now been produced for most of the sub-areas in sociology (Maynard 1990, 270).

7. The historical construction of the concept of gender is thus defined much wider than e.g. in Foucault's postmodern definition (see Connell 1985, 267).

nature of the content of gender: social constructions change over time and place and cannot be defined as constitutive and stable. As Jane Flax (1987) has argued, the analysis of gender may prove difficult in the sense that gender relations enter into, and are constituent elements in, every aspect of human experience. In turn, *both the individual experience of gender relations and the structure of gender as a social category are shaped by the interactions of gender relations and other social relations such as class and race.* According to this definition, gender relations have no fixed essence; they vary both at a given point in time and over time (Flax 1990), but gender is still a constitutive element in society. Not only actors, but also structures, meanings and institutions are seen as gendered (Saarinen 1992, 51).

This 'epochal' change in the definition of gender creates an interesting set of connections between postmodern philosophy and feminist theories. The importance of the epistemological subject and object, i.e. *what are the connections between knowledge and 'women's experiences'*, has been crucial in metatheoretical discussions of feminist theories. According to some approaches 'women's experiences' are the constituting element of knowledge, while on the other side of the continuum approaches are to be found which argue that it is inadequate to see 'women's experiences' as the constituting element of theory. According to Margareta Hallberg, the connections between epistemological discussion and gender have so far been somewhat difficult to establish (Hallberg 1992).

Feminists, like postmodernists, have sought to develop new paradigms of social criticism which do not rely on traditional philosophical underpinnings. According to Sylvia Walby, the main value of postmodern philosophy has been to reveal the potential dangers in theorising gender inequality only at an abstract and general level (Walby 1990, 16). Nancy Fraser and Linda Nicholson, two postmodernists, deny the ontological difference between genders, and argue that postmodernism provides feminism with some useful methodological ideas. In particular, they encourage a wariness toward generalisations which transcend the boundaries of culture and region (Fraser – Nicholson 1990, 3). The relationship between feminist theories and postmodern philosophies has not been without its tensions. To a large extent it is the division between different epistemological approaches which has been, and still is, the crucial question in feminist research. The tension between feminist empiricism, feminist standpoint theories and feminist postmodernism still exists. The well-known classification of feminism into feminist empirism, feminist standpoint theories and feminist postmodernism derives from the work of Sandra Harding (1983, 1986). Instead of epistemological divisions she uses the concept of 'justification strategies'; however, the content is same. This categorisation is not complete in the sense that not all theories fit the classification, but it does seem to cover most of them.

In contrast to the two perspectives discussed above, postmodern approaches reject objectivism and the search for the 'truth', and emphasise partiality and contextuality. The basic ideas of the gender system, i.e. of considering gender as a basic analytical category and seeing society as a gender system, are questioned, and the concept of gender is deconstructed. According to postmodernist views of society, there are no unities or large, all-encompassing structures, but merely fragmentation with various dominant discourses. Knowledge that is subjective and contextual is essential; all-encompassing theories, such as theories of patriarchy and of the gender system, are not seen sensitive to historical and cultural variations. However, in their contingency, postmodern theories, even feminist theories, are sometimes criticised for failing to see structural continuities, e.g. in the analysis of social context of power relations (see e.g. Hekman 1990).

Classifications, such as the one above, are always problematic in that they not only give a static picture but to some extent also simplify things, and thus sometimes create artificial barriers. One essential feature which has been sketched in different metatheories and epistemological theories, concerns how these theories relate to the differences between genders, and how they relate to mainstream (malestream) theories and, moreover, how they justify their critique of the malestream.[8]

3.1.2. Methodological consequences of the concept of gender

Interestingly, the connections between feminist theoretical constructions and postmodern philosophy shed some light on the methodological discussion within feminist studies. Right from the beginning, criticisms of traditional research methods have, however, also generated a questioning of alternative feminist methods. Is there a distinctive feminist method which can be used as a criterion by which to judge the adequacy of research designs, procedures and results? (Harding 1987a). A *methodology* consists of both a theory and an analysis of how research proceeds or should proceed, while a research *method* is a technique for proceeding or way of proceeding in order to gather evidence. But the questioning of feminist methodology and method has also been followed by a questioning of feminist theories of knowledge. My intention here is not to become enmeshed in epistemological discussion: that task is too demanding for this study. Rather, the aim is to present some interesting themes

---

8. A short overview of the two main views has been made by e.g. Ruoho 1990. See also Hekman 1990 of the various elements of postmodern feminism.

which have been of importance to my own thinking and my work.

Even though feminists have argued that traditional epistemologies, whether intentionally or unintentionally, systematically exclude the possibility that women could be 'knowers' or *agents of knowledge* (see e.g. Harding 1987a), epistemological viewpoints are not unilinear in women´s studies, feminist research, or studies concerning women. Discussions of feminist epistemology (e.g. Hekman 1987; Grant 1987; Benhabib 1990; Smith 1990) have presented a challenge not only to philosophy but also to social sciences by questioning the appropriateness of the fundamental dichotomies and rationalism of Enlightenment thinking.

According to this critique, questions concerning the level of analysis, the degree of abstraction, the type of explanation, standards for the assessment of evidence and the tropes discourse should be considered in concrete situations, not as universal discourses.[9] In spite of the complexity of cognition, there is a common feature in most discourses, namely that knowledge is socially constructed and pluralistic.[10] The notion of the subject and the importance of experience are problematic areas in some epistemological discussions: the personal identity/subject and epistemic subject are often regarded as being the same, not different from each other (Ruotsalainen 1992).

The debate on epistemological questions is reflected at the level of methodological inquiry as well. The question that usually arises in this context is whether there is a special feminist methodology and even method. The different answers to this question reflect basic differences in epistemological viewpoints. According to Sandra Harding, for example, it is still a matter of debate as to whether there is a distinctive 'feminist methodology' – which in this context has nothing to do with the level of data collection or the ethics of research practices – if by this we mean the theory and analysis of how research should proceed (Harding 1987a). Harding's view has been criticised by Jane Flax who sees Harding's ideas of the 'objectivity' in the standpoint theories as being connected to the ideology of Enlightenment. The influence upon epistemological thinking of the Enlightenment with its notion of a sharp difference between the universal and particular, culture and nature, soul and

9. See, for example, the essays in Discovering Reality: Feminist Perspectives on Epistemology, Metaphysics, Methodology, and Philosophy of Science, ed. by Sandra Harding and Merrill B. Hintikka (Dortrecht, Holland: D. Reidel, 1983).

10. However, there are a wide number of views on epistemology ranging from the ideas presented in Stanley and Wise's book in 1983 to those presented by Flax (1990) and earlier in Harding (1986). The former views see experiences as being always valid, thus there is no need for us to extend our research analysis and interest beyond everyday experiences (Stanley – Wise 1983). The ideas of Flax and Harding are, perhaps, closer to the 'standard' or mainstream epistemological discourse (Flax 1983, 1990; Harding 1986).

body, reason and emotion (see Alison Jaggar and Susan Bordo 1989), has been criticised by feminism, and by other critiques grounded, e.g., in hermeneutical sociology.

The importance of private and individual experiences which in turn can be reflected into a larger field, has been one of the main starting premises in feminist methods. According to Shulamit Reinharz (1992), a feminist theory of research methods raises questions of *identity* (what are feminist research methods?) and of *difference* (what is the difference between feminist research methods and other research methods; how do feminist research methods differ from one another?) (Reinharz 1992). However, it may be asked whether this is the proper way of asking such questions. Harding sees this, to some extent, as problematic: according to Harding, it is sometimes - falsely - supposed that a kind of relativism would result from feminism using women's experiences rather than men's as an empirical and theoretical resource (Harding 1987a and 1987b).

It would seem more promising to pose the question in the way Liisa Rantalaiho has done. According to Rantalaiho, the usual image of women as being different from men, easily creates the idea that women as researchers are more likely to want to use different (i.e. qualitative) methods to those associated with male researchers (i.e. quantitative methods). Since this view has a basis in reality and is related to a particular way of defining gender, as well as to certain culturally defined ways of defining femininity and masculinity, it is not without a certain logical ring to it. But, as Rantalaiho points out, the importance and meaning of research is to problematise the origins of cultural femininity and masculinity, and to ask how these are produced and assimilated, what is the historical background and social conditions for the culturally defined genders (Rantalaiho 1988, 41). Thus, the focus on specific feminist methods would not be the main issue.

3.2. Shifting definitions – gender and patriarchy as analytical categories

3.2.1. Gender as an analytical category

In chapter 3.1.1., I briefly sketched the development of the concept of gender from the level of a single variable to the level of an analytical category. The idea that social structure and social processes are *gendered* implies that *gender can be seen as an analytic category* (Acker 1991; Connell 1987). Gender is thus not only a social structure but a structure that pervades all social processes and relationships. Joan Scott, for example, defines gender as follows: "The core of the definition rests on an *integral* connection between two propositions; gender is a constitutive element of social relationships based on perceived differences between the sexes, and gender is a primary way of signifying relationships of power" (Scott 1986, 167, emphasis added). The role of gender in the construction of social, cultural and ideological relationships implies that it should be neither considered as one neutral variable among others, nor as a random, untheorisable factor that has no influence on theory construction (Rantalaiho 1988, 39-40).

The shift in the definition of gender in the direction of a conception of gendered structures of society has meant the enlargement and diversification of the discourses of feminist research. This does not mean, however, that there is any general agreement on the contents and emphasis of the various elements which are dominant in the concept. Generalisations about gender may be obscured if judged in terms of a clear-cut Cartesian universe. In fact gender never exhibits itself in a 'pure form', but only in the context of lives that are shaped by a diversity of influences (Grimshaw 1986). The debate about ways of conceptualising gender has been important because it has led to an examination of the system of structures arising from it, as well as an explanation of the patterns of inequality between women and men (Maynard 1990). A critical examination of the concept of gender, e.g. in an organisational context, reveals that much of the literature still refers to it in the sense of role and display. Both of these facets of gender focus on the behavioural aspects of women or men, not on the asymmetrical relationship which constitutes social relationships, social structures and social processes. I will take up further aspects of the gender questions, such as the rationality of feelings of responsibility and of reproduction, which hopefully open up more channels to the concept of gender.

Gender could be differentiated according to its various levels, which both constitute and reproduce various meanings contained within it. For example, Sandra Harding divides gender into three layers. These levels are the structural, the symbolic and the individual levels.[11] *At the structural level,* according to Silius (1992, 27) *gender is both structural in nature and an active producer of structures.*[12] At the symbolic level, various cultural symbols of masculinity and femininity, such as 'positive/positivity' referring to masculinity, and 'negative/negativity' referring to femininity as developed e.g. in the work of

---

11. Scott (1988) further divides Harding's categories into four parts, but as I see it, this division does not bring any new elements to the discussion.

12. The idea of structures and actors within structures is presented in the theory of structuration by Anthony Giddens.

Julia Kristeva, (see Cornell – Thurschwell 1987). This also means that both women and men are created through processes which are relational. The relational nature of gender brings the concept closer to the postmodern feminist theories discussed earlier. Finally, Harding's third level is that of the individual. This level is closest to the notion of a personal gender identity. It provides no single image of how gender identities are created, but rather emphasises socialisation processes which occupy an important position in the construction of gender identities.

The different kind of socialisation process operating in respect of women has been explained by recourse to class analysis on the one hand (e.g. Strandell 1983), or by resort to patriarchy theories on the other. *The concept of the rationality of responsibility* has been introduced as a result of empirically based gender studies (see e.g. Anttonen 1989; Simonen 1990). Broadly defined, this latter approach refers to the way in which women act as care-givers within paid employment as well as in the home. This way of acting does not refer to specific sets of concrete actions but, for example, to the meaning attached to personal responsibility and care-giving in the production of the social structures of everyday life. Taking care of other people's needs leads to a certain way of acting and behaving. However, the rationality of responsibility cannot be thought of as a "women's universal form of acting" (Anttonen 1989, 131-132).

The connection between the rationality of responsibility concept and other social theories has been explored in the works of Jürgen Habermas. According to Anneli Anttonen, "the conceptualisation of women's care work is to some extent analogical to Habermas' idea of conceptualising the lifeworld system in terms of communicative rationalisation", which deals with the communal structures of everyday life (Anttonen 1989, 132). Habermas sees the modernisation of society taking place through the rationalisation of society. The different parts of society are rationalised in different ways: communicative rationality, the idea of the universal language, can be seen as a core element in the rationalisation process. This very strong claim, 'the communicative action requires an interpretation that is rational in approach', is grounded in Habermas's theory of communicative action (Habermas 1988).

Communicative actions combine the different parts of the structures of the lifeworld to each other through different processes. The different structures in question refer to culture, society and personality, while the corresponding reproduction processes concern the reproduction of culture, social integration and socialisation (Habermas 1987, 153-173). Communicative action does not include reproduction in the sense that this concept is understood and defined in feminist theories; i.e. as the reproduction of everyday life. The theory of communicative action only includes the concepts of the material and symbolic reproduction of societies. Material reproduction comprises what Habermas calls "social labour". Symbolic reproduction comprises the socialisation of the young, the cementing of group solidarity and the transmission and extension of cultural traditions. This distinction between material and symbolic reproduction which is argued to be conceptually inadequate by feminist philosophers, is assumed to be natural in form (Fraser 1987, 33). The incompatibility between Habermas' communicative rationality and the concept of rationality of responsibility found within feminist theories is discussed in Seyla Benhabib and Drucilla Cornell (1987) and Nancy Fraser (1987).[13]

The concept of reproduction is a theoretical and methodological concept, which seeks to comprehend society, its construction and the way it functions. Furthermore, it is also an analytical concept, which can be deployed when research is being undertaken into the maintenance of social structures. As an example I may point to the development of occupational qualifications, their maintenance and their status. In an American study concerning female managers, it has been noticed that once a woman manager has become a mother her professional standing is diminished in the eyes of her superiors. This loss of standing also affects the self-image of many women managers with children, as if giving birth somehow magically removes a woman's accumulated knowledge and competence (Nicholson – West 1988). This is not necessarily true in the Finnish context. However, it clearly reflects the value structure of the working life in the cultural context where the study was made.

The use of the family as the central link between gender and society in such studies of professional standing and perceived competence, is closely related to a functionalist way of explaining women's position in society. However, it can also be found in conventional class analysis. The concept of reproduction can also be seen as a special area of social action; a sphere where the reproduction of the labour force and of citizens takes place (Rantalaiho 1986a, 31, 40).[14]

A different way of looking at gender is to approach it textually. This tradition is connected to the postmodern condition in which, in the words of Lyotard, "grand narratives of legitimation" are no longer credible. Grand narratives produce overarching philosophies of history such as the Enlightenment story of the progress of reason and freedom (Fraser –

---

13. Unfortunately I cannot go deeper into the discussion of Habermas's theoretical constructions here. However, the feminist criticism is very well documented and grounded.

14. As I see it, 'diversity in the definitions of reproduction' refers to the growing discussion between feminism and postmodernism, and to the rejection of 'grand theories', universalistic social theories and concepts which have universal significance. Fraser and Nicholson go further and advise social theorists *first* to construct genealogies of *categories* e.g. of reproduction, sexuality and mothering, before assuming their universal significance (Fraser – Nicholson 1990, 31).

Nicholson 1990). Much criticism in feminist discussion has also been directed to this point: one source of difficulty in early feminist social theories was precisely this presumption of a grandiose conception of theory. As Fraser and Nicholson put it, "theory was understood as the search for the one key factor which would explain sexism cross-culturally and illuminate all of social life" (Fraser – Nicholson 1990, 29).

The textual approach, however, reveals several difficulties when, for example, an attempt is made to analyse different gendered structures in society. Gender relations may be produced within the same ongoing practices, e.g. within work organisations. In other words, gender relations need not be produced through patriarchal structures found in social organisations (Acker 1991). Another aspect to this question is presented by Sylvia Walby (1989). Walby argues that patriarchy is created by practices which are best analysed as a set of institutionally rooted discourses, rather than as a free-floating ideology.

The importance of this discussion has been to produce the theoretical basis for an account of women's self-employment, and in offering some theoretical explanatory models as to why women's work, paid work, or working in self-employment, are restricted to certain areas of the economy. One aspect of this explanation concerns the concept of patriarchy which is discussed in more detail in the next chapter.

3.2.2. The unresolved question of patriarchy?

In addition to gender, the concepts and theories of patriarchy have been used in socio-structural explanations of women's position in society, as well as their position in segmented labour markets. The concept of patriarchy is, however, still a subject for theoretical debate (see e.g. Veronica Beechey 1987 for a presentation of the problem of the concept in respect of empirical research; and Malcolm Waters 1989, Sylvia Walby 1989, 1990, Joan Acker 1989 for more recent contributions to this discussion). Largely as a result of the polymorphous nature of the concept, difficulties have also emerged with regard to empirical practice. (For an overview of the different definitions of patriarchy see e.g. Waters 1989, 193-195.) The concept of gender inequality has been used as an analytical alternative to patriarchy theory in many recent treatments of capitalism. It has also been argued that gender inequality is too complex to be traced back to a single structure (Walby 1989). Attempts have been made to use patriarchy theories in the analysis of the labour market structures and their operation. However, such analysis has tended to remain at a very general level, since the operationalization of the concept is problematic at the empirical level (for further discussion of this point see Walby 1986, 50-52).

Most of those who have deployed the concept of patriarchy have started from the assumption that social power structures, within a given society, make possible value hierarchies and hierarchical ways of using power, and so provide a basis for the subordination of women (see e.g. Walby 1986). This concept implies that patriarchy is *analytically separate* from the capitalist system of production, not derived from it. Some researchers see patriarchy as being interwoven with capitalism into a system in which the connection between the material basis of production and men's control over women creates possibilities to control, for example, women's labour force participation (see Hartmann 1983). The subordination of women is seen as indirect and part of a complex system. A number of patriarchy theories have treated patriarchal relations as a constitutive structure of society. The problems with this conception relate to the attempt to widen its scope from specific sets of relations to cover the whole of society and its development.

When patriarchy is defined as arising from within the economy, and interconnected with capitalism, its usage appears problematic. Once the concept is understood in these terms, it becomes ahistorical, and thus difficult to define. Another problem arises from the categorisation of women as belonging to one more or less homogeneous 'class', over which the power of patriarchy is exercised, either through economic mechanisms (Michele Barrett 1985; Heidi Hartmann 1981), or social and material conditions (Brekke – Haukaa 1980; see also Anna Jonasdottir 1988). When patriarchy is defined in terms of social exchange relationships, the importance of the family has often been undervalued, and considered only in respect of its 'reproductive role', or even treated negatively, as a factor hindering the breakdown of patriarchy.

All of these problems connected to the concept of patriarchy have been subjects of discussion for at least three decades now, and irrespective of whether or not patriarchy is reducible to capitalism, strong arguments have been made both for and against a dual system analysis. The dual system strategy used, for example, by Waters (1989) and Walby (1986, 1989) treats patriarchy as a system or structure outside and independent of other systems or structures. This way of theorising patriarchy undoubtedly creates problems. However, as Walby notes, it would be surprising if competing theories of patriarchy did not use the term in slightly different ways, since the meaning of the term has evolved since Weber, who used it to refer to a system of government in which men ruled societies through their position as heads of households (Walby 1990).

Instead of treating patriarchy as one of a number of analytically independent structures, and analysis of linkages between these structures, Acker (1989) starts from the assumption that *social relations are constituted through processes in which the linkages are in-built.* For example, Acker argues that neither gender nor class relations, which may be produced within the same ongoing processes, can be adequately theorised in isolation from one another. However, since Acker´s criticism of dual systems analysis, Walby has developed her concept of patriarchy into a fuller and more flexible formula, which allows for a more developed analysis of changes in gender relations.

In reply to earlier criticism, Walby sees patriarchy as needing to be conceptualised at different *levels of abstraction*. At the most abstract level, she argues that patriarchy exists as a system of social relations. This corresponds to the definition given in the beginning of this chapter. At the next level down, Walby divides patriarchy into *six different structures*. According to Walby, it is possible to identify sets of patriarchal practices within each of these structures which are less deeply sedimented. Walby´s six societal structures comprise: the patriarchal mode of production, patriarchal relations within paid work, patriarchal relations within the state, male violence, patriarchal relations in sexuality, and patriarchal relations in cultural institutions such as religion, the media and education.

As Walby notes, patriarchy is not an historical constant, and thus it is important to differentiate the different forms of patriarchy from differences in the degree of patriarchy, and not to *conflate* these two dimensions. The degree of patriarchy refers to the intensity of oppression within a specified dimension, for instance the size of the wage gap between women and men (Walby 1990).

Further, Walby expands her analysis of patriarchy by distinguishing two forms of patriarchy: private and public patriarchy, which differ on a variety of levels and in regard to the strategies they adopt. In short, private patriarchy is based upon household production, while public patriarchy is based on structures other than those of the household, e.g. employment and the state. However, the private and public forms of patriarchy constitute a continuum rather than a rigid dichotomy. In each type of patriarchy, the six structures mentioned above are present, but the relationship between them and their relative significance is different. Further, there is movement from private to public patriarchy within each of the six patriarchal structures. Walby has traced a shift from an exclusionist strategy to a segregationist one within paid work in British work history (Walby 1990, 179). In order to be able to analyse differences in the forms of patriarchy it is further necessary to divide the public form of patriarchy into two: one founded upon the labour market and the other upon the state.

Walby's arguments are supported by a series of industrial and occupational case studies which document the systematic exclusion of women in Britain from both access to 'better' jobs, and from full participation in the labour market. Crompton (1990, 580), for example, considers this discussion valuable because of its emphasis on the non-domestic constraints which have been placed upon women. All too often, as I will discuss in chapter 4 in relation to economic theories, problems faced by women in employment are perceived as originating solely in the domestic sphere.

The complexity and flexibility of Walby´s theorisation of patriarchy discussed here, shows that even if it is a useful concept for the analysis of women's position in society and, more specifically, women's work, it remains problematic in certain respects. Patriarchy comes in more than one form, and each of these forms may be found in differing degrees. It is important to realise that, for Walby, patriarchy and not gender occupies a position as a primary analytical category. This sometimes creates certain problems when trying to combine the ideas of Walby with those of theorists who emphasise the gender system instead of patriarchy.

However, by developing the theory of patriarchy into a formula which includes different forms and structures, Walby has been able to respond to the criticism of patriarchy, and also to answer the problems of reductionism and essentialism, arguments which have been used against the universalistic definitions of concepts such as patriarchy, male domination and gender. I do not seek to argue here that the concept of patriarchy provides the one and only way of explaining gender relations. Rather, I treat patriarchy as one, undoubtedly important, thread in the theoretical tapestry that I am attempting to weave.

3.3. Concluding remarks: how to study gender?

One conclusion from the above discussions would be to argue that, in order to grasp the whole picture of women's self-employment, it is simply not enough to "add women" on to the existing theoretical discussions on self-employment and entrepreneurship. *The inclusion of women also demands a thorough-going discussion of the theoretical constructions used for the analysis of phenomena, in this case self-employment and entrepreneurship.* This is important since women´s self-employment has not figured as a central theoretical focus for research within women´s studies. Women´s studies and feminist research have been 'accused' of a one-sided concentration upon the Marxist approach e.g. in respect of class research (Goffee – Scase 1985). I consider this to be a logical consequence of the various developmental phases mentioned earlier, even though feminist research - especially in Anglo-Saxon countries - has been rather strongly committed to Marxist analysis, which has also influenced the selection of the research subject (see e.g. Harding 1986). Still, this seems to apply only to the discussions of the 1970s and 1980s. In addition to this, the dominant malestream tradition within research on self-employment has focused solely and squarely on men, and has also generated this knowledge with respect to women. Economic analyses have been seen as valid even if they have only dealt with men, and their activity within the economy. As Richard Swedberg puts it: *"By excluding women from the scientific analysis of how the economy functions, a fine opportunity has been missed to show that the economy can indeed be understood primarily as a social enterprise."* (Swedberg 1987, 65).

Women's self-employment and changes in it can be analysed from several points of view. When the individual level is the focus of research, factors such as education, age, socio-economic status, etc. are taken into account. These factors are sometimes commonly identified as 'occupational obstacles or barriers' which limit women's possibilities to participate in waged work. The implicit assumption in this notion is, however, that working outside the home is somehow 'exceptional' for women. When the general development of the whole group of self-employed women is the focus of research, or cross-national comparisons between the development processes are being made, it is possible to make comparisons between social differences. My study focuses on the developmental features of self-employed women, but I use interviews of individual women's experiences as research material as well, to be able to illustrate the gendered nature of self-employment at the individual level, and not only at the structural level. As I see it, the importance of individual experiences is not only in their individuality but also in the fact that they can be reflected into a broader field of experiences.

At the structural level, according to Silius (1992, 27) *gender is both a structure and an active producer of structures,* as mentioned earlier. How is this structural feature of the concept of gender studied in the context of self-employment? As I see it, when I look at the development of women's self-employment over a period of time and look at the possible changes and variations, or possible rigidity of women's self-employment, at the same time I look at gender as a structure. Thus, both women's self-employment and the development that has taken place within women's self-employment are something more than just a summed number of self-employed women at a given time period. Gender as a structure carries within itself various representations, meanings and concrete actions, which together create the structure and variations – or rigidity – of women's self-employment. How does it come about that textile retailing or grocering are feminine industries, while cleaning business is a male one?

51

Gendering processes in society - by which I mean, for instance, the birth and reproduction of various persistent structures, which (as I will show later in my work) set men and women into various rigid economic positions and different industrial areas, e.g. in self-employment - are not born by themselves. How these gendering processes and gendered patterns are produced and again reproduced, is a complex question which is perhaps answered for its own part by the interview material I discuss in my work.

4 Concepts and theories of self-employment and entrepreneurship

Earlier (in Chapter 1.3., 'On the concepts of self-employment and entrepreneurship') I briefly discussed definitions of the terms 'self-employment', 'small business' and 'entrepreneurship'. In this chapter I shall broaden the discussion into various facets of entrepreneurship and self-employment. My intention is to start from the economics and proceed into main aspects of sociological research; then to discuss the different perspectives and give a comprehensive overview of the variety of ways of describing entrepreneurship; and of how the concept of entrepreneurship/ self-employment has developed into that which is understood today. Secondly, I will describe the sort of results yielded by research into women's self-employment, and present a classification of the typology of women entrepreneurs. I will then proceed to examine more general conditions for women's employment, namely the labour market theories, which also structure the theoretical field of explaining women's self-employment. Finally I shall take up the two concepts discussed in the previous chapter, which I see as indispensable both in arranging those theories discussed and for an analysis of women's self-employment. As Sylvia Walby says: *"While most of the interesting work on gender inequality has been done within feminist perspectives, this is sometimes in reaction to the 'malestream' orthodoxies. It is thus useful to give an account of these in order to understand not only errors of the conventional perspectives in the social sciences but also the shape of the alternative feminist arguments."* (Walby 1990, 2)

4.1. Traditional points of departure

The definition of entrepreneurship is somewhat open and ambiguous, ranging from 'intrapreneurship' (which may be defined as decision-making within the company) to different motivation or action-based theories in the definition of entrepreneurship and, in the most extreme case, to all actions by any individual. Usually, however, entrepreneurship is discussed in the context of small businesses or the start-up process of new businesses. Until recently the concept of entrepreneurship has been connected solely to private ownership and the market economy. However, with the increasing development of joint ventures etc., this view no longer appears so self-evident.

Different discussions of the content of the concept of entrepreneurship are more or less directly related to the various scientific fields of study.[1] These definitions can be divided into psychologically, sociologically and economically oriented definitions. This division is to some extent artificial since the definitions used rarely match precisely the given institutional limits. However, the division is useful as a heuristic tool in this context since many of the definitions used in research follow these orientations. Representatives of classical sociological theory and classical economic theory (Weber, Sombart, Schumpeter and the French Année Sociologique group) are more difficult to put into this division because of the broadness of their approaches. *A crucial factor from the point of view of this study is how women's self-employment can be explained in the different theoretical contexts*[2]. Even if the most essential task of this research may not lie in this theoretical contribution, the analysis of different theories in terms of their adequacy and sufficiency as explanatory paradigms in respect of women's self-employment or entrepreneurship, is crucial. Further, we can see this analysis as essential since the historical connection between different concepts and their use in current research is not always explicitly stated.[3]

4.2. The entrepreneur in classical economic theory – the invisible hand in the economy?

The entrepreneur had an important role in the eighteenth century economy, according to early economists from Say and Cantillon to John Stuart Mill, even if there were differences in the emphasis each writer placed upon that role. Say emphasised the meaning of the entrepreneur for economic advancement, a

---

1. It could be argued that there are as many definitions of entrepreneurship and self-employment – ranging from the highly theoretical debates all the way down to the statistical ambiguities – as there are researchers. See for example Stanworth – Curran 1986.

2. The use of term explanation here refers to historical and general features, not to causal explanation.

3. According to some researchers, research into entrepreneurship is theoretically weak (Lundin 1986). In spite of the problems, this judgement is in my opinion, however, somewhat overstated.

question which was also discussed by the physiocrats of the early eighteenth century (E.g. Quesnay, Turgot) (see Kovalainen 1989b). In classical economics the entrepreneur did not have a "special" position in economic development, but theorists in the mould of Adam Smith did emphasise the division of work as a precondition for growth and welfare in the national economy (Smith 1776/1982, 429-449). The early idea of an entrepreneur as a middleman for goods in the equilibrium economy changed with changes in the economy and economic theory. The focus in economic research changed from that of delivery and accumulation to the question of efficiency. At the same time, price theory grew in importance (Swedberg 1987, 26).[4]

Joseph Schumpeter's view of the rise of entrepreneurship deviates from that of earlier economists. His starting point is the operation of a "circular flow" in the economy; theorised as a form of closed economic equilibrium which does not exist in reality. In the real world equilibrium is interfered with by the entrepreneur, who is the exceptional, energetic agent, who innovates to produce new products and thus develops the economy further. This development is not initiated by consumers through demand but by the active intervention of the entrepreneur. "The producer ... initiates economic change, and consumers are educated by him if necessary; they are, as it were, taught to want new things, or things which differ in some respect or some other from those which they have been in the habit of using." (Schumpeter 1934, 74).

Innovation was the primary adjective which Schumpeter ascribed to entrepreneurship. According to this view, however, ownership did not necessarily mean entrepreneurship, but was more firmly connected to risk-taking. From a sociological viewpoint the entrepreneur did not necessarily have any specific class-position – at least not according to Schumpeter's definition, since entrepreneurship was not a stable position or profession, but more a functional way to channel entrepreneurial ideas into the real world (Kovalainen 1989b).

Later developments in economics focused on different things altogether. At the same time the importance of the entrepreneur was seen to have diminished (Haahti 1989, 205). After the "Methodenstreit" the entrepreneur was given importance in the work of the Austrian school, which emphasised the instability of, and the imperfect state of knowledge concerning, the functioning of the markets. At the same time the role of the entrepreneur in the economy

---

4. With the rise of neoclassical economics so-called institutional factors lost their explanatory power and instead the factors in the price formation rose in importance. This development in economics caused a conflict among economists (so-called Methodenstreit), which encouraged many economists – among whom are to be included e.g. Sombart and Schmoller – to seek alternatives to abstract economic theory (Swedberg 1987, 1989; Manicas 1987).

changed from the original one given to him (economic man) in the classic political economy.[5]

Most of the theories concerning entrepreneurship are combinations of two factors: innovation and uncertainty. Briefly stated, these two factors have three points in common. The first of these points is an assumption that entrepreneurship is the vital ingredient providing for efficient markets (neoclassical economy). The second point involves the ascription of individualistic rather than social causes and influences for the growth of entrepreneurship. Finally, most theories of entrepreneurship are functional, being based upon an assumption of the essentialness of the entrepreneur in the economy (this is especially true of the Austrian school). These three points are crucial in distinguishing the economic and the business economic approach from the sociological one, which is discussed in the next chapter.

4.3. The entrepreneur in sociological research

4.3.1. Connections with economics

The picture of the importance of entrepreneurship in the economy has been presented above all through the writings of Max Weber and Karl Marx. Their influence can be seen more or less directly in all sociological research dealing with entrepreneurship. For Marx, the position of the entrepreneur in society is revealed through a class theoretical approach; other aspects of entrepreneurship have remained outside the mainstream of sociological research. This projects the idea (prevalent in sociology as well as in economics) that large companies and their employment relations and organisational developments reflect better the present situation and future trends in industrial societies (see e.g. Granovetter 1984). An exception to this approach is found in those class and strata studies which connect the analysis of self-employment with broader structures of society and changes within them, or in studies which inspect the development of the welfare society (e.g. Toivonen 1987, 1989; Steinmetz – Wright 1989; Kivinen 1989).

The criteria for defining entrepreneurship in sociological research – at least in the sociology of work – has been the ownership of the means of production combined with a relatively large degree of autonomy in respect of an actor's work tasks. This follows the definition given in chapter 1.3. One important

---

5. In his dissertation Haahti considers the behaviouristic trend in the theory of the firm to be equivalent to coherent theories of entrepreneurship, especially to theories of small businesses (Haahti 1989, 213).

empirical criterion in statistical definitions of entrepreneurship is that an own-account worker does not employ paid employees. Family members may assist in the business, but such 'helpers' are not paid for their work. This ideal type – or definition – of the entrepreneur is not very common: particular studies of women's work and female owned businesses have revealed that the concept of entrepreneurship – or self-employment – is problematic in the sense that not even businesses owned by women fulfil these requirements of autonomy and ownership (Hakim 1984, Dale 1986, Westwood – Bhachu 1988). Despite its problematic nature, this concept has received much attention within both class and stratification research, and its influence has been especially pronounced during the 1980s (e.g. Goldthorpe 1983; Erikson – Goldthorpe 1988; Leiulfsrud – Woodward 1985; Woodward – Leiulfsrud 1987).

According to Jouko Nätti, the discussion of entrepreneurship has come to the fore more as a consequence of the growth and the influence of women's studies and feminist research, and the discussions they have engendered, than as a result of debate generated within a class theoretical perspective (Nätti 1989, 42). Feminist researchers have also criticised labour market theories for failing to include in their theoretical premises any consideration of the possible implications that the rise of entrepreneurship may have on women's position in the labour market. One important development relevant to the discussion concerns the changing patterns of women's employment and position in society in general.

It has been argued that at the level of abstract collectivities, class theories are gender-blind (Crompton – Sanderson 1989). It has also been argued that gender-blindness is not a substantive criticism of either Marxist or Weberian class theory in the abstract (Lockwood 1986). Gender has not, historically, constituted the basis of a structure of social action similar to that of a class or status group, although this should not be allowed to obscure the fact that men have combined to exclude women, and women to resist these practices (Walby 1988).

According to the conventional view elaborated in class and stratification studies, the work of women in the labour market as well as in the home is considered rather unimportant when compared to male paid employment, and keeping this as a starting point, women could be classified as belonging to the same societal class as their husbands (Goldthorpe 1983, Delphy 1981). It has been argued, by Christine Delphy (1981) among others, that stratification is an area where the androcentrism of the subject is most entrenched. According to this view the class-position of the wife is derived from the husband's class-position and thus, like other economic dependencies within the family, reflects reality. The inadequacies of this traditional view have been subjected to severe criticism. Results from a number of studies show, for example, that the consumption patterns, life-styles and standards of living of so-called cross-class families, where wives have attained a higher level of education than their husbands, are defined more through the work of wives than of husbands (Woodward – Leiulfsrud 1987).

Weber's theory of the development of capitalism (especially as set out in 'Wirtschaft und Gesellschaft') includes some of his ideas on entrepreneurship. The position of the entrepreneur in the economy is discussed in many different places in Weber's work. References are made to entrepreneurship in Weber's social economics and in his sociological writings on religion[6]. It is impossible to take up the development of Weber's theory of capitalism here, but my intention is to examine some of the main points concerning the importance of the entrepreneur in Weber's theory and, furthermore, to compare Schumpeter's and Weber's main ideas on entrepreneurship. Weber's entrepreneur does not act outside the economy; his usage of interpretive methodology does not imply that research objects are to be considered in isolation from their environment but rather that they should be seen as part of specific sets of economic actions.[7]

Weber defines economic actions from the sociological viewpoint (as social economic action) but does not abandon the rationality of the economy as a starting point for explanation. Nor does he accept the idea that economic actions can be derived from psychological explanations. *The free organisation of capital through entrepreneurial actions* was one of the most essential components in capitalist economic development (Weber 1923/1961, 232). This organised action takes place through a complex political-governmental system, in which legal control mechanisms are of great importance. The free organisation of capital in the market offers optimal resource allocation possibilities for the entrepreneur: "It must be possible to conduct the provision for needs exclusively on the basis of market opportunities and the calculation of net income." (Weber 1923/1961, 209).

Weber did not try to develop a general theory of action or explanation in respect of individual ways of behaviour, but rather strove "to understand the meaning of single elements together with the concrete causes and effects" (Manicas 1987, 137). Weber's "ideal types" allow for both description and prescription (explanation) while making it possible for us to observe "a single concrete cultural element and the causes and effects for it, and their meaning for

---

6. Swedberg suggests that economic sociology is situated at the interface of these two distinct areas of interest (Swedberg 1987, 30).

7. In this respect Weber's concept of entrepreneur has often been misinterpreted – especially in business economics, where he has been seen mainly as a spokesman for a motivational explanation for the birth of entrepreneurship.

it" (Weber 1975, 65). In the division of rational political action Weber used concepts of goal rationality (Zweckrationalität) and value rationality (Wertrationalität), which with some reservation can also be used when analysing entrepreneurship and different typologies of entrepreneurship.[8] It is worth noting that the Weberian explanatory tradition forms the theoretical premises common to a majority of writers within the Anglo-Saxon tradition of research on entrepreneurship.[9]

In Schumpeter's theory of economic actions the concept of "circular flow" is close to Max Weber's concept of "traditional capitalism", which refers to stable, limited economic circulation without external disturbances. A number of other similarities are to be found in Weber's and Schumpeter's theories. In the first place reference may be made to the importance of "juxtaposition" as a means of theory-building. For Weber, the tight connection (or intertwining) between Protestant ethics and the modern, dynamic capitalist entrepreneur is counterpoised to the picture of Catholicism and the traditional, stable entrepreneur. Schumpeter counterpoises the "circular flow" economy to the developing, changing economy (Macdonald 1965). At the centre of both Schumpeter's and Weber's theories – even if differently emphasised – is the "heroic" entrepreneur, who has all the information he needs in order to act.[10]

A number of other connections between Weber and Schumpeter can be identified. They both reject the idea of the entrepreneur as a person whose main or only driving force is hedonism and greed; a "homogeneous globule of desire of happiness", to quote the words of Veblen (Macdonald 1965, 380). According to Weber, traditionalism is initially the main motive behind entrepreneurship. At a later stage this motive is transformed into a sense of duty divorced from a sense of the religious. Schumpeter sees the rational idea of the possibilities contained in innovations as the main motive force behind entrepreneurship, even if he introduces such unclear concepts as "the will to conquer" into his vision of the entrepreneur (Schumpeter 1934, 78).

The tradition of the Schumpeterian entrepreneurial concept has remained an important factor in business success, especially in those research traditions which emphasise the innovating personality and personal characteristics of the entrepreneur. Examples of this approach can be seen in numerous business

---

8. See the entrepreneur typologies later in chapter 4.3.3.

9. Even though it's difficult to list some studies and leave other out, the above-mentioned starting point can be seen at least in the following research: Bechhofer – Elliott 1974, 1981, 1986; Scase – Goffee 1980; Scase 1982; Stanworth – Curran 1973.

10. Both theories have been criticised for this elitist view. My view is that it is not so much a question of elitism but more of emphasising the role of innovative action as a crucial factor in entrepreneurship.

economic studies (e.g. Ansoff 1979; Carland et al. 1984). However, the Schumpeterian concept of entrepreneurship has often been misused in the sense of failing to follow Schumpeter in connecting, for instance, risk-taking more to ownership than to entrepreneurship. In many studies concerning the entrepreneurial personality, risk-taking has been seen as a *personality trait*.[11]

How does gender relate to these classic ideas of entrepreneurship? In the first place, gender is often considered irrelevant by researchers trying to describe the economy and society at the macro theoretical level in so far as such writers focus on structures and development within these structures, and thus leave economic *actors* as 'shapeless and faceless heroes'. However, we cannot avoid noticing that *the mythical heroic figure*, who is the actor in those theories which take the economic actors into consideration, *is always essentially masculine, and thus excludes feminine ideas.* (For more on the argument of heroic as masculinity, see Sari Näre 1987).

Max Weber did not discuss gender in relation to economic enterprising but he did write about family and marriage in the section titled "The Household Community" in Wirtschaft und Gesellschaft. He inspected family and marriage as social institutions, and examined the emergence of sex-role differentiation and household authority. The household economic unit was "the most widespread" and "continuous" basis of intensive communal action. In Weber's words, the household community is "the fundamental basis of loyalty and authority, which in turn is the basis of many other human communal groups" (Weber 1922/1964, 298). However, Weber did not point out the male bias built into so-called objective culture and reason and logic, which was left for Weber's colleague, George Simmel, to do (see Kandal 1988).

Interestingly, Weber's rationality concept has been applied at the micro level; for example, in analysing women's position within the family (e.g. Ferguson 1984; Harding 1982). Moreover, the analysis of the private and public sphere, and the relation between questions like power within the family and "entering into the markets" – i.e. waged work and the capital markets – have been analysed with the help of Weber's rationality concept. However, a note concerning the *contents* of rationality must be addressed here: The concept of 'rationality of responsibility', briefly discussed in chapter 3, addresses the question of the universalities and categorisations of rationality which e.g. Max Weber produced.

Put very simply, that tradition of sociological research which deviates from Weber's and Schumpeter's ideas of entrepreneurship holds more to the Marxian tradition, and sees small and medium-sized businesses as a part of the capitalist market economy. Within this alternative tradition the major theses concern the

---

11. See for more chapter 4.3.2.

disappearance of the small business strata and the growth of large companies with the development of capital and goods markets. This means that the class-position of entrepreneurs is controversial: small and medium-sized businesses are seen either as competing with large companies or as being dominated by them. The disappearance of small entrepreneurs – either by absorption into the working class or entry into the ranks of the bourgeoisie – has encouraged a view of the petit bourgeoisie as an "intermediate" class standing between the bourgeoisie and the working class (see for example Scase 1982; Steinmetz – Wright 1989; Kivinen 1989).

Attempts to connect the analysis of entrepreneurship with the larger societal structure is primarily found in research on the structure and dynamics of social class or stratum, or in research concerning the consumption patterns of different classes. However, it cannot be said that entrepreneurship from a sociological viewpoint would be focusing on small businesses only as an "involuntary part of the society's mechanism", having a role in certain production, unless we assume that a "sociological picture of a firm would have an emphasis on a traditional business view" (Lahti 1988, 94)[12] This question should be seen as a difference in the levels of approaches, as noted above. For example the entrepreneur´s active role in social interaction is more emphasised in action research (Bertaux et al. 1981; Stanworth – Curran 1973; Kankaanpää – Leimu 1982) than it is in research tradition, which emphasises entrepreneurs as a part of a class or as a social stratum (Szymanski 1983; Steinmetz – Wright 1989; Toivonen 1990).

In the socio-philosophical sense concepts – and symbols – of freedom, independence and autonomy have been brought together in the notion of entrepreneurship. This means, for example, that with the help of the concept of the 'lifeworld' an attempt has been made to connect ways of acting in small business to Weber's and Habermas's concepts of system worlds and thus to show the contrast between lifeworld and systemworld (this kind of schema has been applied by Nooteboom 1988). However, this tradition has not been markedly influential in sociological research on entrepreneurship, even though it appears to be interesting.

---

12. My own translation. In class and strata research much of the analysis of small and medium businesses and their owners has taken place through their class-position. Naturally this viewpoint creates a picture of not having entrepreneurs as actors in their lives.

4.3.2. The personality of the entrepreneur: psychological and social psychological explanations

Theories which focus more on a psychological approach to studying entrepreneurship and the entrepreneur usually seek to connect different kinds of psychological traits and motivational factors in the entrepreneur's personality with her or his success in the endeavours she or he is undertaking. The approach, which emphasises different personality traits as the most important factor influencing the success of the business endeavour, is not the only psychological approach found in research on entrepreneurship, although it is, perhaps, the most influential.

"The psychological complexity" of the entrepreneur – as with the psychological complexity and dynamic structure of any person's psyche – is an accepted factor in research on entrepreneurship (see for example Elisabeth Chell 1986). However, it may be noted that there is a tendency in entrepreneurial research to explain the success/failure of the business with the help of the personality traits of the entrepreneur. Thus in terms of causality the implicit starting point in the research can be assumed to be the connection between personality traits and the success of the business. Psychological models of explanation found in entrepreneurship research may be divided into two different approaches, which are usually described as 'models', namely trait theoretical models and psycho-dynamic models.

The psycho-dynamic models (see e.g. Kets de Vries 1977) stress the importance of early childhood experiences which are said to shape prominent patterns of behaviour amongst entrepreneurs. The picture of the entrepreneur created via these models is one of a person whose family background and other deprivations have been formative in shaping a somewhat deviant personality (Chell 1986). However, it is problematic to emphasise only the importance of childhood experiences, since (to take one example) environmental factors influencing an actor's behaviour and the development of his or her personality usually operate beyond the settings chosen for a piece of research. Furthermore, the characterisation of the entrepreneur can be seen as problematic, as it involves the notion of an apparently exceptional person whose adult life is overshadowed by a difficult childhood. The psycho-dynamic models place emphasis on the development of the personality and especially on the importance of childhood experiences in the moulding of personality. Trait theoretical models stress the static nature of the personality and the stability of personality traits through the subject's different developmental stages (Chell 1986).

According to *trait theories* certain personality traits and certain kinds of constellations of these traits are especially prevalent in an entrepreneur's personality, when compared to other occupational or social groups. This approach has had an especially important role in entrepreneurial studies undertaken within business economics, dating back all the way to David McClelland's (1961) work on 'achievement studies'. According to McClelland, an intense desire for achievement is characteristic of entrepreneurs, and may be combined with the general degree of the development of gross national product in different countries. Need for achievement was defined by McClelland as a special goal-oriented form of motivation which creates a "need to achieve" in individuals, and results in faster development at the nation level (McClelland 1961/1971; also McClelland 1987).

McClelland measured the growth of the economy in terms of growth in generation of electricity. As a means to measure this correlation he used a regression equation which combined 'need for achievement' and the growth in the economy's consumption of electricity. If the real growth was larger than the growth resulted from the regression this was interpreted as meaning a high rate of growth (McClelland 1961, 88-90). However, Schatz has remarked that if the measurement of growth is only the percentage growth of electricity generation, this does not lend support to McClelland's theory (Schatz 1971, 187).[13] The empirical validity of the concept has proved to be problematic, not least because of the research population but also because of the inability to test the concept adequately (e.g. Stanworth et al. 1989).

Another model based on motives is Maslow's hierarchy of needs (Maslow 1943), which also has been applied in entrepreneurial studies. In this model, propensity to risk-taking (see the earlier discussion on the origins of the concept of the entrepreneur), independence, ambitiousness and innovation are seen as being particularly closely connected to the entrepreneur's personality (see e.g. Schwartz 1976, Timmons 1978, and Sirpa Hajba 1987b for a discussion of Finnish research).The propensity to risk-taking has not always been considered an individual, static quality or trait. Indeed more often it has been seen as being contextually situated. This approach is also closer to Schumpeter's original idea of risk as being connected, not within a personality but simply to ownership in general. When women and men are compared according to their risk taking propensity, it is essential to bring out those facts

---

13. The correlation between the level of electricity generation and the need for achievement is .53, while the correlation between the level of electricity generation and the level of national production, which is the most common indicator used to measure growth in the economy, is only .25 (McClelland 1961, 82-85). According to Schatz the problem lies in the causality assumption between the 'need for achievement motive' and electricity generation: the growth of national production (and consequently of energy consumption) is supposed to follow the level of entrepreneurial desire for achievement (Schatz 1971, 188).

which influence the propensity to take risks and the possible differences that may be found in the risk taking behaviour of men and women. This means that research needs to focus on the structural and individual factors rather than merely on a comparison of differences. Women entrepreneurs who have taken personality tests based upon this approach have tended to record lower scores than men in respect of the categories 'motivation' and 'risk-taking' (see Hajba 1987a, 1987b).

Less attention has been given to general criticisms of the notion of achievement motivation (see Lipman-Blumen et al. 1983), especially those which focus upon the theoretical validity of such concepts. For example, empirical testing has not been able to validate McClelland's concept. The concept and the empirical research associated with it do not take into consideration possible differences between men and women, since the concept was originally derived from a population skewed along the lines of gender. It may be argued that in this respect both the definition of the concept and its empirical testing within the McClelland-Atkinson tradition have not corresponded satisfactorily to women's need of achievement. In such cases, research results showing that women differ from men in respect of certain ascribed personality traits, do not necessarily reveal anything more than the problems inherent in the theoretical construction of the concepts employed in the research. For example, Helmreich, Sawin and Carsrud (1986) discovered that social context changed the influence of personality traits on behaviour.

The results of comparative research on personality traits between men and women vary a great deal. There are several reasons for this high degree of variation, one of which concerns the choice of factors used in the research framework, while cultural differences provide for another source of variety. In addition, the trait approach has limitations which are not always taken into consideration in individual research settings. Welsch and Young (1984) found either no differences at all, or only minor differences, in women's and men's personality traits and value structures (see also Fernald – Solomon 1987). DeCarlo and Lyons found that women entrepreneurs differed from women in paid labour in their need for achievement. DeCarlo and Lyons's research population consisted of 122 women entrepreneurs and a comparison group (DeCarlo – Lyons 1979, 29). Most examples of this type of research run up against the problem that their comparisons between men and women always leave out the 'importance of women's and men's cultural experiences' and the possible differences in these experiences (for a discussion of this problem see e.g. Birley 1989, 37).

The approach based on the comparison of psychological traits does not make it possible to take into consideration those cultural and historical factors which mould and influence the way individuals act and react. Further, they leave out questions posed by feminist research in respect of the social construction of gender. The social constructionist approach makes it possible to assess the different theories critically, and also to restructure the trait theoretical approaches.

4.3.2.1. *The difficulties encountered in personality studies.* The previous chapter focused on problems encountered in those studies which emphasise the entrepreneurial personality as the main area of interest. The connection between the success of the business and the personality – or rather the characteristics of the personality of the entrepreneur – has not been unambiguously verified. The same is true for the connection between entrepreneurial personality traits and actual business behaviour. This is because mere personality traits alone provide an insufficient basis for research. Indeed, the factors governing cause and effect are so complicated that direct causal relations are not easily ascertained. The creation of ideal types or typologies can lead – and has in some cases led – to a search for 'the true entrepreneur' (see e.g. Gibb – Ritchie 1982, 41). However, it is clear that in the owner-managed small business sector the importance of the owner and his or her personality is great. According to Carsrud and Sapienza (1989, 7) the relations of cause and effect in the interaction between the entrepreneur and her/his environment are very complicated, and do not necessarily derive from causal connections between personality traits and business success. The measurement of such connections is extremely problematic because of their complexity (Fredriksen 1972).

It may be thought that the cornerstone of this type of research, its philosophical starting point, has been the idea of the omnipotence of psychological traits and factors, and furthermore, of the essentially stabile structure of a given personality type; a structure which is capable of being measured, e.g. with the help of attitude questionnaires. An empirical connection has been found between entrepreneurship and certain personality traits such as innovation, risk taking propensity, ambition and the need for achievement. This examination of a limited number of personality traits does not necessarily lead to a fruitful analysis, since personality should be seen as a dynamic factor, which is not enough on its own to explain the success of individual entrepreneurs.[14] Taken as a totality, personality is seen to refer to a process of theoretical inference. This process of theoretical inference is

---

14. This is indicated in the conclusions reached by Tamminen (1983) in his research on the connection between business success and the personality traits of the entrepreneur. The connection between personality and success may be interpreted in several ways (see Brockhaus 1980).

constructed both by means of observation and by the application of logical thought to a system of structures and processes which give meaning to behaviour (Lazarus 1977, 19).

When considering the value of psychologically-oriented research on female small business owners and self-employed women, one problem to emerge concerns the construction of the theoretical concepts deployed: most of the concepts are biased along the lines of gender, since they are generally based upon norms pertaining to one (male) gender only. Thus the picture of the entrepreneur that is commonly presented is that of a certain kind of male person with certain kind of masculine personality. That this problem has emerged is largely due to research carried out within women's studies (Eichler – Lapointe 1985).

It may be assumed that theoretical models which are based only on one gender cannot provide an adequate picture of reality. Examples of the shortcomings of such approaches are, e.g., McClelland's theory of achievement motivation (1961) and Lawrence Kohlberg's theory of the development of morals (Gilligan 1979), discussed earlier. In Kohlberg's theory, the moral development of an individual is seen to proceed according to universalist, contractarian moral theories (Hobbes, Rawls). Feminist criticism has focused on the very question of the adequacy of this perspective. According to Seyla Benhabib, "the universalistic moral theories in the Western tradition from Hobbes to Rawls are *substitutionalist*[15] in the sense that the universalism they defend is defined surreptitiously by identifying the experiences of a specific group of subjects as the paradigmatic case of the human race as such. These subjects are invariably white, male adults." (Benhabib 1987, 80-82).

4.3.3. From personality measurements to typologies — towards a sociological explanation of entrepreneurship

Instead of leading to the development of a series of trait catalogues, the diversity and inconsistency of different personality traits has led to the construction of several different entrepreneurial typologies. Most of the typologies are either based on the idea of a close connection between the entrepreneur and his or her business, and the role and importance of the entrepreneur in this business (e.g. Scase – Goffee 1980), or then assume that the formation of an entrepreneurial identity (e.g. Stanworth – Curran 1973) is

---

15. Benhabib goes further in defining *interactive* universalism, as opposed to *substitutionalist*, which acknowledges the plurality of modes of being human and the differences among people (Benhabib 1987, 81).

the starting point for typologies. The importance of typologies in entrepreneurial research may be summed up as follows: typologies make it possible to characterise simultaneously the role of the entrepreneur and her/his relationship toward the business. Most of the typologies implicitly assume that both the entrepreneur and the company have the potential to develop and change. Development and change are usually assessed in terms of either the growth of the company or of company profitability. Both of these changes mean that the role of the entrepreneur develops from that of the classical entrepreneurial identity towards the identity of the owner-manager (for a more detailed discussion of this point see Stanworth and Curran 1973; and for a discussion of Finnish entrepreneurial typologies see Kankaanpää and Leimu 1982, Hartikainen 1987).

In the following, I will not develop a detailed analysis of the different typologies, as it is not my aim here to provide an empirical study of women entrepreneurs from the point of view of these different typologies. The large number of existing typologies and their position within specific research settings does not make it possible to compare them directly. Instead of developing a fully-fledged comparative analysis, I will attempt to reveal some of the central features of the different typologies discussed here. As a starting point for the analysis I have taken Weber's concepts of value rationality (Wertrationalität) and purposive rationality (Zweckrationalität) since these concepts are useful devices in the search for features common to the different typologies.

The Richard Scase – Robert Goffee typology (1980) is built upon the form of ownership, and definition of the entrepreneur, involved in business activity. Scase and Goffee cite four different types of entrepreneur, delineated according to the size and the phase of life of the business. First, there is the 'self-employed' or 'own-account worker', for whom the most typical features are the small scale of business activity and the craft nature of the work carried out. Secondly, there is the 'small employer', who usually employs one or two workers while continuing to some extent to be actively engaged within the productive process. The third category is that of the 'owner-manager', who participates to some small extent in firm-based production. The last category of entrepreneur is that of the 'owner-controller', who does not participate in the production process, but manages and controls employees. The size of the business grows progressively from the first to the fourth category.

Even if Scase and Goffee do not place their typology within a continuum, a decrease in value rationality (coupled with a growth in purposive rationality) is clearly to be seen as we move from the own-account worker and self-employed person towards the owner-manager and, finally, to the owner-controller. The possibilities for a self-employed person to follow purposive rational principles are fewer than for an owner-controller. It might be argued that starting a business requires certain value rational premises, which can change into purposive rational values when the business grows and different functions become more specialised with the growth of the company.

The typology developed by John Stanworth and James Curran (1973) is predicted upon an entrepreneurial identity, which they see as changing with the development of the business. The first phase of an entrepreneurial identity is that of the craftsman-entrepreneur; the second phase is that of the classical entrepreneur; and the third that of the manager entrepreneur. The starting point for Stanworth and Curran has been Smith's (1967) counterposition of the craftsman-entrepreneur to the opportunistic entrepreneur. Both the craftsman-entrepreneur and the classical entrepreneur are seen as creating their businesses on the basis of their own skills. This kind of entrepreneurship may be seen as being closer to *value rational behaviour* than to *purposive rational behaviour* where skills and independence are the essential values defining activity. The importance of these values as motivating factors decreases when the business grows and the different functions become differentiated. The manager entrepreneur is closer to the owner-controller in the Scase-Goffee typology as well as being more purposive rational in his actions than are the other two ideal types.

The Goffee-Scase typology (1985) of self-employed women and small business owners starts from a different theoretical premise than the typology dealing with male entrepreneurs described above. When analysing 'general' entrepreneurial typologies, we should remember that they are mostly constructed and empirically tested with male population in view. The basis for the classification of women's economic activity in the Goffee-Scase typology is two-dimensional: attachment to entrepreneurial ideas, and attachment to conventional gender roles. I will come back to this typology in chapter 4.4.

The diversity of the typologies is understandable, given that the theoretical starting point always sets the basis for the typology.[16] Antero Hartikainen has used growth of the business as the main criterion which separates different typologies from one another. According to Hartikainen most typologies include traditional and growth-oriented entrepreneurs (Hartikainen 1987, 57). The selection of growth as the main criterion for the classification moves the typologies in the direction of the business and its life-cycle. The growth of the business, which has often been seen as the most essential factor for a long life-cycle, is undoubtedly one important criterion in the classification of businesses.

---

16. Marjosola's (1979) typology of the founders and Tyrkkö's typology (1980) of the class-position of entrepreneurs are good examples of Finnish research based on typologies.

Carsrud and Sapienza see the standardisation of the life-cycle position as essential for the creation of a business typology (Carsrud – Sapienza 1989, 9). The problems with different typologies and their comparison may be summarised as the theoretically limited basis for the production of different typologies, the brevity of the time period used in their construction, and the gender bias.

The socialisation process both in childhood as well as later in life, e.g. in working life, has an important influence on a person's decision to move from paid labour to self-employment (Stanworth et al. 1989, 20). Recognition of the importance of the socialisation process on decisions made later in life also raises questions about the influence that differences in the socialisation process of men and women may have on the decision to start a business later in life.

4.3.4. Summary

The main criteria for defining self-employment have been in the ownership of means and a relatively large degree of autonomy. Discussions in earlier chapters suggested that concepts of entrepreneurship and autonomy are problematic in the sense that these requirements of autonomy and ownership are not often met. Analysis of the classical texts of Schumpeter and Weber disclosed a misunderstanding in the interpretation: neither Weber nor Schumpeter refer to personality *traits* when discussing entrepreneurship. Secondly, even if these two authorities did not relate gender to the classic ideas of self-employment, and saw the economic 'actors' as 'shapeless and faceless heroes', the notion of mythical hero figure does give the actor the masculine cape, which excludes any feminine manifestations in the idea of entrepreneurship.

The tradition of sociological research which deviates from Weber's and Schumpeter's ideas of entrepreneurship holds more to the Marxist tradition. This means that small and medium-sized businesses are seen as a part of the capitalist market economy. Within this tradition, the major theses concern the disappearance of the small business strata, and the growth of large companies with the development of capital and goods markets. Besides the class and strata analyses, there is also an extensive debate on the various forms of economic development and restructuring of the economy, including factors such as the growth of the 'free market'.

At one level of analysis, the extension of the domain of the 'free market' (e.g. the transfer of state-owned industries and public utilities to the private sector) has encouraged the reconstruction of the concept of entrepreneurship and self-employment. It has also led to the introduction of new managerial structures and 'flexible' employment contracts, etc. Both the discussions and debates around the concepts of 'flexibility' (see chapter 5.), 'flexible specialisation' and 'restructuration of economy' turn themselves into small businesses and self-employment in much higher profile than earlier.

At another level of analysis, the extension has led to discussing particular forms of economic development and organisation in industrial societies. By these particular forms, I mean such terms as 'Fordism' and 'post-Fordism', which are in reality discussed under various schools of thought, such as the French 'regulation school' of Marxist political economy (Aglietta), the 'institutionalist school' (Piore and Sabel), and the 'managerialist school' (Atkinson). I have not introduced them here for several reasons. First of all, the gender is largely ignored in these models. Women's employment patterns, although resembling more and more those of men, are in fact different; labour market positions also differ from those of men. Secondly, models of Fordism/post-Fordism focus mainly on the manufacturing sector, thereby largely ignoring services. This approach has also been criticised for its narrowness: "a manufacturing-based model is a possibly misleading basis for a general account of the changing experience of employment" (see Bagguley 1991, 166).

I also discussed the results of various studies which have focused on the personalities of the self-employed. I noted that it is difficult to produce evidence to support the idea of the existence of a specific personality structure characteristic of the entrepreneur. Still, the idea of the importance of personality in self-employment seems to be pervasive. I discussed two factors related to this importance: the idea of the omnipotence of psychological traits and factors, and that of the stable nature of personality.

To some extent, the various entrepreneurial typologies produced in sociological studies are based on the importance of the person who is in charge of the business: even if the personality traits do not play such a crucial role, they still seem to play a minor part in various typologies and ideal types presented earlier in this chapter. However, it can be stated, as the main result of the various studies, that the demographic and social characteristics of the self-employed seem to enforce the idea that self-employment is by nature more opportunistic than directed by individual abilities. Entry into self-employment is basically a mid-life work phenomenon, following substantial experience in the labour market as an employee. I examined the various typologies with the help of Weber's concepts of value rationality and purposive rationality. It seems that starting a business requires certain value rational premises which can change into purposive rational ones when the business grows.

All in all, 'small business revivalism' and 'enterprise culture' in general have recently been mirrored by a new and increasing academic interest in sociology. There are, however, areas which still remain in the shadows: one cited by Roger Burrows and James Curran (1989) is sociological research on service sector small businesses, since that area of research has apparently concentrated on manufacturing. Another area – which came up in the earlier discussions as well – is women's entrepreneurship, which I will discuss in the next chapter.

The traditional concept of entrepreneurship is insufficient when dealing with women's entrepreneurship, because the majority of the research approaches the subject from classical premises, and classifies women entrepreneurs as **traditional** *if they are in women-dominated branches, and as* **modern**, *if their business activities are extended (from male point of view) outside these traditional female branches* (e.g. Carsrud et al. 1986a). Simultaneously, concepts like risk-taking, self-awareness, smallness, traditionality and several others are attached to descriptions of women's business areas. However, women's businesses should not necessarily be labelled as traditional, or risk- and growth-avoiding. These descriptions often carry meanings attributed to the successful male entrepreneur by 'male' research.

4.4. Research on women's entrepreneurship

4.4.1. Is it all in personality? Some research findings

Until recently, very little literature on female small business owners and self-employed women has been available. As mentioned in the introduction, this is due to the fact that most research into entrepreneurship has been carried out without any attention being given to gender as an issue. Sheila Allen and Carole Truman (1991) note that where studies of women entrepreneurs have been carried out, *"there has been a notable absence of any attempt to achieve representativeness in the range of economic sectors in which women business owners operate"* (Allen – Truman 1991, 115). The general picture that has emerged of women business owners still lacks the credibility that is attached to large data-sets, such as e.g. statistical databases. That said, characterisations of female business owners and the self-employed do include factors such as traditionality, the small size of most businesses, the relative lack of their potential for growth, their above-average concentration in the service sector, and the marked growth in their number in many countries recently (DeCarlo – Lyons 1979; Sexton – Kent 1981; Watkins – Watkins 1984, 1986).

Research aimed at establishing the reasons for the comparatively small number of women among business owners and the self-employed, has usually taken a consideration of socio-demographic variables and personality traits as its starting point. The results have often been contradictory. Part of the research suggests that women do exhibit those qualities and desires deemed typical of the entrepreneurial character: an intense need for achievement, and a high degree of ambition and independence (e.g. Schwartz 1976; DeCarlo – Lyons 1979; White 1986). According to other research results, however, women business owners typically exhibit a personality type that falls short of the requirements of the ideal entrepreneur. In short, women entrepreneurs are found to be not only less motivated in the pursuit of profit and success than their male counterparts, but they also are said to have fewer characteristics needed to be a good and successful entrepreneur (e.g. Hisrich – O'Brien 1981; Hajba 1987b). These kinds of research results, which are based mostly upon a individualist psychological approach, fall prey to the criticisms of feminist scholars. However, some of these research findings have shed light on the barriers and problems women meet in their entrepreneurial careers.

The endeavour to discover the problems women meet in their roles as business owners and self-employed persons has revealed several factors which could be seen as imposing barriers to women's work and entrepreneurial careers (Watkins 1982, 133). Even before the business start- up process has been set in motion, women can face barriers in their occupational careers (e.g. Bowen – Hisrich 1986; Carsrud et al. 1986a; Cromie 1988). The first problems confronting an entrepreneurial career are usually financial in nature (Hisrich – Brush 1987), and as far as women are concerned, financial problems seem to be more clearly related to two things: first to obtaining the right kind of information about financial channels (Hisrich – Brush 1987; Bowman-Upton et al. 1987); and secondly, to an increase in credibility (Sundin – Holmqvist 1989; Carsrud et al 1986b). A highly positive correlation has been found between the number of different social networks and the success of businesses run by women entrepreneurs (Carsrud et al. 1986a; Smeltzer – Fann 1989; Hakim 1988).

According to research undertaken by Sirpa Hajba (1987b) women entrepreneurs have developed their own female entrepreneurial culture, which is in conflict with its male counterpart. Furthermore, Hajba argues that "women who exceed a certain level of 'masculinity' or 'femininity' become entrepreneurs" (1987b, 3). It is, however, debatable whether this situation is due to endogenous personality factors, which are not thought to be influenced by social processes. As I see it, the situation is more related to structural factors than to endogenous personality factors.

A desire for economic independence has been both one of the most important motives for starting a business and an objective to which many other non-economic symbols are attached. The reasons for starting a business vary depending on the group in question. For example, among immigrants or expatriates the most important reason for business start-ups has been the desire to avoid unemployment (Simpanen 1986). In an Irish study, which compared the reasons given by women and men for start-ups, it became apparent that the citing of independence as a primary motive for becoming an entrepreneur reflected not only a desire to gain control of one's own work, but also a strong wish to control one's life as well (Cromie 1987a, 17). Women were more dissatisfied with their work careers than men and saw the business start-up as a better chance to combine family and work. Men were more interested in the potential financial rewards offered by owning a business. Moreover, men's priorities for business start-up were different from those of women. In particular, men were not burdened by a need to combine family and work (Cromie 1987a, 1987b). In this respect *a direct comparison of men's and women's motives for entering business can leave out a number of crucial determining factors including the influence of the internal division of work within the family.*

Carter and Cannon (1988) found that the most important reason for women to start a business was *the need for independence.* Another reason for women's entrepreneurship to emerge from this study was *competition in the labour market and a desire to avoid the effects of that competition.* Of course, a woman's previous work experience, her occupation and pattern of working hours all have their impact on her chances of becoming an entrepreneur (see Fuchs 1982). The gender differences in the motives for business founding are usually connected to the occupation held before the start of the business. According to Carter and Cannon, women entrepreneurs encounter different problems to those faced by male entrepreneurs, but it is still difficult to depict these problems as being solely caused by the gender. Cromie and Ayling (1989) come to the conclusion that where women are concerned, problems faced in the early stages of a business career are more clearly related to gender. At a later stage in a women's career problems become more firmly attached to different business activities (Cromie – Ayling 1989). Since most of the research studies referred to above have a limited research population, generalisations are difficult to sustain.

The importance of autonomy as a reason for starting up a business has been emphasised in a great deal of research into women's motives for becoming entrepreneurs. In a study carried out by Watkins and Watkins, women were found to deviate from men in terms of their work experiences and basic education. In fact neither of these two important factors was seen to lend support to the business start-up process in the case of women, in the sense that the option of becoming an entrepreneur could be seen as a logical extension to the development of a work career. The male model of a business start-up much more closely resembled the traditional 'logical extension' model of a work career in which the business start-up may be seen as a logical extension of a paid work career. For women *the need for autonomy* was a dominant motive for starting a business; this was true irrespective of whether their earlier work careers or education aided their entry into business life (Watkins – Watkins 1986, 193; Birley 1989).

It is clear that such factors as individual motives, family background, the nature and degree of educational attainment, work and labour market experiences do influence the decision-making process, in the case of both men and women involved in small business start-ups (Kovalainen 1990). Moreover, each of these factors has its own specific meaning for men and women. In Cromie's research, for example, children were the most important factor differentially conditioning the behaviour of men and women. It was easier for women with child-care responsibilities to combine work and the family as an entrepreneur than as a waged worker (Cromie 1987a). Thus the concept of independence did not have the same meaning for these women as it had for women without children. For women with children, independence offered a chance to combine work and reproduction, whereas for women without child-care responsibilities the notion of independence more closely resembled the concept used in 'traditional' entrepreneurial research (locus of control, Fernald – Solomon 1987).

4.4.2. Typologies of women entrepreneurs

Typologies of women entrepreneurs are useful in so far as they show that not all women are the same. At the same time, however, such typologies are limited to the extent that they remain descriptive generalisations of women's experiences of running a business. It has been noted that there is considerable scope to develop more detailed analyses of the female entrepreneurial experience. One of the most important issues to have emerged in recent research on entrepreneurs has been the importance of life-cycle factors for women (Allen – Truman 1991, 120). Life-cycle factors have a particular significance for women, since the way in which they become entrepreneurs and run their businesses cannot be *isolated* from their domestic circumstances.

Female entrepreneurial typologies are based usually on rather small samples, and hence do not provide generalisable information. Most of the typologies also use empirical evidence gathered from male entrepreneurs. This means that research results reflecting the situation of women entrepreneurs are often interpreted as being 'deviations from the normal scale'. Typologies are used differently by different researchers. The most common ways of using such typologies involve either the employment of an empirical type of classification, which means that the typology is based on the measurement of one or many separate variables, or reliance on a theoretical type of classification, which means that the typology is created indirectly with the help of theoretical concepts. Both approaches are commonly used in entrepreneurial studies, and both theoretical background knowledge and empirical measurement influence the form typologies take. A number of typologies concerned with women business owners and self-employed women may be classified as theoretical in nature, and these typologies have brought new theoretical questions into traditional empirical research settings. This has also made it possible to include ingredients from other approaches, in addition to a purely economic approach.[17]

Goffee and Scase's typology for women entrepreneurs is based on a rather small sample (N=54), but it is theoretically interesting since the basic idea behind it was to see *how women react to a situation of subordination and to consider the impact of any such reaction.* The essential division within the typology corresponds to the different ways women in the sample worked out their own solutions to their situation. Their responses may be classified as either *collective* or *individual* in character: starting one's own business was considered to be an individual response to the social subordination of women, whereas working in the women's movement or some other type of organisation was classified as a collective response.

On the basis of interview data, Goffee and Scase classify women's experience of business proprietorship according to two sets of factors. The first of these factors is women's attachment to entrepreneurial ideals, and the second is the extent to which women are prepared to accept conventionally defined male-female relationships. (Goffee – Scase 1985, 54). Goffee and Scase's classification is presented in figure 4.1.A. In this classification, *'attachment to entrepreneurial ideals'* refers to a set of attitudes characterised by the following features. First, a belief in economic self-advancement. Secondly, an adherence to individualism in terms of 'self-help', 'personal responsibility' and 'self-reliance'. And finally, an attachment to the work ethic and a belief that enjoyment of the fruits thereof (i.e. company profits) constitute 'just rewards' for those who have made the necessary sacrifices. Conventional gender roles are defined in this schema as acceptance of women's subordination to men alongside a willingness to see women's social position defined by men.

17. See for more British research e.g. Sallie Westwood and Parminder Bhachu 1989, and Annie Phizacklea 1989, and for Finnish research Marja-Terttu Uimonen 1987.

(Goffee – Scase 1985, 1987a, 1987b).

Goffee and Scase assume that if an attachment to entrepreneurial ideals and an acceptance of conventionally defined gender roles affect the behaviour of business women, then it is possible to describe these women in terms of a typology organised around those two concepts. The first category in such a typology may be referred to as *'conventional women'*, who are strongly committed both to entrepreneurial ideals and conventional gender roles. Goffee and Scase argue that these women entrepreneurs often work in areas where they can easily combine traditional 'female roles' with business activities. These traditionally include such businesses as restaurants, coffee shops, catering firms, cleaning companies, secretarial and nursing agencies and hairdressing salons. The growth of the business is not the most important factor for these women; profit-making is usually achieved through cost-effectiveness, not through the growth of the business or diversification of business activities. Women who are strongly attached to conventional gender roles, and who are highly committed to entrepreneurial ideals, do not readily see themselves as "real entrepreneurs" but rather more as a helping member of the family, if the spouse is in business as well (Kovalainen 1990). This reflects the pervasive nature of the image of 'real – male – entrepreneur' discussed earlier in chapters 4.2. and 4.3.

A second category of women entrepreneurs is that of *innovative* proprietors. Innovative proprietors may be defined as women who are highly committed to entrepreneurial ideals, but who nevertheless reject prevailing notions of 'the female role' (Goffee – Scase 1985, 55). According to Goffee and Scase, the business occupies a central place in the lives of these women. As a consequence such women are strongly motivated to develop the growth and profit potential of the businesses, often at the cost of their own social life. For these innovators, business ownership offers an opportunity to continue or create the kind of rewarding career that would otherwise prove more difficult or impossible in paid employment. Most of the businesses in which Goffee and Scase found their innovators were within postwar growth areas of female employment[18] such as business related services (marketing, advertising, public relations etc.)

A third group of women entrepreneurs was found to be strongly attached to the traditional female role and to have only a limited commitment to entrepreneurial ideals. Goffee and Scase use the term *'domestic proprietors'* to refer to this group. Proprietorship offers these women opportunities for non-monetary self-fulfilment and personal autonomy within the limits drawn by their domestic responsibilities. The importance to these women of their

18. In Finland this growth took place considerably later, mostly during the 1980s.

traditional role means that their own special areas of business activities such as arts and handicrafts, health foods, beauty care, dressmaking etc. are close to those of 'conventional proprietors'. The relative lack of importance attached to the scale of business profitability on the one hand, and the high degree of emphasis placed upon personal self-fulfilment on the other hand, indicates that the scale of such businesses is usually quite small.

The final group in the typology may be described as *radical proprietors* since they have a low degree of commitment to both entrepreneurial ideals and to conventional female roles. Members of this group are usually highly-educated and have met barriers in their previous work careers. The attraction of owning a business for these women lies in the fact that it seems to offer them a means to overcome their subordination in the labour market; thus business is not seen primarily as a means to maximise profits. These enterprises tend to be associated with the women's movement and to be in such diverse spheres of activity as publishing, printing, the craft trades, education, and manufacturing. (Goffee – Scase 1985, 57).

The influence of role models and the outcome of a commitment to them can be seen in everyday practices and ways of acting in various situations. According to Goffee and Scase the 'innovator' does not think that gender has any 'special role' in business life, and in consequence, it seems that she subscribes to many of those attitudes generally associated with the 'classical' male entrepreneur. Interview responses suggest that the innovators were even prepared to sacrifice personal relationships and to exploit conventional notions of femininity for their own business ends. (Goffee – Scase 1985, 79; Cooper – Davidson 1982). Goffee and Scase also analyse female entrepreneurs from a feminist perspective: they conclude that the innovators do not change the system; *"they beat it by joining it"* (Goffee – Scase 1985, 138).

Radical entrepreneurs do not apply traditional business values to their business activities. Rather, in their view the business should be seen as part of a personal aspiration to overcome a situation of subordination. The only apparent contradiction here is in the case of radical proprietorships, where the attempt to overcome subordination does not follow the pattern set by the innovators, by 'beating men at their own game', but instead by trying to create an autonomous position in the business world.

Even if Goffee and Scase take into account the familial position of the women they interviewed, this fact does not assume the same form found in the typologies developed by Stan Cromie (1985), and Elisabeth Sundin and Carin Holmqvist (1989), in which women's positions did differ significantly from one another, especially in terms of their family commitments. In Cromie's study (N=34), the 'innovators', 'dualists' and 'returners' were the three categories of women entrepreneurs that differed from one another in terms of having or not having children. Having an own business acted as a career continuum for waged work in the innovators' group. The need for autonomy and achievement was the primary factor leading to the start-up process, not the existence of pressures or barriers within waged work. Women who wanted to combine family and work by starting a business were classified as 'dualists' in Cromie's study. The will to combine these two spheres of life placed restrictions upon women's choice of business: usually they opted for a business in the service sector, either in the area of personal or business services. Contrary to Goffee and Scase's classification, Cromie did not find a category of 'radical proprietors' in his sample (Cromie 1985). Again, the researched group of women was rather small.

As noted earlier, *life cycle factors are an important research area largely ignored in most studies of women entrepreneurs, and especially in standard typologies of business women and self-employed women* (see also Allen – Truman 1991). The main reason for this lacuna lies in the 'male' centred bias of such studies, which tend instead to focus upon the comparison of certain restricted characters and traits, and the economic success of the business. Sundin and Holmqvist (1989) have gone the furthest in their typology in revealing the complexities of the situation facing women in business. Their starting point is the way of life shared by women entrepreneurs ('independence' as a way of life, 'the waged worker's way of life' or the 'way of life appropriate to a career'), marital status and attitude towards gender roles (traditional/modern). (See figure 4.2.A.)

Women who follow a 'traditional independent' way of life do not differentiate between work and leisure, often working within the family business. Naturally enough, working in a family business involves some intertwining of work and leisure, even if female work is categorised as assisting family members. This means that such women are statistically 'invisible' as entrepreneurs. Marital status is important in the sense that for unmarried women who follow a similar kind of close relationship between work and leisure, the decision to follow this life-style is made irrespective of their own desires. Women who live a 'modern', independent life, may work in the family business, but unlike women who consider themselves to be assisting family members, these women see their activities as essential and important, to such extent that work is not only seen as a means to something else but also as an end in itself. (Sundin – Holmqvist 1989).

'The life of the waged worker' is assumed by women who combine work and family through self-employment. It is clear, however, that for many of these women *self-employment is largely seen either as a means to adapt their working lives to their family situations, or as a way of coping with a changing situation of waged work.* The business itself does not figure so prominently in the lives of 'the waged worker entrepreneurs'. A career-orientated way of life can be either 'traditional' in the sense of providing support to the husband's career, or 'modern' in the sense of building up one's own career. The most essential innovation in this typology is that it takes into account the family's life situation, which brings dynamics into their classification, and makes it possible to chart the movement of women from one category to another within the typology.

4.4.3. Concluding remarks

The above-mentioned typologies suffer from the same general problems confronting all typologies: namely *the static depiction of a situation and the absence of a time span against which to measure changes diminish the reality of the typologies.* A further problem with these entrepreneurial typologies concerns the small size of the samples and the relatively small number of variables used. In respect of the smallness of the data base, only the Sundin–Holmqvist typology is based upon a regionally and industrially representative sample (N=1 014). The Goffee–Scase typology is based on interviews made with 54 women, all from industries where women are well represented. Moreover, accurate generalisations cannot be made where the data has been obtained from a non-random sample (e.g. Cromie 1985) if the entrepreneurs in the sample are in different phases of their entrepreneurial careers. Another weakness in these typologies is that *the economic necessity of entrepreneurial actions is not necessarily taken into account.* Instead, the reality of economic necessity is replaced by an ideology of free choice for those who start their entrepreneurial activities.

In the following I redefine all three of the above-mentioned typologies by using two dimensions, which include a measure of different economic necessities, independence and life-style as well as the extent of the dependence or independence of the traditional role models and role ideals of each gender. At the general level, the first of these two dimensions is from *'necessity to freedom'*, while the second is from *'dependence to independence'*.

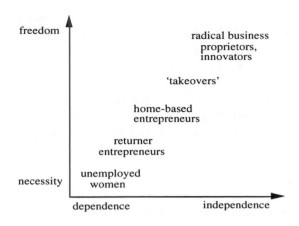

Figure 4.1. Summary of the typologies presented in chapter 4.4.

In figure 4.1., unemployed women or women who were outside the labour force before starting up a business are located at one end of each dimension. *Economic necessity* may be seen as the driving force for business start-ups. Such businesses tend to be small-scale, based on special (often handicraft based) skills. Most often business success rests upon some form of special 'feminine' knowledge, as found, for example, in cooking, child care and other home activities, which are not usually counted as occupational qualifications. Another typical feature is that entrepreneurial activity usually takes place at home, does not need special investments and is not growth-oriented. All this refers to the fact that independence, both as a way of life, and also in terms of economic rewards, is very low; women who subcontract as a self-employment position belong to this end of the continua.

Research reports from many countries (e.g. Great Britain and Germany) indicate that most ethnic minority businesswomen and self-employed women could be included within the above category (Westwood – Bhachu 1989). The lack of waged work possibilities and the 'need to survive' can also create regional forms of "home-based entrepreneurship". *In this respect, marginality is not necessarily a subjective experience* (see also Kovalainen 1990). The group described above would include most of Cromie's earlier mentioned 'returner entrepreneurs' as well as 'home-based entrepreneurs' in Goffee-Scase typology. Being an entrepreneur does not

80

necessarily mean that traditional role models and stereotypes are present, not even where women work in traditional female-dominated areas. On the contrary, qualitative research has shown that women working in ultra-traditional enterprises can turn to modern solutions to their problems in terms of the lifestyles they adopt outside their businesses (Uimonen 1987).

At the other end of the continua the areas of independence and freedom include women entrepreneurs who are classified as *'radical business proprietors'* by Goffee and Scase, as well as Cromie's *'innovators'*. Women who see entrepreneurship as a way of life, even if their own businesses are not necessarily growth-oriented or situated in an unconventional area, could also be placed at this end of the continuum. So-called *'takeovers'* (involving entrepreneurs who have earlier worked as waged workers in the same business) lie between these two ends of the continua. But it should be remembered that although women may seem to lead independent lifestyles and run businesses which make such lifestyles possible, in reality they are not necessarily independent. Indeed, business activity may be tied to subcontracting or to a narrow area of competence which does not necessarily make independence possible. This may even lead to a worse situation than that experienced by the waged worker (Allen 1983).

One issue which has emerged in research on women's entrepreneurship concerns the typical business culture that women are said to have in their business activities. Not only is this culture held to differ from the dominant male business culture, but it is also regarded as being closer to 'female culture' in general than to 'male business culture' (Hajba 1987b). Issues related to business culture include, for example, patterns of growth and change, the emphasis placed upon high levels of profitability, and the degree of importance attached to achieving set goals (Tamminen 1981). 'Female culture', on the other hand, has been seen as connected to traditional roles and role stereotypes, so that the male definition of business culture stands in almost complete contrast to it.

Some researchers believe that as entrepreneurs women have to use male entrepreneurial culture to confront traditional female roles and female culture (Hajba 1987b; Sundin – Holmqvist 1989). The juxtaposition of these cultures has also been seen as creating a female entrepreneurial culture, which breaks down both cultures and can be situated between the two. The contrasts between these cultures are seen as one reason why women do not become entrepreneurs, and also as a reason why they start their businesses in traditional female areas that are often regarded as marginal compared to traditional male business areas (Hajba 1987a, 55).

As I see it, the idea that cultural differences between women's business activities and men's business activities constitute a reason for the small number of women entrepreneurs does not tell the whole story. *The question of cultural differences should be seen as part of a larger question concerning the generalised gendered segmentation of the labour market into male- and female-dominated areas of work.* The cultural model of explanation regards gender as a learned role or behavioural pattern which simultaneously characterises individuals and the whole gender group. The group is supposed to be similar in respect of this quality (cf. the different definitions of gender outlined in chapter 3.) to the degree that a number of conditions have been met. The first of these conditions is that the basis for behaviour is assumed to reside in the psychological characteristics classified as female, and the second, that this cultural-behavioural model is assumed to account for the failure of women to become entrepreneurs or start up their businesses to a great extent in traditionally female areas. *This means that the commonly-used concept of gender is in fact ahistorical, characterising an individual or a learned pattern of behaviour in a way that fails to take change into account.* Hence, instead of drawing attention to social and economic structures, the focus is given to individual or group qualities and cultural patterns of behaviour. Finally, these qualities and behavioural patterns are also treated as causal factors.

I see this cultural approach as highly problematic. As mentioned earlier, the analysis of women's entrepreneurial activities cannot be separated from the analysis of women's labour force participation, any more that it can be separated from an analysis of wider aspects of economic development. This is the case, I will argue, because women's self-employment is not a single phenomenon, which is divorced from economic reality; rather, it is clearly an issue relevant to any economy. Thus, it is not only an issue of individual differences in the definitions of female and male, or female and male culture.

The separation of women's labour markets from men's labour markets is naturally reflected in the separation of women's entrepreneurship from men's entrepreneurship. Thus it is a question of factors exercising an influence both on the structural level (the level of the whole economy) *and on the individual level* (the existence of barriers to entry into male-dominated branches). (cf. Julkunen 1985; Kauppinen-Toropainen et al. 1986). Less attention is given to the frequency and extent of women's labour force participation in studies of women's entrepreneurial activities, even if individual studies (cf. Cromie 1987b; Kovalainen 1990) have revealed that it is precisely waged work experiences which have been the essential factors in the business start-up process. *Conceptualisations of gender-divisions within waged work must also take account of conditions within the entrepreneurial sector.* The aim must be to ensure that different spheres within this sector are opened up equally to both women and men. In the following I will try to provide a general picture of those theories which seek to explain women's labour force participation as well as of the growth of occupational segregation.

4.5. Labour market models — an alternative framework for self-employment?

What factors account for women's inferior labour market situation? Is it a question of the behaviour of women at work, which creates a disadvantaged position within the labour market, or is it more a question of structural selection mechanisms directing women, with similar qualifications to men, into inferior positions? Different explanatory models approach this question in different ways. According to the starting premises in the models, they may be divided into two groups: explanatory models which concentrate on individual characteristics, such as educational qualifications, and models which concentrate on the structural mechanisms of the labour markets and the economy.

I will try to outline a general overview of the basic premises of different theories as well as of the research results gained from empirical research.[19] The purpose of this chapter is to explore the issue of economic labour market theories and their implication for thinking about the birth of women's self-employment. Economic research on the labour market has been governed by neoclassical labour market theory which assumes free competition to be central to the organisation of the labour force. The 'institutional school', with its development of segmentation theories, has been seen as the main competitor to the neoclassical approach. The institutional school entered into sociological discussions and research on the labour market in the 1970s (see Jouko Nätti 1989, 7).

Explanatory models concentrating on *individual employment characteristics* approach the differentiation of labour markets from the point of view of the socialisation and educational processes that individuals go through, and the different qualifying factors these processes bring with them. In the socialisation to gender roles, in particular, attitudes and behavioural models are seen to be stable and influential as far as individual action is concerned. This influence is especially marked in educational and occupational selection processes. Furthermore, socialisation at school and in home has been seen as creating the

---

19. My intention here is not to create a thorough picture of the different forms of explanation. A description of the general premises of explanatory models can be found in any labour economics textbook.

basis for segregation at work. Role models maintain the division of work outside the family so that men and women themselves seek respectively men's work and women's work (Marini – Brinton 1984).

Discrimination at work is not necessarily direct: frequently, indeed, it is indirect, so that part of the available employment is associated with low wages and low occupational status, in which the possibilities of advancement and the content of the work are restricted (female or women's jobs e.g. nursing jobs, clerical work and teaching occupations). Forms of discrimination may also differ according to the occupational image: studies of predominantly male occupational groups (e.g. lawyers, physicians, engineers etc., see Harriet Silius 1992; Elianne Riska – Katarina Wegar 1989; Veronica Hertzberg 1989) indicate that images of work and occupation change as women enter these groups in increasing numbers. It seems that women themselves specialise within certain areas (or alternatively choose areas) which no longer enjoy a high status in terms of wage or occupational career advancement once the number of women increases substantially (Riska – Wegar 1989).

Individually-oriented explanatory models have been criticised for their tendency towards functionalist, and especially reductionist, forms of reasoning (see e.g. Alanen 1986; Walby 1990). By emphasising the individual processes of socialisation and ignoring the social circumstances under which socialisation takes place, socialisation theory also reduces sociological explanation to psychological processes (Alanen 1986). For example, as an explanation for women's situation in the labour market or in the self-employment, the socialisation model is condemned to adopt determinism, although it may suffice as an explanation for individual behaviour. *Generally speaking then, the socialisation model should be seen as a product of social 'forces', rather than as a determinant of social phenomena as such* (see e.g. Baude et al. 1987, 34).

I can take an example of this. According to Silius, a young person's own cultural behavioural models continuously disrupt the socialisation models adhered to by adults, and this phenomenon – the discarding of old models and the emergence of new ones – occurs in working life as well (Silius 1989, 151). Sundin and Holmqvist see both structural and individual explanatory models as necessary to an explanation of the differences between male and female entrepreneurs. However, this does not mean that the division of work, or differences in entrepreneurial activities between men and women, may only be explained by reference to individual psychological starting points. Neither does it imply that individual strategies adopted in business can only be explained by structural or cultural factors. These two approaches need to be combined in order to arrive at a satisfactory account of gender-based differences in entrepreneurial activity (Sundin – Holmqvist 1989, 132-134).

Structural models of explanation concentrate on those institutional barriers in work organisations or in the labour market and the economy in general, which make it more difficult for women to enter certain occupations or achieve specific occupational status. These structural barriers usually include factors of an intra-organisational cultural nature (e.g. values and traditions), which restrict women's freedom to apply for certain positions in the organisation (e.g. the requirement for overtime work, one-gender recruitment, the lack of identification models for women etc., see Kanter 1977; Roos 1985). Even if the number of women within a certain occupational group has grown – as has happened in Finland in occupational groups such as physicians, lawyers, engineers – both horizontal and vertical segregation seems to have remained within those occupational groups as a result of changes in job descriptions and a differentiation of occupational images (e.g. Riska – Wegar 1989). Moreover, problems exist in the study of organisational structures and the use of micro-level concepts for the purpose of structural explanation. Such attempts usually end up within a reductionist model of explanation. One way to avoid this outcome when research on gendered organisational structures is being undertaken is to use concepts like hierarchy, bureaucracy, rationality and modernism, and analyse them in relation to gender (Joan Acker 1987; Marta Calás – Linda Smircich 1992).

4.5.1. The neoclassical theory

It is possible to reduce the core presuppositions of the neoclassical theory to the basic premises of the socialisation theory. However, the starting point for the neoclassical model, the assumption of profit-maximising, differs considerably from the main tenets of the socialisation theory. According to the early neoclassical theory of supply, maximising leisure and income are the main factors in explaining labour force participation (Hemmilä 1988; Amsden 1980). The reason for this is that *the primary analytical category in neoclassical theory is the individual who exercises freedom of choice and, in the process, behaves rationally to maximise utility*. The major determinants of an individual´s behaviour are income and prices. Neoclassical theory assumes that the essence of rational individual behaviour may be captured by a model which utilises a limited number of universal economic variables, and that this model can be projected over time and across social strata. Accordingly, this means that "the human subject of neoclassical investigation is a timeless, classless, raceless and cultureless creature; although male, unless otherwise specified" (Amsden 1980, 13).

The neoclassical account of women's employment and occupational segregation draws attention to wage differences between men and women. These differences are also used, indirectly, to explain occupational inequality. Neo-classical analysis presupposes either the existence of perfect competition where earnings correspond to the value of the marginal productivity of labour[20] or, alternatively, the existence of a monopsony situation in which the company enjoys a monopoly status as an employer within the labour market.[21]

The so-called *'overcrowding approach'* explains the low productivity of women's work by its excluded nature, i.e. by a combination of the oversupply of, and lack of demand, for women's labour. The reason for low wage rates among women is to be found in the same 'excluded' nature of their work. In part it is due to demand factors; the supply of women's work is restricted to only a few occupational areas. This restriction has two important effects. First, wage rates in these 'restricted' occupations are not very high; and secondly, wage rates in the other group of occupations, i.e. in the male labour market, are higher than would have been the case if this gap in demand for the labour of men and women within the labour force did not exist (see Barbara Bergmann 1986). Jobs in the women's labour market attract markedly lower wages than similar jobs in the male labour market. According to the overcrowding approach, demand creates the appropriate supply situation, i.e. the observed differences between the labour of men and women. This means that this approach implicitly assumes that all workers are identical in their potential productivity.

In contradiction to the overcrowding approach, the *'human capital approach'* sees no potential transferability between the male and female labour markets. Instead, it considers each labour market to be independent of the other, at least in the short run. Within the male labour market, wages get set in such a way that they balance the supply of men with the demand for their labour – in jobs that have been reserved for men in each occupation. Within the female labour market, the same process takes place. Human-capital requirements affect the supply of labour to jobs in each occupation within both male and female labour markets. Differences in wages reflect differences in productivity, and a worker's productivity reflects the 'human capital' investment (for example the education) that she or he has made.

The nature of the work force resembles the investment in capital goods: a person makes an investment decision to acquire educational 'capital', and once

---

20. There are two different schools of thought within this approach: "the overcrowding approach" and "the human capital approach".

21. To some extent, the women's labour market situation often resembles a monopsony situation, where her place in the labour market is established on the basis of her husband's work.

this goal has been achieved, our rational decision-maker moves onto the labour market to realise her/his investment. Occupational segregation, for example, in the form of differences in wages may be understood as a reflection of the supply of labour. But why is it that men with less valuable qualifications than women are able to obtain higher wages in the same labour market? Paradoxically, it seems that the answer to this conundrum is that women and men do not operate in the same labour markets at all: supply and demand in the male labour market decrees one set of wages, while supply and demand in the women's labour market decrees a whole set of different, and lower, wages.

For the first time in the history of economics the human capital approach discussed the influence of the family on women's labour force participation (Gary Becker 1965/1980). In large measure the origins of the differences in the labour market positions, and of men and women, are due to differences between the genders in respect of their propensity to encourage working at home. It should be noted in this context that *economists* frequently use the concept *'homework' when referring to household work, i.e. unpaid domestic labour,* whereas *sociologists* apply the term *'housework' to unpaid domestic labour* and reserve the term *'homeworking' for paid labour which is done at home* in the fulfilment of an employment contract. I will clarify the concepts below using brackets to indicate their 'sociological meaning'.

From the point of view of the rationality maximising principle, it is very useful for the family if the wife stays at home or works only temporarily outside the home (Jacob Mincer 1962/1980). This line of argument was the first to include homework (i.e. unpaid domestic labour) as part of the dichotomous choice between market based work and leisure. Women's labour market behaviour could be explained as a form of rational profit maximisation lying between market-based work, work in home (i.e. unpaid domestic labour) and leisure.[22] The effect of substitution upon income has become important as a factor explaining women's growing participation in the labour force: As Alice Amsden notes, "while higher income encouraged women to expand their leisure time activities, higher wages pushed them in the opposite direction and out of the home" (Amsden 1980, 14).

Becker's general theory of the allocation of time analysed the family both as a production unit and as a consumption unit in business terms: Marriage is conceptualised as "a two-person firm with either member being the 'entrepreneur' who 'hires' the other for ... a 'salary' ... and receives residual 'profits'" (Becker 1973). Women hire men as breadwinners since men earn more than women in the market; whereas men hire women as housekeepers

---

22. Mincer's research results showed that in addition to the husband's earnings, a wife's own wage rate (price of labour) would influence how she chose to spend her time.

since women bear children and are superior at rearing them. The analysis of the family as an economic unit means that there is an assumption about the division of work within the family. As Mincer and Polachek write: "That the differential allocation of time and of investment in human capital is generally sex linked and subject to technological and cultural changes is a matter of fact which is outside the scope of our analysis" (Mincer – Polachek 1974/1980, 170).

The household maximises its well-being when there is a negative correlation between the spouses earnings: one spouse (she) specialises on housework while the other spouse (he) concentrates on market-based work (Becker 1973). This division of labour is thus consistent with economic maximising principles.[23]

The question how a family's internal division of labour is arranged and how it may change over time is beyond the scope of this analysis. The primary analytical category in neoclassical theory is the individual. Thus the division of labour markets is due to the individual factors: "Given the sex linkage, we focus on the relation within the family between time allocation and investments in human capital which give rise to the observed market earnings of women" (Mincer – Polachek 1974/1980, 174). This model assumes that individuals exercise freedom of choice and behave rationally to maximise utility. The only constraints in the exercise of freedom are individual in nature (e.g. income and prices). The choice of occupation (at the individual level) and the existence of occupational segregation (at the societal level) are seen as a *consequence of individual preferences.*[24]

The order of cause and effect in neoclassical theory is open to criticism: the connection between waged work and the family exists. However, it does not necessarily follow that a women's position in the labour market is defined by her position at home; indeed, the contrary is also the case (Walby 1986, 70). This notion is supported by a simple empirical fact: the supply of women's labour has not declined during the current economic recession, as was the case earlier (with respect to the Finnish data see Ingberg et al. 1986), even though the degree of women's labour force participation follows economic fluctuations more than is the case for men (Lyytikäinen 1984). One important area for

---

23. A positive correlation between the spouses wages is found in many studies (e.g. Aarnio – Eriksson 1987). This refers to the fact that households do not behave as economists suppose. In addition, this refers to the fact that there are factors, such as social class, which explain more of the social dynamics within households than human capital theory.

24. Arrow has criticised the above-mentioned by noticing that the economic arguments put by most of the theories concern anonymous persons: "Variation created by sex, race or nationality are not included in these models, thus it is not surprising that those theories do not have much to say about the differences created by sex, race or nationality." According to Arrow these factors should not be included at all (Arrow 1976, 236).

further criticism has been the lack of consideration given to the impact of unemployment as a factor explaining women's labour force participation, despite the fact that great emphasis has been given to the impact of unemployment in the case of men.[25]

Despite the revelation by neoclassical theory of the extent of the impact of the family on women's labour force participation, the internal dynamics of the family is left unexamined – even though it has an important effect upon individual decisions with regard to how to participate in labour market work and to allocate time between different activities.[26] In this context, the family is considered to be an homogeneous economic unit.

Both models described above are based on an assumption of perfect competition where the employee wage corresponds to his/her marginal productivity, and wage differentials reflect differences in marginal productivities. Monopsony does not require perfect competition, but the extent of monopsony is decisive as to how large the difference between the level of wages and the real marginal productivity of labour is, i.e. the less elastic the labour supply, the lower wages are found to be, assuming that the firm maximises its profits and the supply curve for labour is on an upward curve (Blau – Jusenius 1981, 189; Bergmann 1974/1980). The monopsony model explains wage differences between men and women by the lower elasticity of women's labour supply, which means that firms have more monopsony power over female labour markets than they do over male labour markets.

From a sociological point of view, the rationalistic nature of the basic premises of neoclassical theory, as exemplified in the importance afforded income and prices as the main restrictive and decisive factors in individual's behaviour, is also one of the main 'weaknesses' in the theory. This weakness is most apparent in the neo-classical analysis of real life incidents. The failure to consider structural features, such as the family or unpaid domestic work, changes in income etc., leaves essential factors outside the analysis of the neoclassical model. Changes in behaviour – whether due to social, cultural or ideological reasons – are assumed to be constant, or causally derived from the above-mentioned factors; or they are attributed to 'tastes' which can be divided into price and income variables (Stigler – Becker 1977).

According to Walby (1986), in order to explain women's labour market participation the neoclassical theories (Mincer, Niemi) begin from women's household responsibilities (human capital approach). Theories accept the importance of the production aspect of unpaid work carried out in the home

---

25. E.g. Mincer. Later, however, Mincer did bring the possibility for unemployment also as an affecting factor in the case of women (See Walby 1986, 72).

26. This point is clearly evident in sociological studies of life history, see e.g. Strandell 1983.

while either leaving out unemployment totally (Mincer), or explaining unemployment derived from women's position in the family and *voluntary* shifts between labour reserve and market work (Niemi 1974/1980). They do not regard them as being derived from the structure of the labour markets or of patriarchal labour relations, as sociological theories do. Human capital theories assume that labour market segregation should decline as women's possession of human capital rises towards the average for men. However, there is little evidence that this is the case (see Catherine Hakim 1979).

4.5.2. The labour market segmentation theory

Another important approach which has been used to analyse women's employment from the point of view of how the labour market is organised is that of labour market segmentation theory. Dual and segmented labour market theories are primarily concerned with explaining divisions within the working population and with examining the functions of such divisions for employers. As Walby notes (1986), confusion sometimes exists between the concepts of segregation and segmentation. Segregation is the concentration of persons by ascriptive criteria such as gender and race in particular sectors of employment. Segmentation is the differentiation of the labour market into distinctive types of employment, which may or may not be filled disproportionately by members of different gender or ethnic groups. Thus *"theories of a segmented labour market are one type of approach to the question of the explanation of the segregation of genders and ethnic groups into different types of occupations"* (Walby 1986, 18).

Contrary to the neoclassical approach, which focuses upon the individual, the institutional approach takes the family as its starting point, for an exploration of the connection between women's household responsibilities and paid work.[27] The institutional approach does not view the labour market either as one single market, or as a sort of stock exchange market, where buyers and sellers meet, and in which all work is open for buying and selling. The institutional approach did not set out to broaden the analysis of the relations between the family and the capitalist economy, as Marxist approaches have sought to do. Instead, its starting point was the empirical knowledge of the fact that labour markets function differently in different spheres of the economy. Factors affecting the organisation of labour markets can be individual characteristics such as race, gender and age, or institutionalised factors such as

---

27. However, we have to remember, as stated earlier, that women's labour force participation is explained in the neoclassical theories starting from different selections within the family. The individual is primarily in the focus of the research.

tendencies to build up closed occupations or branches (Hemmilä 1988, 24).

A number of slightly different segmentation theories may be included under the term 'institutional approach'; minor differences in segmentation theories are to be found which vary according to the aspects they emphasise. All these different theories share a common origin: they were developed by economists as part of a critique of human capital theories of job differentiation. Segmentation theories hold that the labour markets are segmented into various parts which are essentially different from each others. Moreover, the mobility between different parts is also seen as being relatively minor (Nätti 1985; Smith 1989). Segmentation theories look for side explanations for observed segmentation; they maintain that employers require different types of workers or a differentiated labour force, and that people enter the labour market with different characteristics, and thus heterogeneity in demand creates heterogeneity of supply (Nätti 1989).

Wage differences are explained by reference to occupational inequality. According to these theories, large differences in productivity exist between different industries and companies, and these differences in productivity are larger than the differences between employees. This set of assumptions provides the rationale for abandoning human capital type approaches. Male and female qualifications may be the same, but the employment segregating practice common to company policy on hiring personnel creates a situation where women are forced into customary occupations for the female gender. In early dual labour market theories, women were usually seen as a single group belonging to a secondary sector within the labour markets. Opinions about the usefulness of such segmentation theories in explaining women's employment have varied. Even if these theories provide some insight into women's experience in the labour market, they have been criticised for creating an image of women as 'secondary workers', which is open to objection on empirical grounds. The more recent research has shown the complexity of women's labour force segments (e.g. Dex 1986).

The reason for the above-mentioned segregation is to be found in the existence of two labour markets, a primary and a secondary labour market, which are a product of the duality of the economy. The hypothesis of a dualistic economy has been presented in the work of many economists (in the USA e.g. by Bakke, Dunlop, and Kerr, and in Europe e.g. by Sengenberger, Loveridge, and Mok). *The main idea is that large companies constitute the core of the national economy, while small and medium-sized companies make up the periphery of the economy.* This duality within the commodity and capital markets reproduces duality within the labour markets: larger firms within the core economy hold on to workers who have specific knowledge and skills, and they develop specific strategies for the workers they wish to integrate into the firm. These workers are referred to by Doeringer and Piore (1971) as 'primary sector' workers.

Primary sector workers receive various benefits: jobs with higher pay and greater stability, education and career circulation, benefits which maintain the company's position within the primary labour markets (Nätti 1989). By contrast, the secondary sector workers are less well educated, often unskilled or semi-skilled, and move between industries and occupations, from one low-paying job to another. According to Barron and Norris, so-called endogenous factors, such attitudes towards one´s own work, also seem to be influential in the process of becoming a secondary sector worker (Barron – Norris 1977; see also Hemmilä 1988, 25).

The division of labour markets into two sectors, primary and secondary, has been further developed by, e.g., Lutz and Sengenberger, who abandon the idea of a strict dualism in the economy, since a dualist approach is best applied to production of goods, and is relatively inappropriate when it comes to labour divisions. Lutz and Sengenberger divide labour markets into three parts which, in practice, are combined in different ways. These parts consist of: first, general labour markets, secondly, labour markets for skilled workers and thirdly, firm centred labour markets (Kasvio 1985, 38). Most women are classified as belonging to the general labour markets, whether or not specific skills are demanded of them. The labour markets for skilled workers develop when the supply of labour is continuous, and demand is non-continuous (as is the case for construction workers). Firm- or company-specific labour markets can be compared to labour markets found within companies where, with the help of staff education, promotions etc, the labour force is mobile within the company.

Inter-company labour markets lead to a twofold pattern of occupational segregation: on the one hand, new employees are recruited from outside the company to fill certain positions, while on the other in-company staff promotion is established as the norm for other occupations (Blau – Jusenius 1981, 193). Competing market forces are most strongly felt in the first category of occupations. Inter-company promotions usually require "company specific" knowledge. In this case, wage rates, the hierarchy of work and its allocation are defined by the rules, customs and praxis of the company rather than by market forces.

Crompton and Jones argue that occupational segregation takes place at two levels: first at the horizontal level, which broadly corresponds to occupational segregation. This means that women and men work in different types of occupations. Another level of occupational segregation is vertical segregation, in which men and women work within the same branch but carry out different tasks, with women occupying a lower level than men (Crompton – Jones 1984, 248). Horizontal and vertical segregation is also documented in Finnish research: totally segregated occupations (in which 90-100 per cent of all workers are of the same gender) constitute almost half of the Finnish labour force, while so-called 'balanced occupations' (in which 40-60 per cent of all workers are of the same gender) employed only 10 per cent of the labour force in Finland in 1986. Vertical divisions are present at the workplace level: men and women carry out different tasks within the work unit. Most vacancies seem to be earmarked for one gender or the other (Bergmann 1986, 133).

The critique of dual theories focuses upon both theoretical and empirical issues. From the standpoint of neoclassical theory, dual labour market theories over-emphasise limited empirical evidence. The way the dual labour market theory conceptualises women's employment is also problematic. Moreover, there are further problems with regard to the operationalisation of the segmentation concept: it may be conceptualised at various levels including those of industry, branch, firm, organisation, work place and qualifications of the worker. These levels are asymmetrical with regard to the exercise of power and additional in respect of other dimensions (Työvoimaministeriö 1985).

A further problem is that the theory has been formulated implicitly from the standpoint of the skilled male industrial worker. This means that it succeeds better in analysing production work in the manufacturing sector than in the service sectors. Furthermore, the line between primary and secondary sector workers is poorly drawn in dual labour market theories: the concept of the primary worker is fleshed out much more fully than the concept of the secondary sector worker (cf. Kendrick 1981).

A less commonly heard critique of dualist theories focuses on the fact that market conditions prevailing within both commodity and labour markets arise independently of strategic decision-making at the company level. According to Craig, Garnsey and Rubery, the *demand factors* creating segmentation within the labour market cannot be separated from *supply factors* creating segmentation within the labour market. To back up this assertion Craig et al. present findings which show that in spite of the various industrial occupations found within different industries comprising the primary sector, secondary-type traits are related to these occupations, to the extent that so-called 'secondary-type' employees are hired (Craig et al. 1985).

It may also be argued that segmentation theories do not describe those labour markets which are segregated along gender lines and, as Julkunen notes, *the labour market position of women is on average more 'secondary' than is the case for men, and furthermore, women change their labour market position more easily than men do. This fact is not necessarily taken into account in dual market theories* (Julkunen 1985). Nätti has studied the segmentation of the labour markets in Finland, and according to his results, it seems that both gender and the socioeconomic position effect one's position in the segment. In addition to this, the position of men is stronger than that of women within every segment (Nätti 1989, 42). This finding is in accordance with the results obtained from similar research carried out in other studies (see Martin – Roberts 1984; Zighera 1989; Lillydahl 1986).

A more serious critique focuses on the theoretical premises of dual labour market theory. *"The dual labour market theory is permeated by an uncritical acceptance of a masculine model of the labour market in which gender is both too present (although untheorized) and too absent"* (Beechey – Perkins 1987, 137). It is "too present" in so far as women are conceptualised too simplistically. Women are treated as if they were an undifferentiated group, as if e.g. women were the same, with the same class background, familial status, education and skills, etc. The question of why most workers within the primary sector are male is not posed, since an analysis of this question would require an analysis of the official and unofficial processes in which men obtain, and maintain, control and authority over primary sector jobs (e.g Koch 1989, 13; Beechey – Perkins 1987, 137). For example, the classification of work as skilled work or unskilled work is not just dependent on the contents of the work, but also on the negotiating strength and gender of the group (Nätti 1989, 42). An analysis of the processes of discrimination whereby women have generally been excluded from primary sector jobs by employers (and this has happened often with the consent or collusion of trade unions) would inevitably be part of the story. This issue is discussed, for example, by Edwards (1979). According to Edwards *differences between the genders are not reducible to differences between segments but, rather, the analysis of women's position should be related to the history of capitalism and patriarchy.* (See also Nätti 1989, 43) Theories employing a concept of social gender as well as theories of patriarchy concentrate on the analysis of these processes and mechanisms. I will return to the concept of patriarchy in the next chapter.

Gender is also absent in other respects, because the characterisation of the secondary sector generally implies that the attributes of secondary sector jobs are objective. Veronica Beechey and Tessa Perkins take the following example: the notions of skill and training are seen as absolutely central to the way in which the distinction between primary and secondary sector workers can be drawn. The theory assumes that what counts as skilled work can be treated positivistically – as an objective phenomenon which is unaffected by employers' conceptions or by the bargaining power or social status of those

94

who characteristically do it.

However, it should be quite clear, from recent empirical research at least, that *gender enters into the very definition of skilled work and that it also plays a part in what counts and does not count as training*. The fact that women's skills and training are systematically downgraded is well documented. As Beechey and Perkins remark, as soon as one begins to introduce an analysis of gender and of employer's attitudes and discriminatory practices into the framework of analysis, important new questions emerge, and ideological constructions and social processes have to be introduced into the theory whose predominantly economic foundations are thus called into question (Beechey – Perkins 1989, 137).

A 'second generation' of labour market segmentation theories has been formulated by a number of researchers, including the Cambridge Labour Studies Group. This group has developed an analysis of labour relations based upon three main innovations (Rubery et al. 1984). The first of these innovations involves broadening the analysis to take account of the impact of *power relationships* upon the structure of labour markets. Briefly put, this means that the consequences of conflicts of interest are now being given serious consideration. The second innovation is that a consideration of the technological conditions under which labour markets operate has also been introduced into the theory. This means that it is these conditions, rather than the traits of individual workers, which are seen as the causal basis for segmentation. The third innovation is that greater attention is given to supply-side factors, and this in turn has led to a more developed theory of social reproduction. The Cambridge Group has brought the question of labour force supply and demand back into the centre of sociological discussion. This means that it is not only the price system which affects the price of labour but also, and to an even greater extent, social and political changes, including those in family organisation and migration procedures. The Cambridge Group argues that it is through the system of social reproduction – the family system, the welfare state system and the education system – that the labour force becomes differentiated.

As Beechey and Perkins note, the Cambridge group's revised analysis of social reproduction is undoubtedly a very important contribution to the analysis of labour markets (Beechey – Perkins 1987, 139). However, Beechey and Perkins continue that the theoretical approach of the Cambridge Group is problematic in the sense that *it explains why women are secondary workers only in terms of an analysis of social reproduction, ignoring therefore the gender construction of jobs within the production processes itself*. Even if the Cambridge Group's theoretical construction takes the sociological view of social reproduction more fully into account than the earlier labour market theories have tended to, *it still does not take account of the way men's and women's experiences of work may differ 'substantially despite similar structural situations'* (Scott 1986).

Even if there is now a wide variety of segmented labour market models to choose from, most of them suffer from an overdependence on narrowly economic assumptions, and from trying to conflate a wide variety of forms of work into the 'primary-secondary worker' distinction. It could be concluded, as the Cambridge group argues, that 'further progress in the development of segmented labour market theory can only be made by much more detailed investigation of the determinants of the demand for, and supply of, labour.' (Labour Studies Group 1985, 123). It seems that detailed investigation as proposed above will need further analysis of work organisations and, e.g., part-time jobs. Walby and Bagguley argue further that changing gender relations in local labour markets show that existing theories are flawed especially in addressing the theorisation of gender relations (Walby – Bagguley 1990). Instead of segmented labour market theories, which conceptualise and operationalise occupational segregation with the help of different indices (e.g. the index of Dissimilarity; the sex ratio index etc.), they suggest a theory which explicitly deals with the specificity of gender relations as autonomous, or relatively autonomous, relations vis-à-vis capital, and theorises gender relations as a result of the interaction of patriarchal and capitalist relations (Walby – Bagguley 1990, 79).

That the labour markets in Finland are gender segregated is clear: men and women work in different occupations and have a different occupational status. The unequal situation is also reflected in the inequality of earnings, and this inequality cannot be explained by differences in education, since irrespective of their level of educational attainment, men earn more than women.[28] However, when it comes to growth of earnings, men clearly do better than women. Counting on this information alone it may be assumed that the labour force participation of women has several features in common with the secondary labour market segment (Nätti 1989).

Though the gender effect in respect of assigning workers to different segments was present in the Finnish empirical data, the effect was not found to be as strong as in foreign studies (Nätti 1989). Depending on the model used, gender not only explained the pattern of segmentation but also the duration of employment, and willingness to change the workplace and work orientation. According to Nätti, gender is the factor that best explains career advancement

---

28. Women's general education is higher than men's in all the Nordic countries except Norway (Anttalainen 1986, 142).

and internal mobility within labour markets. Gender explains the employee's position within the labour segment in which men in each socioeconomic group are more likely than women to be found in the so-called core jobs, and women are more likely to be found in the so-called marginal jobs. *Core jobs* signifies jobs in the primary sector, in branches which are relatively free from the influence of wider economic trends. *Marginal jobs* are found in the secondary sector, and there jobs are more sensitive to general economic trends. An essential factor distinguishing primary and secondary jobs is the benefits which are associated with each (Nätti 1989, 37, 65, 88-90).

As I mentioned in chapter 4.5.1. the concept of gender has not been integral to the dominant traditions of economic theorising. For example, the basic assumptions of neoclassical economic theory are questionable to the extent that the real economy and women's labour market situation is taken into account (e.g. Santamäki 1986; Ilmakunnas 1989, 12). According to Nätti, labour market segmentation theories and social class theories can be regarded as parallel, or even partly overlapping, ways of understanding how labour markets function (Nätti 1989, 139).

However, the position in which labour market employees find themselves reflects a state of affairs which is already an established fact prior to their entry into the market: *the different kinds of selection processes governing occupational education direct men and women into different occupations and also into different occupational statuses within the same occupation* (Riska – Wegar 1989; Silius 1989). Women who have the same education as men are more likely than men with the same education to end up doing menial jobs: such women are less well paid and have inferior possibilities for occupational advancement.

All the above-mentioned points indicate the need for more research to uncover the practices in, for example, the employment selection process through which women are concretely discriminated against. Barron and Norris (1977) have shown how these mechanisms function in the case of women, and results may also be generalised to cover other marginal groups in the labour markets. *Taking such criticism into consideration, it could be argued that women's labour market situation or the existence of so-called 'atypical employment models' is not reducible to economic factors alone.* Labour market studies usually define atypical employment as employment that is temporary, part-time, or occasional in nature, or that involves self-employment (Nätti 1990). This means that in order to understand gender segregated labour markets and a gender segregated economy, the structure of employment has to be analysed from a sociological standpoint as well.

4.5.3. Concluding remarks: the insufficiency of labour market models?

In the preceding chapter I have discussed various ways of explaining women's position in the economy from the point of view of the labour market theories. That means, briefly, that only women's 'official' market work is taken into consideration in these settings. I have not extended the discussion by bringing in the empirical data concerning Finland, but refer here to a few studies made (e.g. Kolehmainen 1991; Pusila 1992) which note that there have been changes in segregation, and that segregation seems to have widened both in male and female labour markets. This means that various processes have taken place both in the labour market and in the economy in general. It is interesting that even if the degree of segregation tends to vary a great deal between countries, it has been noticed that in countries where women's labour force participation is highest, occupational segregation is greater. This has led some researchers to the tentative conclusion that increased female labour force participation rates may intensify the 'overcrowding' process, whereby the concentration of women workers in certain sectors and occupations results in increased competition and a decline in women's relative pay (OECD 1986b).

What is problematic in the above-mentioned ways of theorising employment relationships in the economy – or more specifically in the labour markets – is that inequality between genders is not considered to be theoretically sufficiently important. However, *the division of labour within a company or national economy is not structured simply according to different economic interests, whether those interests are based upon class or the individual, but also by social and cultural factors.*[29] Even if my own data on the structural development of self-employment for women in Finland does not allow an examination of the above-mentioned theories, I have reviewed them here in order to highlight the essential elements of the alternative ways of explaining women's self-employment.

As noted above, the human capital approach regards the genders as being separate in respect of their position within the various labour markets, a situation that need not imply a high degree of inequality between women and men, whereas the Marxist analysis of labour segmentation mainly derives the differences between genders from the capitalist mode of production. But, as Walby notes, most Marxist analyses have not addressed the issue of gender segregation in employment, although much of Marxist theory is devoted to

---

29. In terms of its emphasis and findings, research carried out on women in paid employment has had important consequences for both theoretical debates and empirical research agendas. It has also led to a re-defining of areas of interest in sociology, not least in the sociology of work and unemployment.

explaining inequality (Walby 1986). Nevertheless, a few exceptions to this absence within Marxist scholarship may be noted (see e.g. Edwards 1979).

Marxist research has, however, questioned both human capital theory's assumption that people act on the basis of rational calculations of economic benefit, and the sufficiency of the capitalist mode of production as an explanatory model in explaining differences in the educational, occupational and working possibilities open to women and men (see e.g. Beechey – Perkins 1987). Because various economic theories operate on the supposition that a genuinely free market exists, it is difficult to explain employer preferences for men when women workers might be the more economically rational choice in certain job categories. The human capital approach which treats the time women spend outside paid employment as voluntary, and which further views their standing in the labour market as being determined solely in terms of the human capital they bring to that market, has also been criticised for ignoring the inequality of power within the household that may determine the distribution of paid employment, domestic work and leisure.

Shirley Dex notes that *theories of segmented labour markets have been particularly crude as far as women's work has been concerned, since the initial theories tended to put women into a single category along with blacks, that is, in the secondary sector* (Dex 1987). However, various studies which examine women's lifetime occupational mobility suggest that a more complex structure of market segments exists for women. Dex presents one response to labour market segmentation and women's employment in her study. In this study women's primary sector is divided into a non-manual and a manual sector, which together include teaching, clerical, nursing jobs, plus a semi-skilled secondary sector which includes factory work (for more, see Dex 1987). The concept of women as a reserve army of labour is fundamentally flawed; indeed, arguments about women as a reserve army have now been more or less abandoned (see Walby 1986, 74-80). Walby has argued that women do not 'flow' on to the labour market when there are shortages, precisely because of the pre-existing segmentation by gender in both local and national labour markets. However, once gender is treated as a set of social relations that are spatially and historically varied, it becomes possible for the analysis to focus upon the kinds of shifts in patriarchal relations which alter the forms and relations under which women labour, both in the household and in the workplace. These shifts constitute the core of social restructuring (Bagguley et al 1990, 30)

The sufficiency of these explanatory models is essentially connected to the question of gender and to the possibilities of relating the concept of gender to other social structures in order to increase their explanatory power. These are questions that, in the main, have been posed by feminist scholars. The concept of gender is thus sketched as an essential part of the structure of a society. It is also closely linked with methodological discussion, since the concept of gender cannot be considered as a single variable which can be standardised in research. This is the most common way gender is dealt with in labour market theories: according to Aino Saarinen (1992)[30], earlier research into sex gender roles and equality which flourished in the Nordic countries in the 1970s, is a good example of this type of approach.

The theories of women's work presented above suggest what might cause the differential in women's and men's labour market positions, and what maintains them. One of the suggestions is that we examine the structural characteristics of employment for patterns that place women at the bottom of the economic hierarchy. Finally, the extent to which the explanatory models discussed above are considered to be adequate depends upon the meaning given to the concept of 'work', and the history of the development of distinct areas of women's and men's work.

The structural divisions between home and waged work, public and private, are usually made so routinely that they seem to be self-evident. Conventionally, work is regarded as an area clearly demarcated from domestic or social life, as one side of the opposition 'work-home'. However, the above-outlined theories of the labour markets fail to point out the ways in which the informal economy has co-existed with the development of the formal economy. The separation of women's and men's work in respect of the labour market and the home, and within wage labour, has evolved historically. A complex set of historical and technological changes has identified, for example, clerical work as 'women's work' in the modern era.

One of the underlying themes that is to be taken into consideration in untangling issues of structural effects of the labour market, is that of caretaking and the use value and exchange value of that caretaking. The caretaking roles of women overlap dimensions of both paid and unpaid labour. Some researchers have commented on this overlap as the 'seamlessness' of women's lives, as they move from caretaking in their homes to caretaking in the labour force. The caring occupations within the welfare state have been characterised as "an extension of the housewife's work. Housework and child care, the political mothering that women perform, have been considered as a private matter and as a sort of labour of love" (Simonen 1990, 140). The 'grey zone of caring', understood as Leila Simonen defines it, takes the question back to the problems

---

30. Saarinen (1992) has discussed the question of what do the changes in the category of gender mean more thoroughly in her dissertation. See Saarinen 1992, 48-60.

inherent in the definition of work.[31]

4.6. The linkage between gendered self-employment and gendered waged work

How are changes in women's labour force participation connected to changes in women's self-employment? Reasons for the growth and changes in self-employment are naturally present and influential in the development of women's entrepreneurship as well. However, while the majority of both women's business activities and women's labour force activities are concentrated in the service sector, it is possible to connect changes in entrepreneurship not only to changes in the general structure of the economy, but also to changes in women's labour force participation. Furthermore, it could be assumed that women as a group would benefit from the growth of the service sector because of the growth in employment and entrepreneurial opportunities for women. But, as the evidence has shown, this is not necessarily the case.

According to Kelly (1991), the barriers to success in the core branches of the economy and at the middle and upper levels in the peripheral economy have contributed to an increase in the number of self-employed women in the USA. In explaining this feature, we are led back to the more individual factors, although not solely so. When the rigid and persistent industrial division by gender in self-employment is taken into account, the individual factors are left with insufficient explanatory power. In Nordic countries, feminist researchers have clarified the structuration of gender within the society by the concept of gender contract (Julkunen 1992; Silius 1992; Rantalaiho 1993).

Factors such as patriarchal structures in society and "patriarchal ideology about women, family and careers have strongly shaped our collective definition of how women relate to the economy" (Kelly 1991, 132). Despite the frequently presented evidence of the rapid rise and breakthrough of female entrepreneurial power, the fact seems to be that the growth and the number of women entrepreneurs follows the traditional industrial patterns of women's waged work. This is not, however, the case for men, as they operate on a broader scope than women.

The growth in women's labour force participation has been argued to directly increase women's potential for business ownership and self-

---

31. Simonen uses the concept to refer to political (unpaid care, labour of love) and social mothering (salaried care work), and relates it to the Nordic type of societies with well-developed welfare states.

employment (Goffee – Scase 1985). Goffee and Scase see the mechanism working in various ways: First, the gender division in the labour market and the unemployment in the branches dominated by women has increased self-employment in the sense that *unemployment has pushed women into entrepreneurship.* This does not necessarily mean a traditional business start-up, but it can mean that women give up the status of a legal worker with benefits and move into possibly very specialised and dependent subcontracting. This does not fulfil the characteristics of entrepreneurship in other than a statistical definition (Allen 1983; Hakim 1984). Allen and Truman suggest that apart from women who assist in their male partner's business by doing clerical and office tasks, there are many examples of women's enterprises which may never appear in official statistics (Allen – Truman 1991, 116).

Another, perhaps more indirectly effective mechanism is related to the structure of labour markets, but it has more effect at the individual level: work satisfaction and the importance of work contents are minor in the low wage occupations where relatively little occupational skills are needed. This is usually characteristic of women's occupations (Webb 1982). Dissatisfaction with waged work has been noted to increase the will to start up one's own, in the case of men (Bechhofer et al. 1974), but this has also held true for women (Cromie 1985; also Allen – Truman 1991).[32] One of the ways to avoid the subordinate labour market position and career creation is to start a business of one's own (Stanworth – Curran 1973; Goffee – Scase 1983).[33] The marked increase in the participation of women in self-employment also perhaps suggests the probability of an increase in the importance of non-pecuniary factors.

Furthermore, one of the factors that are influencing the growth of women's self-employment is the change in women's labour market participation behaviour: e.g. in Great Britain the model of women's labour market participation has changed from the 1960s up to today. Women do not, after marriage, stay at home to the extent they did before, but seek to place themselves in the labour market either in full-time or part-time work (Martin – Roberts 1984). In Finland, women's participation in the labour force has not been channelled into part-time work, even though the model for labour market participation has changed somewhat from the 1960's until today. There are

---

32. In a study by Aronson (1991), demographic factors of self-employed women and women in waged jobs were compared. The data showed that self-employed women differed little from their wage and salary counterparts in their observable social and cultural characteristics, 'human capital endowments and market opportunities' (Aronson 1991, 92).

33. This avoidance of subordination has been reported to happen at the individual level as well (Kovalainen 1990). However, a statistical approach does not tend to bear out everyday reality.

several reasons for this; most often women's early entrance into the labour force at the beginning of industrialisation has been seen as creating the present waged-labour models and patterns. (e.g. Jallinoja 1984, 252).

The question of how gendered occupational structures arise and are reproduced has remained insufficiently answered. How is it that self-employment more acutely reflects those gendered patterns existing in waged work? Is it not the case, as noted in the analysis of conceptual contents of entrepreneurship and self-employment, that entrepreneurship would bear in itself a promise of Eldorado, that it would be a step into freedom from constraints such as subordination and marginality? As the empirical evidence will show that this is not the case, it recalls the explanatory power of patriarchal and gendered structures of the economy.

4.7. Concluding remarks: a fragmented picture

To conclude this chapter, I have argued that the emerging picture of self-employment is in many ways insufficient, not only from the point of view of lacking empirical data on self-employed women. In this main chapter 4, I have so far discussed three large 'fields' which I see as the most important ones when focusing on women's self-employment. A crucial arranging theme for the discussions has been how women's self-employment can be explained in different contexts. I will briefly summarise the main conclusions.

The 'Woman Question' or the 'Personal Problem' in classical theories? Self-employment in traditional approaches

This chapter begins with the discussion and the critique of the existing approaches in self-employment and entrepreneurship, starting with the early economics, and then proceeding into the classics of economic sociology, namely Schumpeter and Weber (chapters 4.1 – 4.3.1). The traditional criteria for defining entrepreneurship in sociological research have been the ownership of the means of production and a relatively large degree of autonomy regarding work tasks. It was noticed in the discussion that gender is not explicitly related to the classic ideas of entrepreneurship. On the contrary, in the classical texts the entrepreneur is defined as a mythical heroic figure – and thus essentially masculine. The image of this heroic entrepreneur has also remained unchanged in this type of literature.

The analysis then proceeds via more psychologically-oriented approaches into the 'contemporary' sociological perspectives on self-employment and entrepreneurship (chapters 4.3.2 – 4.3.3). Here I question the approaches which have concentrated on 'the psychological complexity' of the entrepreneur. As a conclusion, it was noted that it is difficult to produce evidence to support the idea of the existence of a specific personality structure which would be characteristic for entrepreneurs. However, personality and its traits and women's 'differences' compared to men come up often in the study of self-employed women. Instead, various typologies constitute a more sociological approach to self-employment: they usually take both the entrepreneur and the different business activities into the same focus. Several typologies and their qualities were discussed.

Or Is It All in Personality? Inspection of self-employment in psychological and social psychological approaches

I then proceeded to another important area which is the main focus of my research: namely the studies dealing with women's self-employment (chapter 4.4.). I evaluate studies which were based mostly upon the individualist psychological approach – the dominating approach in the studies of self-employed women. Even if some of them have been able to reveal the psychological barriers and problems women meet in the entrepreneurial life, they still fail to give general pictures or a general mapping of the specific problem areas for women. I discuss shortly also the business start-up process, since it has often been presented as merely a logical extension of a paid work career. Based on my results from another study (Kovalainen 1990), this does not seem to be the case.

Another strand of studies on women and self-employment deals with the various typologies based either on empirical or theoretical types of classifications. Describing altogether three different typologies, I noted that even if women's familial positions are taken into account, the complexities of the situation facing women in business are rarely considered in these typologies. What was found to be common to all these typologies is that, together with rather small samples, the "reality" of typologies diminishes with the static nature and the absence of time-span. Finally, I redefined all three of the pertinent typologies, using two dimensions which included a measure of different economic necessities, of independence and life-style (the 'necessity to freedom' dimension). In addition to these, they included the extent of the dependence or independence of the traditional role models and ideals of each gender (the 'dependence to independence' dimension). It seems that all 'classes' of self-employed women in the typologies I discussed could be included on this scale. Basically, the main questions which are not explicitly stated in the typologies were the two dimensions I stated above. Economic necessity and dependency on traditional role models seem to be the pervasive categories.

Or Would the Answer lie in the Markets? A consideration of gender as an analytical category in labour market theories

I also addressed the question of how the inferior position of women in the labour market is explained, and briefly discussed the various theories and their basic premises explaining the gendered division of labour. This analysis creates the third aspect in women's self-employment in chapter 4.5. As I see it, and as others have also seen it, the feminisation of the labour force is not merely a 'new' variable affecting a set of fixed factors, like the organisation at the labour market, state policies or other similar things. Rather the relationship between different factors is reciprocal as all factors change simultaneously.

On the basis of examining various theories exploring the structure of the labour markets, it seems that existing approaches to theorising women's labour force participation all have limitations, some more 'severe' than others. Furthermore, it seems that these limitations can be overcome only if the category 'women's work' incorporates all female activities – paid labour, within the sphere of market relations, and unpaid domestic labour, within the sphere of the reproduction of individuals. I propose to condense the differences discussed in several theoretical approaches into three categories.

First, the most common approach has been *essentialist* – or deterministic – in which gender differences are seen as deriving from biology. Such studies base their understanding of women's labour on a notion of the *female condition*. This 'condition', which is determined mainly by biological difference, and is thus ahistorical, designates that women's primary social responsibility is for biological reproduction: thus, wage-earning women are studied as a particular sub-set of the general category of wage labour. "What women do is a deviation from the norm, and explained as a consequence of the supposed essential differences which biology makes" (Daune-Richard 1988, 261).

Another approach to women's participation in the labour force which makes an essentialist distinction is the one which conceptualises 'gender as a variable'. This means that sex is taken as a classificatory model. The variable 'gender' is introduced at a certain point in the analysis, although the units of observation have not been initially constructed on the basis of gender, but on the basis of men. In other cases, the variable 'gender' is treated as a *subordinate* one to theoretical premises.

A third major approach for understanding women's labour force participation was also outlined in the discussion in chapter 4.5. This approach appears to a large extent in studies which are close to neo-Marxism. These studies discuss either the interconnection of production and reproduction, or extend reproduction to cover all various activities that *socially* organise the reproduction of individuals. I could state that as a result, there is an increasing need to understand gender as a social category, which is defined in terms of social relations understood as a gender system. Altogether, I outlined the different ways women's labour force participation has been conceptualised in several theoretical approaches, and came to the conclusion that, as a result, the attempts to deal with waged labour and domestic labour separately, and to ignore gendered social practices at the work place, are serious obstacles to any valid analysis of female labour.

To be able to move beyond the deficiencies of the earlier studies of women's self-employment, I have tried to work out a more comprehensive way of inspecting it. Because of the nature of this study, however, I am unable to grasp all the various facets influencing women's self-employment, e.g. the interconnections of practices and meanings of women's roles in domestic and paid labour. Instead of looking at the actors, I have concentrated on structures. However, to complete the discussion which I started in chapters 2. and 3., I move on to inspect gender and patriarchy as analytical categories.

Categories of gender and patriarchy

Earlier, in chapter 3, I discussed gender as a category and the concept of patriarchy. First of all, the idea that social structures and social processes are *gendered* has implied that the *concept of gender is elaborated as meaning more than a socially constructed identity and image, namely an analytic category* (Acker 1991; Connell 1987). Gender is thus not only a social category, but pervades all social processes and relationships. Constructing analyses which are founded on the concept of social relations implies that we make use of analytical categories which grasp their gendered character.

There are several implications of this notion, and the epistemological one is that analytic categories do not have one simple function, nor do they merely rest on an empiricist observation of behaviour. Social facts as such cannot be taken as 'given': the meanings of practices are as important for our understanding of events as the practices themselves. For example in an organisational context a lot of literature still refers to gender in the sense of role and display, not to asymmetrical relationships which constitute social structures.

Post-modernist arguments for the fragmentation of the concepts used in 'modernist' social theory have produced a tendency to shift the central theoretical concepts away from 'structure' into 'discourse' or texts. The criticism in postmodern feminist discussion has also referred to the failure of grand theories and key factors as explaining sexism. This failure has been one of the main sources of criticism towards the theories of patriarchy as well, as Walby states: "Post-modernist analyses are often constructed in reaction to totalizing frameworks, which attempt to reduce the complexity of the social world to one or two structural principles" (Walby 1992, 39). The tendency to shift from large-scale theories into various small-scale discourses concerning women, gender and feminity has, however, major problems which were not discussed in detail in chapter 3. The fragmentation of the 'grand theories' may bring out pictures with more nuances of the various situations in women's lives (issues of ethnicity, race, subcultures etc.), but at the same time this fragmentation may also ignore crucial questions like the question of power, which has been an important question in the construction of both gender and patriarchy; and which is also more or less directly observable when sketching the place of self-employed women in Finnish economy.

The viewpoint of the welfare state

So far in my work I have not discussed the welfare state and the question of how women's self-employment is connected with the changes and development of the welfare state. That connection exists in several ways. One is that the state, by providing public services, creates possibilities for women – and men – to participate in paid employment. In fact, the construction of the welfare state – the construction of social reforms and changes, that is – has to a large extent taken place with the help of women in Nordic countries. In Finland, though, women's integration into the labour markets took place before the major social reforms.

As several social policy researchers have noted, the welfare state has been the best ally for women[34]. Both child care and the care of elderly people have become professional work which has made it possible for other women to enter paid employment in other sectors of state. But, as several feminist researchers have pointed out, "the world's best reforms for women" can – and in reality do – produce gendered consequences and gendered practices in society (Julkunen 1992).

The main quantitative indicator for the growth of the welfare state has been

---

34. Raija Julkunen has described the state as a "collective wife and mother" (Julkunen 1992, 44).

the growth of social expenditure in the GNP. In Finland the social expenditure share of GNP was 25 per cent in 1988, against 36,5 per cent in Sweden and 26 per cent in Norway. However, there are differences in the ways the social welfare has been organised within the Nordic countries, so the quantitative measure does not tell the whole truth. Even though the Nordic model of organising welfare policy is considered to be 'the best possible for women', it has been open to criticism during periods of economic recession (Langan – Ostner in Julkunen 1992), and therefore the Nordic welfare state model includes also a threat to women.

In Nordic countries, feminist researchers have clarified the structuration of gender within society by the concept of *gender contract* (Julkunen 1992, Silius 1992, Rantalaiho 1993). According to Rantalaiho, the concept of gender contract reveals the implicit, 'hidden rules' in the world we live in, and points to how we live in a world of taken-for-granted gendered structures (Rantalaiho 1993, 4). The gender contract[35] includes continuous conflicts and renegotiations and, especially during economic recessions, when there are pressures to cut down public and social expenditure, the gender contract is redefined and renegotiated over and over again.

One way of assessing the position of self-employment (or markets) in relation to the welfare state has come up in discussions of the crisis in the welfare state. The concept of 'welfare pluralism' includes the idea that the state does not have to take care of all social services; instead the markets, and various institutions such as the church, etc. can replace it more efficiently (Anttonen 1989). This has been one of the arguments in recent public discussions on behalf of the need to cut down public expenditure in Finland. It can be questioned though, as Raija Julkunen (1992) has done, whether cutting expenditure in the public sector really produces competitive advantage to export industries as it has been argued. Or, as a consequence of the cuts, does the number of self-employed in the social and welfare services actually grow? And what are the consequences of this development, for the social and welfare services and for those in self-employment? While the clearcut divisions between public and private, market and state seem to blur[36], the discussion becomes more complicated and more difficult to handle.

As Aidan Kelly (1991) has argued, the 'problem' of the welfare state for the enterprise ideology is that it involves public expenditure that is a burden on tax-payers and business organisations. This 'burden' could be diminished by

---

35. See for example Harriet Silius' (1992) research on the different facets of the gender contract in Finnish society in the case of women lawyers.

36. This is taking place at least in Finland at the moment: the state support to the private bank sector is estimated to exceed 50 billion FIM this year.

reducing the publicly produced services and offering grounds for privately produced services instead. This idea is based on the belief that privatisation is an unproblematic answer to the problems of state welfare provision.

Naturally the answer is not that simple. The privatisation of the welfare services involves complex shifts away from the welfare state model. According to Kelly, privatisation can mean a shift from an all-public to an all-private model of funding and provision. Privatisation can also mean that the state increases its funding and provision in the private and voluntary sector. In Britain, there has been movement towards privatisation along all fronts. (Kelly 1991)

There are, as yet, no comprehensive studies made on the exact shifts between publicly produced social services and the growth of self-employment in Finland.[37] When we look at the slight growth in self-employment in social and personal services, and follow the recent discussion of the alternatives to employment available to women, and even the 'official' (ie. state-supported) encouragement given to women to start their own businesses, it seems that the trend towards the 'welfare pluralism' is on its way. Questions which remain unanswered are, first of all, the position of women in self-employment and in paid employment: what will happen to women who are now employed in the public services, producing public health care, child care, teaching, elderly care, 'social mothering'? The decline in the number of publicly-produced services means a decline in women's paid employment, but not necessarily a rise in women's self-employment. Thus, the position of women in society, and the gender contracts, will be changing. Another question is to what extent will this development increase inequality in society as a consequence of the breaking down of the welfare services?

---

37. There are some studies concerning the recent changes in Finnish society on the way. Leila Simonen has outlined the possible outcomes as a step to a new era of modernising the whole welfare structure. She sees the redefinition in the relations of gender and citizenship as the crucial one in Finnish society. (Simonen 1993)

5 The settings for women's self-employment

In general, it may be argued that the development of entrepreneurship varies considerably both within and between different countries. Nevertheless, a "new rise" in the number of entrepreneurs has been evident in most OECD countries in recent years. In the 1980s, the relative extent of entrepreneurship, measured as a proportion of the total employed population, clearly grew in such countries as Great Britain, the United States, Canada, the Netherlands, Spain, Italy, Ireland, and Belgium (see table 1.1.A.; also OECD 1986a, 44-48). Moreover, this trend has been accelerating in many countries although exceptions are also to be found. In Finland the relative weight of entrepreneurs as a proportion of the economically active population was in the 1980s actually less than at the beginning of the 1970s (Toivonen 1990, 336).

The extent to which the rise of entrepreneurship in the 1980s can be considered really "new" is, of course, debatable. However, the fact remains that this trend displays certain new features as well as encompassing a number of industries which formerly were not associated with self-employment. I will argue here that the attempt to classify the nature of self-employment into "new" and "old" forms of entrepreneurship is unhelpful, since the phenomenon of self-employment as such is so complicated that it cannot easily be reduced to such bipolar categories.

In chapter 4. it was noted that it was rather common in the 1960s, and even in the 1970s, for economists and sociologists to pay attention to the characteristics and motivations of those who become self-employed. Recent discussions fall mainly under one of two approaches[1] : either they focus on individuals with particular abilities, or else they see self-employment as being more or less 'opportunistic', rather than the result of 'special' abilities that differentiate the self-employed from waged workers. In this chapter I will discuss factors which can be classified as being more structural and environmental in nature. I have classified them according to the themes which

---

1. By 'recent' I mean mainly research carried out at the end of the 1970s and during the 1980s.

have emerged in general discussions.

5.1. Cyclical changes

In general, the growth in the number of self-employed and own-account workers has been explained by recourse to various structural and environmental factors. Two broad groups of explanation for this growth may be identified: first, explanations that refer to *cyclical changes in the economy,* and secondly, explanations that refer *to structural changes in the economy.* According to theories of cyclical change, the growth in the number of entrepreneurs may be connected to the mild economic recessions, which have the effect of encouraging larger companies to withdraw from markets marginal to their core activities and thus create possibilities, in the form of 'market niches' for smaller firms (see e.g. Graham Bannock 1981).

This not only leads to a rise in the number of small firms during periods of economic decline. According to this thesis, a fall in the rate of economic growth and rising unemployment leads to increased efforts on the part of workers to create their own jobs. The total of 'temporary self-employed', which Joseph Quinn (1980), for example, has distinguished from the 'career self-employed', increased during a period of mild recession until opportunities for waged work improved again.

On the other hand it has been noted that changes in the level of employment may produce an 'underemployment' effect in smaller firms. This means that the number of hours worked diminishes radically in small companies and among the self-employed in certain industries, such as construction (Linder 1983, 264; OECD 1986a, 53). Empirical verification for the cyclical model is rather difficult to come by. And, in general, it may be assumed that the extent of cyclical change is usually insufficient to explain the observed growth in the number of entrepreneurs in the OECD countries. This is because growth has taken place as much as a function of time as a function of employment (OECD 1986a, 53). *It could be concluded that the case for considering the business cycle to be a major determinant of change in self-employment is not strong.* Several studies covering individual sectors and industries have examined self-employment as a response to economic changes. The results of these studies have been inconclusive. The effects of cyclical changes upon the extent of self-employment have not been studied in the Finnish context.

5.2. Displacement

A decline in entrepreneurship is often causally linked to a general rise in the level of unemployment, in the sense that unemployment is usually associated with a general decline in the economy. A decrease in a country´s GNP indicates, on the one hand, that the general demand in most sectors of the economy decreases along with the number and scale of investments (Wilken 1971, 7). On the other hand, unemployment is seen to result in an increase in a certain kind of self-employment, which is related to the cyclical features in economic development discussed earlier.

First, it has been argued that high unemployment "forces" people to create their own jobs (the so-called 'push-factor'). This means that during periods of high unemployment, relatively highly-skilled unemployed people with entrepreneurial acumen will find themselves drifting into long-term unemployment. In particular, this occurs in those economic areas which experience high seasonal unemployment and which require special occupational skills – more than high capital investments – that are in scarce supply compared to the demand. Once more, various kinds of construction work may be cited as an example of this kind of work.

Secondly, economies which have a strong public sector can more or less direct the course of development within business formations by their control of governmental support. This support may be provided, for example, in the form of entrepreneurial courses and investment loans, tax incentives, start-up money and different kinds of support programmes aimed at small business. The background for such support is partly ideological: being based both on the idea that small and medium sized businesses employ relatively more people than large businesses (Bannock 1981), and on the idea that the regional importance of this effect are significant. It also has been stated that small and medium-sized businesses avoid certain problems affecting larger organisations, since trade union activity and organisation tends to be of less significance (Rainnie – Scott 1986; Rainnie 1989).

So far, however, the thesis that unemployment is an important factor accounting for the recently recorded growth in self-employment is not necessarily supported by the statistics on changes in the size of the employed population – at least not in the case of Finland. The mathematical probability that a given unemployed person will start a business has not been very high,[2] since most of the start-ups in the Finnish business sector have come from individuals moving directly from employment to self-employment. The reason for this situation is that the number of entrepreneurs is not only much smaller

---

2. Toivonen 1987, 16; also OECD 1987a, 9.

than the number of employees in absolute terms, but also in relative terms; the probability is much smaller that an unemployed person will start up a business, than that he or she will return to some form of waged work. Nonetheless, many writers have postulated the existence of a positive relationship between the level of unemployment in the economy and the rate of new firm formation, even if evidence provided by empirical time-series seldom supports this thesis fully[3] (Johnson 1991).

Recent changes in labour market policy in Finland have led to a strengthening of measures designed to provide funding (in the form of a start-up allowance) for unemployed people who wish to start their own businesses. The eligibility criteria for this allowance are as follows: the applicant must be registered as unemployed, she or he must have sufficient training or experience to be judged capable of self-employment, and the applicant must produce a viable plan for the business.[4] So far, industries where women constitute the majority of the employed have not been included in many of the state support systems. Instead, the support has been more or less directed towards various manufacturing industries. Service industries have not been included in, for example, regional state support systems. *Thus, fewer women than men receive state support for business start-ups.*

In Finland, public health care and the social services constitute the major employment sector for women. At the end of the 1980s, 42 per cent of women in paid employment worked in the public sector. However, the Nordic model of welfare is undergoing a process of structural change: economic decline has created intense pressure to cut back on public sector spending. More generally, not only is the whole of the public sector in Finland built upon the mobilisation of women for paid employment, particularly within the public sector, but so is too the whole of the Nordic welfare system. Thus a decline in employment in the public sector means both that proportionately more women will become unemployed, and that this will occur alongside a disintegration of the foundations underpinning the Finnish welfare system.

As Julkunen (1992) has noted, the recession which was visible in the early

---

3. Evidence from the empirical time-series is relatively sparse largely due to the paucity of aggregate time-series data on firm formation rates and/or employment. Hamilton (1989) has demonstrated a positive relationship between company registrations and unemployment for Scotland between 1950 and 1984, and Hudson (1984) found similar results for Great Britain as a whole. However, as mentioned above, work by Binks and Jennings (1987) has questioned the direction of causality within this relationship,.

4. Unemployed persons admitted to the business start-up scheme receive an allowance equivalent to 50 per cent extra unemployment benefit for 15 months. The maximum amount paid per day during the operation of the business has been 180 FIM (US$ 45) (1990).

1990s raises a question mark not so much over the future of economic growth as over the future of the Nordic social policy and welfare system. The change in emphasis from a system of provision based upon the public sector to one based upon the private sector is not comparable to changes taking place between other industrial sectors. In reply to the question, "what will be the impact of the privatisation of public welfare and social provision?", Julkunen argues that it will result in more women becoming displaced (Julkunen 1992). Even though the state supports women's self-employment in sectors where they so far have been employed in waged work, Julkunen maintains that is not likely to offset the overall negative impact of privatisation upon women's employment at the national level. The transition from a Nordic welfare system towards a British system of welfare service provision neither breaks down the gender-specific forms of labour market segregation, nor does it give women better opportunities in society. Instead, it leads to an increase in inequality, and a deterioration in the labour market position of women.

Even though self-employment is presented as an alternative to unemployment, it is unlikely to guarantee a standard of living similar to that achievable through paid employment. In cases where rising unemployment has led to an increase in self-employment, this increase in self-employment has tended to be only temporary in nature. In practice, the category 'temporary self-employment' implies both incomes insecurity and the likelihood of an increased resort to 'moonlighting'. Overall, studies of worker adjustment to permanent displacement have provided little support for the existence among displaced male workers of a strong interest in self-employment as an adjustment strategy (e.g. Johnson 1981).

5.3. Structural changes in the economy

As argued above, the coincidence of an economic recession with a growth in the number of the unemployed is not necessarily a clear indication of a cyclical cause-effect -relationship.[5] The growth trend for new businesses can equally be attached to another, more *structurally-based, explanatory model* of the changes taking place in post-industrial society. Support for this latter approach also comes from the notion that the cyclical explanation model does not sufficiently explain the changes which have taken place in the society. In most countries,

---

5. Although in certain industries (e.g. construction), where the investment costs born by own-account workers and small businesses are relatively small, the cyclical changes in the economy are naturally reflected in the number of businesses much more readily than in other industries, which have higher investment costs.

the largest part of the new entrepreneurship found outside agriculture is concentrated in *the service sector* and not, as might be supposed, in manufacturing. And, moreover, it is *the service sector which is the most sensitive to economic fluctuations*, even if with some time delay.

A structurally-based model of explanation receives support from statistics on the growth in the employed population, and from the growth in the extent of entrepreneurship by industry in most OECD countries. Although both the size of the labour force and the number of entrepreneurs have either declined or remained stable in manufacturing during the 1970s and 1980s, the number of entrepreneurs in the service sector has grown in most countries (OECD 1986a, 51-52; also OECD 1987a).[6] In Finland the economic importance of business services has grown substantially over the last few decades. Growth was especially rapid during the latter half of the 1980s, so that in 1988 11 per cent of all enterprises were in business related services. The majority of these enterprises (74 per cent) were small companies employing under 5 per cent of the employed population (CSOF 1990b).

To a large extent, growth within the service sector is accounted for by the growth in the provision of so-called personal services. This trend in Finland is also common to all other industrial countries. Growth of this kind usually takes place as the result of a shift from the primary sector to the tertiary sector involving a relative as well as an absolute decline in the size of the secondary sector. Finland is an exception in this sense, since the service sector was already larger than the manufacturing sector in the 1960s, at a time when the primary sector – agriculture – was the largest employer (Toivonen 1988). This structural model of explanation is supported not only by evidence of a growth in entrepreneurship in general but also by OECD employment research: The service sector has been the largest employer in most OECD countries since the 1970s.

But the service sector is not a single unified entity and neither are all industries within the service sector similar in respect of their features and the possibilities they offer for self-employment. Steinmetz and Wright (1989) show that the incidence of changes in self-employment by industry is quite varied even within the service sector. Turning to Finland (chapters 6. and 7.), there are some signs that this has taken place so that more men have become self-employed in female-dominated sectors than vice versa.

---

6. According to Toivonen the growth of the new entrepreneurship has taken place within industries, which does not necessarily imply structural change in the economy as a whole (Toivonen 1989).

5.4. Technological changes

Technological innovations are closely connected to different structural explanation models in the sense that technological changes in production are usually stable in nature. Innovations also increase the possibilities open to small and medium-sized businesses. For example, one of the fastest expanding industries in Finland, measured by the rise in the number of entrepreneurs, is that of business services (embracing accounting firms, advertising companies, etc.). This rise is seen, more or less, to be a direct consequence of technological development (in respect of personal computers). The cost of innovations varies considerably depending upon the branch. Moreover, the developmental phase of the economy affects the ability of innovative companies to break into the market. It has been noted that during periods of economic recession more companies are established within stable or even 'declining' industries than within innovative and newly established industries (Binks – Jennings 1987, 34).

The importance of technological innovations for the development of the economy has already been discussed by Schumpeter (1951/1989). Roy Rothwell and William Zegweld (1982, 61) have shown the importance of small companies and entrepreneurship for the production and spread of innovations (see also Marchesnay 1990). According to Roy Rothwell and William Zegweld, the strategic importance of small businesses in general can be crucial in situations which concern the development of new technology and its implementation, as well as in situations where the markets develop quickly (e.g. in biotechnology, microelectronics, etc.). However, the need for large investment does diminish the development of small businesses in these areas (Alic 1986; Rothwell 1989, 51; also NSF 1979).

Small and medium-sized firms cannot merely be considered to be a passive buffer within the economy. Depending upon the industry, small businesses can be important innovators. The capital intensive industries do not have opportunities for company formation since large scale production investments are beyond the means of small companies. Scase and Goffee distinguish four industries in which small and medium-sized businesses in general can be found: the textile industry, the printing and publishing industry, subcontracting in plastics, instruments and tools and finally, consumer goods trades with low costs and high labour content, products involving strong elements of fashion and specialisation like furniture and clothes (Scase – Goffee 1980, 21). Growth areas for small enterprises in the economy still involve elements of labour intensiveness, subcontracting, small-scale technological innovation and market variability. Of these different factors the degree of labour intensiveness has been cited as the most important factor.

5.5. New forms for the organisation of work

5.5.1. Subcontracting

On the other hand, account must be taken of the fact that the majority of the production markets of the industrial societies are governed by large companies, rather than small or medium-sized ones. This means that contrary to the research setting for the majority of the literature of the 1970s, small and medium-sized companies should not be seen as a sector in competition with the large company sector. Rather, it should be regarded as an ancillary sector, providing complementary services similar to those of subcontracting businesses. Small and medium-sized enterprises form a more flexible part of the economy than large companies, and this flexibility has been seen as giving them better changes to survive periods of economic recession. According to Suzanne Berger (1981), subcontracting, especially in manufacturing, is relatively large in France, Italy and Japan. Furthermore Berger argues that the small business sector in these countries provides a buffer against uncertainty for large companies during periods of recession. A rise in wage costs has also accelerated the shift of production abroad in the form of subcontracting.

Not all work is done on the basis of subcontracting, but any attempt to reduce indirect wage costs increases the importance of alternative forms of wage labour. It is also worthy of note that the number of people who work at home is estimated to have grown considerably in many countries (Hakim 1984; Dale 1986; Allen – Wolkowitz 1987). A number of special features emerge in respect of the nature of work and arrangements between homeworker and employer when different countries are compared. In Italy, for example, the unofficial or underground economy (grey sector) is estimated to constitute a rather large part of the whole economy (Berger 1981). The majority of the work undertaken in the grey economy consists of different kinds of subcontracting[7] carried out in the home. Part of the work which was earlier carried out in the factory has been shifted to the home with the help of family members, including children (see e.g. Annie Phizacklea 1989). The employer may rent out machines required for the completion of the work, but often the employer expects the worker to use her/his own sewing machine or steam iron etc.

---

7. Overall, the evasion of taxes and the avoidance of regulation are also seen as some of the major reasons for unrecorded self-employment.

5.5.2. Homeworking

The definitions of home-based work, or homeworking, vary to some extent. Sheila Allen and Carol Wolkowitz (1987) define homeworking as waged work which is carried out on domestic premises. This definition of homeworking excludes self-employed persons, artisans and artists. Minna Salmi, in her dissertation concerning the extensive resort to homeworking in Finland, has a different starting point. Salmi (1991) uses location and duration of the work contract as the main criteria by which to define homework. Thus, the self-employed are also included in her material, although the focus of her research is in the everyday life of those who work at home. Where self-employment is the main focus of interest, the main criteria for the definition of home-based work are independence and autonomy. Homeworking is usually defined broadly to cover all those workers who work from home including the self-employed, freelance workers and independent contractors.

Irrespective of the country, it is commonly assumed that most homeworkers are women (Allen 1989a; Salmi 1991). For example, in Japan almost all home-based workers, who mostly do phase work or assembly work in the electronics industry or the textile industry, are women who are classified as own-account workers in the statistics (OECD 1986b, 64). However, this is not the case in Finland. According to Salmi, once childminders are excluded from the statistics, as many men as women are to be found in the homeworking category (Salmi 1991, 68). This is partly due to the large proportion of own-account workers, and the predominance of men in that category.

In discussions of the employment position of homeworkers, it is commonly noted that even if, in a statistical sense, they share essential elements with own-account workers, homeworkers can very seldom be thought of as 'real' entrepreneurs in anything other than a statistical sense. Very often the special and narrow nature of subcontracting and home-based assembly work make it impossible to accept other work assignments. Naturally this diminishes the actual number of entrepreneurs if the basis of the definition is the independence of self-employment.

As a form of production and as a form of paid work most homeworking is hidden. This deception is not only characteristic of homeworking but also of women's self-employment in general. In Finland, homeworkers comprised 2.5 per cent of the economically active population in 1985. According to Salmi (1991), this is not exceptional when compared to figures for other countries (Sweden 2.5 per cent; US 2 to 5 per cent; UK 2.8 per cent).

The occupational groups containing the largest proportion of homeworkers in Finland are childminders (41 per cent of all in homeworking are

Table 5.1. Socio-economic status of the homeworkers (%)

Status	Total labour force			Homeworkers				
	All	Men	Women	All	Men	Women	Child-minder	Other
Wage workers	86	84	88	57	26	69	93	36
Self-employed	8	12	4	32	59	21	7	41
Employers	2	3	1	3	9	1	-	2
Assisting family members	4	1	7	8	6	9	-	21
Total	100	100	100	100	100	100	100	100

Source: Salmi 1991, 65 ; CSOF 1988a.

childminders), real estate workers (8 per cent), animal attendants (3.5 per cent) and hairdressers (2 per cent). Salmi briefly discusses the division of homeworkers into employees and self-employed. Once the largest number of homeworkers, the childminders, are excluded from the analysis, the majority of (the remaining) homeworkers in Finland fall under the classification of own-account workers, i.e. self-employed persons without employees. Indeed two out of every three homeworkers are self-employed (childminders excluded; see table 5.1.). In the case of homeworking women, Salmi notes that there are three times more women in the 'assisting family member' category than there are in all other employment categories. Salmi refers here either to family ownership of businesses, or to those women who are in charge of the paperwork associated with their husbands´ firms. (I will discuss the position of assisting family members in chapter 7.)

Further, one factor which has had an effect on the number of small businesses and on the birth of new firms is *that of structural change within the markets.* An example of this is the increase that has taken place in franchising activity in recent years. The most important factors for small firms, from the point of view of costs, are the vertical market structure and centralisation. These two factors influence the selection of enterprise form (McGee 1989).

The argument usually advanced is that by granting franchisees a licence to use a proven business format, the hurdle of finding a specific and viable business idea is surmounted, thus offering many an opportunity to 'be their own boss' (Felstead 1991, 68). Since risk avoidance has been shown to be the most important factor in the selection process of a business formula, franchising is usually regarded as a safer option. This is so, even if the degree of business independence varies depending on the formula chosen (Knight 1984, 61). The growth of franchising has also increased the number of self-employed (Bögenhold 1988, 1989; Felstead 1991). This increase has also been affected by the increase of alternative forms of business such as co-operatives.

Freedom from external control is often taken as one of the defining characteristics that also differentiates small firms from the larger units of large companies – as well as the self-employed from employees (see Rainbird 1991). However, as has been pointed out on many occasions, even the degree of independence enjoyed by the conventional small business is always less than total, and often difficult to assess accurately in practice (Felstead 1991). The ability to exercise business independence, to 'be your own boss', are not dichotomous notions, but relative concepts which some small firms enjoy to a greater degree than others. There are different levels of independence and fluidity depending, for example, on the formula chosen for the contracts in franchising.

5.6. Institutional influences

The desire to minimize corporate taxation can induce larger companies to split themselves up into smaller independent units in countries where legislation makes such a procedure possible. An example of this sort of behaviour was provided by the so-called "Lump" system of subcontracting in the construction industry, which allowed the subcontractors to defer payment of taxes until after the work in question has been completed while also permitting some tax reductions (Bolton Report 1971). This has been seen as a means to increase significantly company formation in those activities where subcontracting was possible. The general impact of the taxation system can also be indirectly seen in the small firm sector: in some countries the taxation of income from self-employment is much lower than the taxation of waged income. The observed difference in taxation levels is largely due to differences in the kinds of deduction permitted (OECD 1986a, 56).

In the context of the growth of the small business sector there are two main ways to explain changes in the level of state intervention, or in the lack of such intervention. First, reference may be made to the ineffectiveness of public sector services. This argument is commonly used when publicly produced services (e.g. the health services) are being privatised (this is the so-called 'economic model of explanation'). Secondly, reference may be made to the failure of the state system to solve bureaucratic problems (this is the so-called 'political model of explanation'). Both of these types of explanation implicitly are used to legitimise the privatisation of the public sector.[8]

Privatisation results in a shift in the ideology of the welfare state that parallels the move from a *regulated market economy towards an individualistic market economy, where the emphasis is on the private business sector and the importance of the public sector is diminished through the privatisation of services.* Countries which have gone furthest in the direction of privatisation have privatised not only state-owned companies but also services such as certain health care and education services and housing services (UK, US) which previously had been publicly produced and thus did not express market values.

According to researchers in social policy this is not only a question of the economic system or of the political system and its functions, but also of a desire to dismantle the welfare state system. Privatisation makes possible both a growth of private services and, at the same time, for example, the transfer of certain services which earlier were provided by the state social system, back to the home and the responsibility of individual women, in the form of unpaid labour (Anttonen 1989, 66). But at the same time privatisation also creates possibilities for new alternative models for the provision of social services (Riska 1981). In Finland, however, it is difficult to see, for example, how self-employment could offer these women who lose their jobs in the public health care services the opportunity to attain the same standard of living and continuity of employment. And it is questionable whether self-employment could provide the same standard of care any cheaper than the existing public services.

Besides current moves to restructure the welfare state and to alter the level of state intervention and the nature of policy implementation, changes are also taking place at the level of general values. In opposition to the corporatist trend of the 1960s, increasing stress is being laid on individualism, which is creating a generally favourable climate for self-employment. The new emphasis on privatisation cannot be distinguished clearly from political and ideological changes which have strengthened due to the importance of right-wing politics. The growth in the standard of living has coincided with the crisis expressed in terms of inefficiency, low status, etc., of the public sector services, and this has increased the demand for the private sector services e.g. in health care.

---

8. However, it should be noted that the public-private distinction has not *one* but *several elements* (see Lane 1985, 8). In political sociology, the term 'government and its organisations' is preferred to the term 'public-private', However, the term 'public sector with public finance' is sometimes used.

5.7. Summary

The discussion of factors mentioned which influence the growth of the small business sector of the economy, in respect of the reduction of costs through the application of new technological innovations, the growth of subcontracting and the growth of government support, are all factors which may be thought of as being common to the growth of both men´s and women´s self-employment. *However, it may be assumed that there are further factors which have been especially important for the growth of women´s self-employment, and yet other factors which have clearly supported the rise of men´s self-employment more than women´s self-employment* (Aldrich et al. 1989). One example of this latter group of factors is state support to manufacturing industries which, at least in Finland, is directed more to the predominantly male metal industries and manufacturing than to predominately female handicraft and service-related businesses (Wickmann 1989a; Kovalainen 1989a).

The growth of women´s labour force participation has been seen as a development that has widened the possibilities open to women to engage in self-employment. Goffee and Scase (1985) argue that women´s self-employment generally follows the breadth and distribution of women´s paid work. If the availability of state-provided care and other public services is restricted, entrepreneurship may offer an opportunity to 'earn a living' and to regulate, for instance, their working hours in a more flexible way than women could within paid work. Nevertheless, it has to be remembered that the work of the housewives is regulated in accordance with the timetables of their husbands and children (Simonen 1990). In this sense the regulation of such women´s labour is not within their own control.

When discussing the flexibility of women´s working hours and of those hours women work in the home, it should be borne in mind that this flexibility is not always voluntary. In everyday life the line between voluntary and involuntary flexibility is constantly changing. However, the possibility of greater flexibility which has become more concrete as a result of information technology is becoming more general, and as a result the growth of home-based business has been one of the main factors in the growth of women´s self-employment in the USA (SBA 1986). The need for flexibility has also been seen as a major reason for the growth of women´s self-employment in those OECD countries where it has been growing the fastest (OECD 1987c).

Clearly, restructuring refers to a complex set of different economic, social and political changes. Reference to some of these changes is contained within the notion of *'the enterprise culture'*: individualism, independence, flexibility, anti-collectivism, privatism, self-help and so on. It has been argued that *the discourse of the business (or enterprise) culture presents itself as the justificatory language of social integration for a world characterised by an economic insecurity unknown in the more corporatist and collectivist world of the 1960s and much of the 1970s* (Burrows 1991; Pollert 1988). However, it is clear that rise in the standard of living together with the crisis of the public sector services in many OECD countries, from the 1970s onwards, has increased the demand in the private sector, e.g. in respect of health care.

In this chapter I discussed a variety of mainly structural and institutional factors which have contributed to the increase in self-employment. No single factor stands out as being crucial for the recent growth of self-employment. Nor is it exactly clear how some of the factors discussed here have affected the shift from paid employment to self-employment, as some of the factors are clearly contradictory in nature. It is also difficult to say whether the growth of self-employment represents a lasting restructuring and change in the nature of the labour market, or indeed, a lasting change in behaviour of the labour force. It may be, as some researches have implicitly suggested, that *changes have occurred in factors which are less accessible to measurement, such as shifts in cultural attitudes, attitudes toward autonomy, flexibility in working hours, willingness to take economic risks, nonpecuniary factors and finally, work itself.*

Part III

PART III

6 The tale vs. the reality – a sketch of self-employed women in Finland

6.1. Women's work and women's business

Two points may be made about the discussions referred to above. First, the picture of self-employment that emerges is many-sided in nature and characterised by a masculine set of discourses. Secondly, self-employed women have been presented in these discourses as being both separate and excluded from the whole phenomena of self-employment and entrepreneurship. Self-employed women have not been 'present' when self-employment has been discussed in general, while their economic importance has been equally invisible. As a consequence, women´s self-employment is discussed in the literature only in the context of individual choices, and of the freedom and restrictions met in waged work.

Statistical data on the development of aggregate self-employment provide only a limited view of the labour market situation of Finnish women. One way to disaggregate the statistical data is to consider the changing pattern of self-employment across industry groups. Other ways to disaggregate data on the self-employed also exist, including disaggregation according to occupation.[1] However, to a large extent, the occupational structure of the self-employed reflects the distribution by industry. Moreover, precise judgments about the skill level of the self-employed cannot be drawn directly from the type of information provided on, e.g. major groups in occupational classification reports, when judged at aggregated level.[2]

The purpose of this chapter is to examine where Finnish self-employed women are located and, where possible, to consider changes between industries over time. In chapter 7., I will concentrate on the development of

---

1. However, industry was selected as a basis of disaggregation for several reasons, one of the most important being that reasonably comparable time series data for the future cross-country comparisons are more easily obtainable on an industry basis.

2. One reason for this is that International Standard Classification of Occupations was not designed to describe detailed skill levels.

female non-farm based self-employment in Finland, and I will look at the development of those industries in which female entrepreneurship measured as the share of all self-employed is important.

6.1.1. Features of women's self-employment in some OECD countries

One of the reasons why the rise of entrepreneurship has been so remarkable, has been in its historical unexpectedness. The declining trend in the number of small firms and self-employment in most industrial societies was seen as an indicator of economic progress itself, as discussed earlier. "The remarkable renaissance", as Curran and Blackburn label the rise of the small business sector in the 1980s in Great Britain, has been widely documented (Curran – Blackburn 1991).[3] However, according to Curran and Burrows, there have been some tendencies to overstate the growth of women's share of self-employment and small business ownership (Curran – Burrows 1988, 29). This seems to be the case for many OECD countries, as Allen and Truman suggest, even if self-employment and small business ownership have increased for both men and women, and there is no certain evidence in official statistics to suggest that the ratios between men and women have changed (Allen – Truman 1991, 115).

The rising trends, however, have been noticed, and documented, in Japan and in the USA as well as in Canada, where the small business sector and the importance of small businesses in the economy have originally been much larger than in Great Britain. The importance of the small business sector in general is also emphasised by the fact that, according to the statistics, the net growth of new jobs is concentrated into the small business sector of the economy, and that this birth of new jobs has a more significant role in employment than the possible expansion taking place in 'old' or declining industries (OECD 1987c).

Entrepreneurship has generally been concentrated into certain industries, such as the retail and wholesale and hotel and catering industries, which vary in OECD countries from 25 per cent to 50 per cent, the average being 37 per cent. The entrepreneurs in the retail trade consist of 18 to 30 per cent of all entrepreneurs in countries where a more detailed classification by industries is available. *Both the retail trade and various personal services are among the two most important areas for women entrepreneurs in Finland.* The importance of

---

3. Self-employment in the UK rose from under 2m in 1979 to almost 3.5m in 1989 according to Labour Force Survey data (Department of Employment, 1990). Undoubtedly the rapid rise is partly due to restructuration taking place in British economy (see e.g. Bagguley et al. 1990).

the real estate and business related services and personal services has risen during the last decade in most of the OECD countries (OECD 1986a, 1987b). The number of entrepreneurs in manufacturing varies strongly between countries, largely depending on the economic structure in the country. The share of entrepreneurs in manufacturing is lowest in the USA, Great Britain and Canada, whereas it is highest in Japan, Germany and in the Scandinavian countries.

The number of entrepreneurs can be seen as reflecting the relative size differences between industries measured by employment (OECD 1986a). However, two branches manifest themselves as the most important ones, when measured by the number of employed in the same industry. These two are the retail and wholesale trade and the catering and hotel services. They are followed by construction industry, and the insurance and real estate businesses. The number of employed in manufacturing industry has declined rather evenly in all other OECD countries except Japan. There have been shifts within various industries, so that in most OECD countries the number of employed in high-technology businesses has risen in spite of the capital intensiveness of the branch (OECD 1987b).

The development of entrepreneurship in Scandinavian countries varies somewhat from that in other OECD countries. In all Scandinavian countries the turning-point in the development of the number of self-employed seems to settle into the beginning of the 1980s. In Sweden, the number of self-employed shot up after the decline of the 1970s, partly due to governmental support. In the 1980s, most of the growth has taken place in service industries (OECD 1986b). Depending on the time-period, the rise in the number of self-employed can be placed at the end of the 1970s and the beginning of 1980s, and this seems to be true especially for the business related services (Lindmark 1982, 11).

In Norway, during the period 1973-1984, the decline was strongest in the share of entrepreneurs in both mining and in manufacturing, whereas the number of entrepreneurs rose rapidly in service industries, concentrated mostly in business related services and in personal services at the beginning of the 1980s. Women's share of all entrepreneurs outside agriculture was, according to the statistics, 14 per cent in 1980. It rose from the year 1970, when the share was 10 per cent; correspondingly it was 12 per cent in 1960, and 15 per cent in 1950. Development in Denmark was rather similar to Norway. (OECD 1986a, 1987b, 1987c)

Women's self-employment and business ownership has concentrated in industries where women form the majority of employees, especially in distribution, hotel and catering services and other services. All in all, the trend sketched above would suggest that women's business opportunities will widen in the future, even though the present data of the Finnish experience does not necessarily support this. This persistence of the gender-typing of industrial branches and occupations needs to be further examined.

According to the statistics it seems that the highest growth figures for women's self-employment can be found in countries where the importance of the public sector in the economy is minor, and general economic development has been positive (Canada, USA), and the lowest are in countries where the public sector is large (Denmark) or agriculture and manufacturing are dominant industries (Greece), or where the economic structure is biased as being one-sided or dominated by one industry only (table 6.1).

As can be seen from table 6.1, in two countries only, Japan and the USA (underlined figures in the table), female self-employment in relation to male self-employment exceeds the corresponding labour force participation rate. *Women's self-employment in relation to women's waged labour seems to be greatest in countries where the employment in the public sector has not risen very strongly* (OECD 1987c). In addition to the relative shares, the growth rate

Table 6.1. Share of women and men in non-farm paid employment and self-employment, in selected OECD countries (%)

	year	Men self-employed	employed	Women self-employed	employed
Austria	1984	68	59	32	41
Belgium	1983	74	66	26	34
Canada	1984	63	57	37	43
Denmark	1983	83	52	17	48
France	1983	75	59	25	41
Germany	1984	84	70	16	30
Greece	1984	84	70	16	30
Italy	1983	83	67	21	33
Japan	1984	64	64*	36	36*
Netherlands	1984	78	67	22	34
Norway	1984	71	55	30	45
Sweden	1984	72	51	28	49
UK	1983	75	58	25	42
USA	1984	55	67	45	33

* accurate percentages are 64.4 and correspondingly, 35.6.

Source: OECD 1986a

130

of female entrepreneurship is essential: For example in the Netherlands, female entrepreneurship has risen over 200 per cent from 1971 to 1985, when waged employment has risen by only 38 per cent (OECD 1987c). This gives an instance of the fact that female self-employment has grown in the fast-growing service industries, and this private entrepreneurship seems to compensate partly for the lack of public services in those countries, where the public sector is not very large.

In Scandinavian countries women's self-employment mainly follows the development of women's labour force participation, so that industries where women's share of the labour force is high also have a relatively large proportion of women entrepreneurs. Of all Scandinavian countries, the number of women in service occupations has grown most rapidly in Sweden, where the total growth of the female labour force has shifted into personal and business related services. Industries like the retail and wholesale trade, have employed women during the last decade to a much smaller extent (Nordic Council of Ministers 1989, table 18). In service industries the proportion of women has tripled during 1960 and 1985. In other Scandinavian countries the rise has not been so rapid, although women's employment is also mostly concentrated in the service industries in Denmark, where 58.3 per cent of women work in service industries.[4] In Sweden the corresponding figure is 55.4 per cent.[5]

The comparison of Scandinavian countries reveals that in Denmark, women's self-employment is lower than in other countries. However, government support to women's self-employment and education are perhaps highest in Denmark (Bryt Nytt 1988). Entrepreneurial education and government supported services like educational support, advice and consultation are much more integrated with the *government's labour policy* there than in other Scandinavian countries. This means that the support given also aims at different kinds of goals. Furthermore, in Denmark the relationship between the feminist movement and women's self-employment seems to be more intense than in other Nordic countries. This may increase the general interest in alternative forms of entrepreneurship – within the terms of Goffee and Scase – and also raise interest in ordinary forms of self-employment and lower the 'threshold' to becoming an entrepreneur. (Wickmann 1989b).[6]

---

4. According to 1981 statistics.

5. According to 1985 statistics.

6. In other Nordic countries there are no separate support systems for self-employed men and self-employed women, even if there has been some experimental, separate courses in Finland, Norway and Sweden.

6.1.2. Features of women's work in Finland

The changes in the structure of the economy have also meant changes in women's labour force participation. Women's labour force participation rose from 57 per cent (1950) to 72 per cent (1985) (CSOF 1956, 1988a). These figures show that women have been active in the labour force in Finland during the whole industrialisation period. The latest rise in women's labour force participation did not start much before the 1970s, whereas the decline in men's labour force participation had already started in the 1960s. The connection between the growth of the service sector and the rise of women's labour force participation exists, because the growth of the private and public services created new jobs which very soon became occupied by women. The largest growth has taken place in public services (table 6.2.).

The rapid economic change and the importance of the manufacturing sector is partly reflected by the fact that as late as the 1960s, 53 per cent of all women in employment worked in the traditionally male-dominated branches (e.g. technical occupations, manufacturing occupations, farming occupations) and 47 per cent in female-dominated branches (service-related occupations, nursing and health care occupations, teaching, clerical work). However, the high percentage in male occupations is mostly due to the importance of farming in the industrial division, even in the 1960s. The strong reduction in farming is already visible in the 1970s' statistics.

In 1980, only 18 per cent of all men in employment worked in female occupations, whereas 32 per cent of women worked in male occupations. However, this should not be interpreted as women having broken down the occupational segregation; on the contrary, the move has been in the opposite direction: relatively more men than before are in the service sector. Partly this is

Table 6.2. Number of women and their share of all employed in public services in Finland, 1960-1990

	1960	1970	1975	1980	1985	1990
Women's number (in thousands)	124	192	256	332	398	455
Women's %-share of employed in public services[*]	39.5	50.3	55.7	60.0	63.1	64.5

* state-governed companies not included

Source: Julkunen 1992, 44.

132

influenced by the decline of traditional male occupations (in manufacturing industry) and partly by the growth of the service sector, in which new occupational groups are being born. Instead, women's share in manufacturing occupations and in the male occupational sector has remained stable almost from the 1950s onwards, with almost every fifth worker in these occupations a woman.[7]

When we inspect the occupational substructure, we notice that the following branches are clearly feminine: *over 90 per cent of all employed have been women* in household-related and beauty-care occupations, in washing and ironing work, in cutting, upholstering and sewing occupations, in secretarial work, and in accounting and cashier tasks in 1985. *Further, 81-90 per cent of all employed are women* in medical and nursing jobs, in waiters' jobs and in cleaning, postal and office work. *The fewest women employed* are in the legal, wholesale and agency occupations, in the securities business, in guardian and military occupations, in construction and manufacturing occupations.

The most essential changes both in men's and women's occupations took place in the mid-1970s (CSOF 1973a, 1983, 1988a), whereas it seems that there were not so many changes in the 1980s. Changes have taken place in nursing and caring occupations where women's share of all employed rose in the 1980s, and in some manufacturing occupations in which men's share of all employed has risen. However, here we have to remember that the degree of segregation by *industrial sector* is less than by broad *occupational grouping*. It is noted that this is because women tend to be concentrated in a small range of occupations within different industries.

Table 6.3. Share of women in female dominated occupations[a] and share of men in male dominated occupations[b], 1950-1985 (%)

	1950	1960	1970	1975	1980	1985
Women in female dominated occupations	79	82	79	78	84	85
Men in male dominated occupations	92	90	86	87	87	87

a = women's share 51 – 100 % of all employed.
b = men's share 51 – 100 % of all employed.

Source: Anttalainen 1986.

---

7. 23 per cent of all employed in technical, science, manufacturing, traffic and governmental occupations were women in 1950s, whereas in 1980s the corresponding figure was 22 per cent.

When we take the changes in the occupational structure into account, the differentiation in occupational segregation by gender has become stronger in Finland, except in the farming sector. (Anttalainen 1986, 69; table 6.3.) The phenomenon was strongest in administrative, retail and service occupations from 1960 to 1980; the changes between 1980 and 1985 were nowhere near as great. The feminisation of the occupational structure, which is to say that women's share in almost all occupational areas and in almost all occupations has grown, and the simultaneous segregation by sectors are most often interpreted as meaning gender polarisation in the occupational structure (Anttalainen 1986, 75; Walby 1986; Hakim 1979).

When we inspect the whole occupational structure it seems to be evening out, since women's share has risen in almost all occupations. The conclusions drawn by Anttalainen (1986) are undoubtedly true, when the information pertaining to the reason for the rise in the women's share is drawn in to this picture: the rise in the women's share is due *both* to the rise in the number of women *and* to the decrease in the quantity of men. When the statistics are compared, it seems that men's occupational activity is greater than that of women, tied to the gender division of the occupations (Anttalainen 1986). This is also supported by educational statistics. The circumstances which prevent women from entering male occupations are complicated, and are both individual and structural by nature. Different economic theories explain the effects of these factors in different ways.

The difference between genders emerges, as well as occupational differentiation, in the occupational *status difference*, which measures the inequality in perhaps a more significant way than the division of labour in different sectors and occupations. Occupational status in itself carries meanings of status, respect, and potential for career advances. The clearest difference between men and women was previously most marked in agriculture, and the difference is still very clear in managerial positions. Agriculture differs from other industries in the sense that women's position as entrepreneurs has been minor; in statistics farmers´ spouses are classified as helping/assisting family members, while husbands are classified as self-employed. However, in other industries women's share of all self-employed is greater than in agriculture.

In many OECD countries women have formed, and still act as, a sort of "threshold labour force", which works as a buffer in the labour markets and thus increases flexibility (Työvoimaministeriö 1985). When we examine disguised unemployment, we can see it – with only a few exceptions – consisting of women and young people. This development has been different in Finland: Women's labour market participation has traditionally been rather high, and growth has not occurred in the same way in the period of after World

War II as it did in many OECD countries. The demand for women's labour has been seen to be connected to structural changes in the economy in the short term, and to fluctuations in the economic situation in the longer term.

On the other hand, Ingberg et al. (1986, 24) note that, in the case of women as well, the regularity of the economic fluctuation has been broken during the last few years and the flexibility of the supply of women's labour has decreased (see also Owen – Joshi 1987): this means that women do not return to the home as reserve labour e.g. after the birth of children. Taken altogether, *women's labour market behaviour patterns have come closer to men's labour market behaviour patterns.* In spite of this, labour market segregation does not seem to change.

6.2. Changes within industries or between industrial structures?

In the following chapters I will describe some of the developmental features in women's self-employment and entrepreneurship in Finland from the 1960s to the 1990s. Part of the research literature connects the growth in women's entrepreneurship to the "new rise of self-employment", which has developed in a parallel fashion in many countries (see e.g. Aldrich et al. 1989; Cromie 1985). However, according to Toivonen, this 'new rise' of self-employment is not so much due to the structural changes in the economy as to internal changes within industries in most of the countries where entrepreneurship has grown in the 1980s (Toivonen 1990, 336).

The question to which I have tried to find a tentative answer is whether the aforementioned is analogous in the case of women, whether the changes in women's self-employment are due to the *internal changes* within industries, or whether they are more *structural by nature.* Shift-share analysis is used here as an exploratory method to determine whether the changes in women's self-employment are connected to general changes in employment.

Shift-share analysis has generally been used in comparative studies of regional development and of occupational change, and also in comparisons of class structures (Toivonen 1990). Most applications of shift-share analysis have been reported in regional economics (Green – Allaway 1985). It has also been used to assess the influence of a region's industry-mix on its growth in employment, as Tervo and Okko note (1983, 115). Toivonen has used shift-share analysis in the inspection of new entrepreneurship and the changes in the economy under study that concerned 12 of the OECD countries.

The shift-share analysis makes it possible to analyse whether the changes (rise/decline) in women's self-employment are due to changes in the number of women employed within an industry, or whether the change has taken place between industries, which refers more to structural changes in the economy. Observed changes in the proportion of female self-employment in total employment may be arithmetically broken down into three components by means of shift-share analysis.

The strategy of the analysis brings out three shift components, namely the *structural* component, *internal* component and *interaction* component. The structural component is counted assuming that the share of women's self-employment within economic sectors had remained unchanged, but also assuming that the distribution of women's employment between industries changed as expected. The structural component thus measures the employment change expected if all industries had developed exactly on a par with the national averages for these industries.

The internal shift component is counted under the assumption that the share of industries in women's employment had remained unchanged, but assuming that the share of self-employed women within industries had changed as it actually did. The interaction component is a residual term whose interpretation is rather more complex. As Toivonen notes, the component can be expected to be large if the shares of industries of total employment and simultaneously the shares of self-employment within industries both change considerably (Toivonen 1990).

The net change is the difference between the actual and hypothetical number of self-employed women. The latter is that which would have resulted from the employment increase if the share of self-employment had remained unchanged. Simply put, the shift-share calculation thus compares expected with actual growth.[8] The net change or net shift will be positive if the component exerted an influence in the same direction as the actual net change, whereas a negative shift naturally implies a move in the opposite direction to the actual net change. However, we have to remember that the usefulness of the shift-share analysis is subject to limitations that must be understood prior to an application of the technique. There are a number of caveats surrounding the interpretation of the output of the shift-share analysis. It should be recognised that the percentage net shift figure has meaning only within the analysis group and the time frame used. Since the time frame is important, there should not be any external influencing economic forces, such as e.g. changes in the labour market.

Since shift-share calculations involve only two points in time, the time frame of the analysis is critical. In order to inspect, in particular, the change that took place in the assumed 'new self-employment', I chose two time periods for comparison. First, 1980 was selected as the base year for the comparison, and

---

8. Detailed computing formulae in appendix.

Table 6.4. **Net changes in female self-employment and its components** (%)

years	structural shift	internal shift	interaction shift	total	net change (000)
1980-85	7.9	169.8	–77.7	100	7.27
1985-90	29.5	84.5	–14.0	100	16.23

Source: CSOF census data for 1980-1990.

I compared the changes from 1980 to 1985. Secondly, I compared the most recent changes from 1985 to 1990, in order to find out whether development at the end of 1980s would be different to the earlier part of the decade. The internal and structural changes were calculated at one-digit level of ISIC.[9]

When the structural change component is counted, it is assumed that the division of self-employed women has been unchanged in different sectors of the economy, but that the change in the numbers of employed women is real. In the counting of the internal change component it is assumed that the division of labour in different industries has remained unchanged but in the case of self-employed women the actual change is taken into account. The interaction component is thus the difference between the net change and the structural and internal components.

Both the structural and internal change have had a positive influence on the increase of women entrepreneurs. However, for first time period inspected here, the internal change is much stronger than that of the structural component, thus referring to the importance of internal changes within industries, not to any changes in the industrial structure. This means that, for example, in 1980-1985 the percentage growth in women's self-employment should have risen by almost 170 per cent if the percentages within industries had grown as they did but, simultaneously, the industrial structure as a whole had remained unchanged. The interaction component is relatively large for 1980-1985, and it has negative influence i.e. a simultaneous change in industrial structure and occupational status.

In 1985-1990, the importance of the structural shift seems to have grown, in comparison to an earlier period. Furthermore, the impact of internal and interaction components in the analysis has changed. The decline in the impact

---

9. Industries included were all activities outside agriculture (mining, manufacturing, electricity, gas and water, construction, wholesale and retail trade, restaurants and hotels, transport, storage and communication, financing, insurance, real estates, business services, community, social and personal services, other activities).

of the internal shift, even if it is still more important than the structural shift, means that the growth of self-employment within industries did slow down during the latter part of 1980s, in 1985-1990.

Change in the structural shift, i.e. the changes in the industrial structure, have had rather a strong influence on increasing the percentage of women's self-employment. This seems to be true, even if employment in the public sector grew during the 1980s, and this would possibly have lessened the impact of the structural component. In other words, the time period chosen for the comparison, as well as the frequency of the classification, can have some effect here. The interactive change had a slight negative influence on the development in the number of women entrepreneurs. In other words, the internal change in different branches has had a greater effect on women's rising self-employment than the structural change across industries, even though the latter has also been positive.[10]

The shift-share analysis reinforces the idea that the internal shifts have been more significant than the structural shifts in the change of the percentage of women's self-employment in Finland in 1980-1990. This result is in general agreement with the conclusions of Toivonen (1990). There has been growth in the importance of the structural component during the latter part of 1980s but, in general, the internal component still plays the major part in the percentage change of women's self-employment. *Thus, the changes in the proportions of women's self-employment are only partly due to changes in industrial structures of the Finnish economy.* A more disaggregated analysis would possibly reveal a more complicated picture with more exaggerated nuances. However, since the focus of my study is not to explore whether women's self-employment, and changes within it, are more internal or structural by nature, I have used the shift-share analysis more as an exploratory device. The results support the idea that the structures of the economy are rigid, since the changes in women's self-employment are taking place more within than between industries. Thus, I draw the conclusion that patriarchal structures do receive support from the shift-share analysis.

---

10. Because the number of self-employed women was lowest in 1975 in wholesale, the retail trade and restaurants and hotels, whereas in 1980 the number of self-employed women was lowest in manufacturing, the years 1975 and 1985 were also selected for a tentative comparison. This calculation reinforces the earlier result regarding the importance of the internal change, even if it is not as large as before.

6.3. Self-employed women in Finland – what do they look like?

The general division of women´s self-employment follows in outline the labour force participation of women, such that in industries which are dominated by women as employees, there are *relatively* more female entrepreneurs as a proportion of all women economically active than there are male entrepreneurs as a proportion of all men economically active. However, in those industries where men as employees are dominant, there are *practically no* female entrepreneurs at all. Undoubtedly, Elisabeth Sundin and Carin Holmqvist are right to argue that social invisibility is characteristic of women´s self-employment (Sundin – Holmqvist 1989).

By social invisibility Sundin and Holmqvist mean mainly two things. First, the statistical invisibility that emerges, for example, in the category of 'assisting' or 'helping family members'; most of these women are working in the same business as their spouses. Secondly invisibility in industries in which female entrepreneurs are found but which are not considered to be important to the economy (Sundin – Holmqvist 1989). The importance of female entrepreneurs means here the importance of their productive capacity or the relative size of their share of national productivity or of the labour force. Even if women's businesses form a growing part of the economy measured both by production and by share of employment, the invisibility thesis seems to hold true.

Owing to the lack of detailed data for 1990 in the population census for that year, the years 1960 and 1985 were chosen for the purposes of a comparative analysis in tables 6.5. and 6.6.[11] Although some increase in the number of self-employed women was registered in several non-farm industries during the time period of 1960-85, marked variations remained between industries (table 6.5.). In relative terms, the largest increase took place in the main industries where self-employment has generally grown, such as finance, insurance and business related services[12], and personal and private household services. By contrast, in manufacturing, the percentage of women who were self-employed was relatively high in 1960, but had declined by 1985, largely due to changes in the internal structure of manufacturing.

A relative growth has occurred in the percentage of women who were self-employed in industries such as the retail trade, restaurants and hotels, even though the absolute number of all self-employed has declined. A decline has also occurred in the percentage of employment accounted for by women in the

---

11. The category "self-employed" includes all self-employed people, i.e. own-account workers and employers, plus assisting family members.

12. Sometimes referred to as 'new' self-employment.

Table 6.5. Women in self-employment in non-farm industries, 1960 and 1985 (%)

Industry	1960 All self-employed	1960 % women	1985 All self-employed	1985 % women
All non-farm main industries	113 080	29.0	114 170	29.6
Manufacturing	25 690	48.9	15 650	24.6
Construction	10 580	0.9	16 040	1.3
Wholesale, trade, etc.	30 500	38.3	29 810	41.5
Wholesale, retail trade	28 100	34.3	25 360	37.1
Hotels, restaurants	2 400	84.0	4 450	66.9
Transport	23 940	1.2	17 600	4.0
Finance, etc.	4 150	15.4	8 850	26.6
Business related services	1 750	15.9	7 750	28.0
Services	18 220	46.1	26 220	54.4
Health services	3 670	67.0	3 930	55.2
Personal and private household services	11 920	41.5	15 170	56.3
Other services	2 630	37.6	7 110	50.0

* I have omitted the mining industry from this and the following tables since it is not an important industry in the Finnish economy, measured in terms of the number of employed or self-employed. Census data for 1990 is used in the study where comparisons are possible.

Sources: CSOF 1963, 1988a

'restaurants and hotels' industry, in spite of a rise in the number of the self-employed. If industries such as 'trade' and 'finance, insurance, and real estate' are included in a broader category of service industries, there has been a positive change in the industrial location of women in respect of self-employment. A more detailed examination of the statistics on services, on the basis of their division into goods and non-goods services, reveals a number of minor changes.

Interestingly, an examination of the group of wage and salary employees (i.e. manual workers and clerical employees) would suggest that – in relative terms – women´s share of employment has remained more or less stable in core industries such as manufacturing, trade and the health services. In reality, major changes and restructuring have taken place within these industries as well. However, women´s share of employment has not declined to the same extent as their share of self-employment.

Table 6.6. Women in paid employment in non-farm industries, 1960 and 1985 (%)

Industry	1960 All in paid employment	1960 % women	1985 All in paid employment	1985 % women
All non-farm main industries	1 094 840	45.6	1 897 030	50.0
Manufacturing	387 650	38.2	535 680	37.0
Construction	106 680	10.9	150 810	9.5
Wholesale, trade, etc.	201 760	60.9	292 090	60.5
Wholesale, retail	172 490	55.8	87 040	38.9
Hotels, restaurants	29 270	90.7	149 400	66.6
Transport	103 680	25.2	153 400	29.0
Finance, etc.	30 680	61.2	144 500	39.7
Business related services	5 700	41.2	79 280	47.0
Services	264 290	64.2	620 550	70.0
Health services	59 290	87.7	133 400	86.7
Personal and private household services	56 660	92.2	32 930	51.8
Other services	148 440	44.0	452 210	66.7

Sources: CSOF 1963, 1988a

Table 6.7. Self-employed women and women as assisting family members in non-farm industries, 1985 and 1990 (%)

Industry	1985 All self-employed and assisting family members	1985 % women	1990[*] All self- employed and assisting family members	1990[*] % women
All-non farm main industries	134 310	35.3	162 130	36.5
Manufacturing	18 280	31.8	22 840	26.2
Construction	18 670	5.4	24 240	4.2
Wholesale, trade, etc.	37 010	49.2	49 390	42.1
Wholesale, retail trade	31 480	46.1	42 470	37.9
Hotels, restaurants	5 530	69.0	6 920	68.3
Transport	19 220	9.3	22 580	8.3
Finance, etc.	12 830	24.5	17 250	33.0
Business related services	8 550	33.0	11 760	31.9
Services	28 300	56.3	25 830	65.9
Health services	4 310	58.5	4 780	56.3
Other services	23 990	56.0	21 050	68.0

[*] minor changes in industrial classification.

Source: CSOF 1988a, 1990a

Major changes – that are not necessarily visible in statistics based upon the industrial division presented in table 6.6. above – have taken place in the pattern of women´s labour force participation during the 25-year period 1960-1985. The most important of these changes are those in the labour force participation of women during their most active years, educational changes and those in the occupational structure. The statistics from the latest 5-year period for which detailed data exists, (1985 to 1990), show that the proportion of self-employment accounted for by women – including assisting family members – has declined substantially in some industries, such as the retail trade, which have traditionally been a source of 'female businesses' (table 6.7.). This development and the reasons for it are discussed in chapter 7

6.4. The principal industrial distribution and trends

In 1960, 18 per cent of all self-employed people in Finland were women.[13] More than half of these women were active in agriculture. The importance of agriculture for Finnish society in the 1960s is also visible in the distribution of women entrepreneurs: including agriculture, almost all self-employed women were active either as own-account workers, or as assisting family members. Of the non-farm self-employed women, 22.8 per cent were employers, and 71.2 per cent were own-account workers without paid employees. Almost all women classified as assisting family members were active in agriculture, i.e. in reality they worked on the farm, taking care of various agricultural activities, without receiving a wage in return for their work. In the history of Finnish women, the phenomenon of female self-employment is not new; it has only been invisible in the statistics, as Pirjo Markkola shows in her research on Finnish women in agriculture at the turn of the century (Markkola 1989).[14]

By the mid-1980s, this picture had changed in several ways: in 1985 women´s share of total self-employment rose slightly above the level of the 1960s to represent 22.5 per cent of all entrepreneurs, including those active in

13. The absolute number of self-employed women was 71 500 in 1960, including those active in agriculture. The number of self-employed women outside of agriculture was 32 800.

14. Markkola shows that to be able to earn a living from agriculture at the turn of the century, many women in the Finnish countryside were active in some sort of subsidiary production, for example, cloth spinning, or working for others every now and then. Even if I have, in this study, restricted my interest area to women's non-farm self-employment, it does not mean that women classified as farmers of assisting family members in agriculture would not have other self-employment activities than farming. In this case it could be said that the statistical category of self-employed in agriculture hides a variety of business activities.

agriculture.[15] Of these women, 21.8 per cent were employers, whereas 78.2 per cent were own-account workers. With respect to entrepreneurs outside of agriculture, 29.2 per cent were employers, and 70.8 per cent were own-account workers. Most of the women who are classified in the statistics as assisting family members are still active in agriculture – this has not changed over the years – but their number has decreased somewhat.

As the figures above indicate, there has been a minor quantitative change in the number of female entrepreneurs. However, even if the relative distribution of female self-employment within industries has changed as a consequence of the diversification of the economic structure, there are two typical features, which have not changed over this 25-year period. These two features are: *the larger number of women who are active as own-account workers rather than as employers, and the concentration of self-employed women in a limited number of service sector industries*.

The growing importance of services, which is also visible in female self-employment, is generally connected to the overall long term rise in the labour market participation of women, and in countries such as the UK and the US, in the mix of full time and part-time jobs. In Finland, the number of female entrepreneurs has declined in manufacturing and risen in the wholesale and retail trades, in catering and hotel services and in personal services. This development contrasts with the line of development common to many other OECD countries.

The more detailed division of the statistics into those for own-account workers and employers does not change the picture of the relative distribution of self-employed women across different industries. The relatively large number of own-account workers in relation to employers suggests that *female entrepreneurship is concentrated around small-scale business activities*.

When the distribution of female self-employment by industries is compared with the corresponding distribution of male self-employment, a clear difference can be seen in the relative distribution of own-account workers and employers. First, a relatively smaller proportion of women are employers than men. Secondly, it is very interesting to note that women's relative share of the total of self-employment in manufacturing has diminished from 44 per cent to 25 per cent. Contrary to this development, women's relative share of all self-employment in the 'wholesale and retail trade, restaurants and hotels' increased from 33 per cent to 42 per cent (see table 6.8.). In the 'finance, insurance, real estate and business related services' industry, the relative share of all self-

15. There were 51 300 self-employed women, including those active in agriculture, in 1985. In the same year there were 34 550 women outside of agriculture engaged in activities classified as self-employment.

Table 6.8. The relative distribution of self-employed women and men by main non-farm industry, 1960 and 1985 (%)

| | percentage of all self-employed | | | | | |
| | 1960 | | | 1985 | | |
Industries	women	men	all	women	men	all
Manufacturing	48.9	51.1	100	25.0	75.0	100
Construction	0.9	99.1	100	1.3	98.7	100
Trade	38.0	62.0	100	42.0	58.0	100
Transport	1.2	98.8	100	4.0	96.0	100
Finance	15.0	85.0	100	27.0	73.0	100
Services	46.0	54.0	100	55.0	45.0	100

Sources: CSOF 1963, 1988a

employment in industry accounted for by women has to a large extent remained the same, being 26 per cent and 27 per cent in 1960 and 1985 respectively. However, this development has not been linear and there have been a number of remarkable internal changes within the principal industries. This development will be further discussed in chapter 7.

As table 6.8. shows, men still constitute both a relative and an absolute majority of non-farm self-employment. By 1985 the development of female self-employment measured as a proportion of total self-employment has been clearly positive in the 'wholesale and retail trade, hotels and restaurants'. The proportion of self-employment accounted for by men had risen by 1985 so that the relative proportion of total self-employment accounted for by own-account workers declined, while the proportion of self-employment accounted for by employers grew in construction, transport and the service industries.

When the relative proportion of self-employment accounted for by women entrepreneurs is compared with the proportion of self-employment accounted for by male entrepreneurs a difference is apparent in industrial distribution: *men are active in **all** industries in a self-employed capacity, both as own-account workers and as employers.*

Instead of clear, uni-directional changes in industrial distribution, multi-directional changes affecting female self-employment have taken place within different industries. This makes it more difficult to chart the development of female self-employment over time. A detailed picture of the changes in the number of female entrepreneurs by industry between 1960 and 1985, as well as in 1990, is discussed in chapter 7. The general economic decline in the

Table 6.9. Women's self-employment by industry, 1960-1990
(%)

	1960	1970	1975	1980	1985	1990[*]
Manufacturing	34.5	18.4	11.7	9.6	11.4	11.5
Construction	0.1	0.2	0.2	0.3	0.6	1.0
Trade	35.6	43.8	42.6	44	36.7	39.0
Transport	0.9	1.6	2.6	2.6	2.1	2.0
Finance	3.3	1.9	2.9	4.0	7.0	3.7
Services	25.6	34.1	40.0	39.5	42.2	42.8
Total	100.0	100.0	100.0	100.0	100.0	100.0

* there are minor changes in industrial classification and figures are thus not directly comparable with the figures from earlier years.

Source: CSOF 1988a, 1990a

1970s may be seen as a reflection of a decline in the number of female entrepreneurs in the 1975 census. According to the statistics (table 6.9.), this decline in manufacturing continued even into the 1980s.

With the exception of manufacturing, a clear rise in the number of entrepreneurs has taken place in all major industries between 1980 and 1985. Even though statistical series for the year 1990 are not directly comparable because the available information on the self-employed includes assisting family members, this development seems to have continued up until 1990. Assuming that the relative share of total employment accounted for by assisting family members in 1990 is the same as in 1985, the decline in the share of female self-employment within manufacturing industry also seems to hold true as far as census data for 1990 is concerned (see table 6.7.).

When the assisting family members are assumed to be on the same level in 1990 as they were in 1985, it seems that women´s share of all self-employment has only grown in the broad category of trade and also of services, including business services. However, it should be noted that the category of assisting family members is problematic and difficult to estimate in many senses, and is usually examined separately from the categories of 'employers' and of 'own-account workers'. In addition, the changes in the industrial classification between 1985 and 1990 can have effect here.

6.5. Longer hours for less pay?

The 'from rags to riches' ideology often connected with self-employment is not necessarily confirmed by the evidence on the working conditions and experience of the self-employed. However, the evidence available is not as extensive as for wage and salary employees. Reported working hours for the self-employed are longer than those for waged and salaried workers (i.e. manual workers and administrative employees). The extent of this difference between the employed and self-employed varies: according to OECD reports, in countries such as Denmark, Finland and France (all countries where self-employment is a relatively small part of total employment) the difference is close to ten hours, while in Japan it is almost nothing (OECD 1992). The difference is very evident in the case of self-employed men, whereas in the case of self-employed women it is not so marked. This is to a large extent due to the fact that in many countries a relatively large number of self-employed women work part-time.

However, in Finland, the difference between the weekly hours of work of those in paid employment and the self-employed follow rather similar patterns. To some extent, part-time work is more usual for self-employed women than it is for women in paid employment: 16 per cent of all self-employed women work less than 30 hours per week, compared with 11 per cent of all women waged workers, and respectively, 8.6 per cent of all women salaried employees. However, over 79 per cent of the self-employed women work much more than a 'standard' working week of 35-40 hours, while the majority of waged women workers work a 'standard' working week of 35-40 hours, and do not exceed this to any notable extent. Part-time work is not very common among self-employed men, and the majority of self-employed men work more than 41 hours per week (table 6.10.). Taken together, and in spite of the claimed growth in atypical forms of employment, such as part-time work, the majority of employees (both women and men) in Finland still work a 'normal' 35-40 hour week. This has not changed during the last 5 years, 1986-1990 (see table 6.1.A).

The variety of hours worked by assisting family members is greater than either that of employees or of the self-employed. The term 'assisting family member' speaks for itself, since over one third of the men and over half of the women who are active as assisting family members work part-time in the family business, that is under 29 hours per week. Twenty per cent of both female and male assisting family members work less than the 'normal' working week of 35-40 hours, whereas 20 per cent of male, and 10 per cent of female assisting family members work more than 50 hours per week.

146

Table 6.10. Distribution of manual workers, administrative employees and self-employed by hours worked per week, by gender, 1990[*]

	Under 29 hours	30-34 hours	35-40 hours	41-50 hours	Over 50 hours	Total
			Percentages			
Manual workers						
men	3.1	2.4	90.7	2.4	1.4	100
women	11.1	3.8	83.3	1.2	0.6	100
Administrative employees						
men	4.1	3.7	83.1	6.3	2.8	100
women	8.6	7.6	78.9	3.8	1.1	100
Self-employed						
men	7.1	4.0	23.2	23.7	42.0	100
women	16.0	4.5	22.3	26.2	31.0	100
Assisting family members						
men	36.0	8.0	19.0	14.6	22.4	100
women	52.6	4.0	18.0	15.4	10.0	100

* agriculture included.

Source: CSOF 1992c

There has been a clear shift in the situation of female assisting family members towards shorter weekly hours of work in family businesses. In 1986, 20 per cent of female assisting family members worked over 50 hours per week, whereas in 1990 the figure was just 10 per cent. A similar change has also taken place in the case of male assisting family members, but not to such a large extent.[16]

If agriculture is excluded from the analysis, as in table 6.11., where the distribution of weekly hours of the self-employed and of assisting family members is analysed according to the main industries, the division of hours worked is more even. However, this statistical outcome may be caused by the assisting family members being included in the analysis. The majority of the self-employed and of assisting family members (82.9 per cent) in the retail trade, hotels and restaurant businesses work over 50 hours per week.

---

16. The reason for the apparently smaller shift in respect of men is the inclusion of the agricultural sector in the figures contained in table 6.10., and table 6.1.A. in the appendix.

Table 6.11. Hours worked per week by self-employed and assisting family members, by industry, 1990 (%)

Industry	Under 29 hours	30-34 hours	Percentages 35-40 hours	41-50 hours	Over 50 hours	Total
Manufacturing	9.6	4.4	31.5	25.7	28.8	100
Construction	4.9	3.4	37.6	25.2	28.9	100
Wholesale, trade etc.	5.2	1.6	20.7	28.9	43.6	100
Transport etc	10.5	5.5	24.0	23.5	36.5	100
Finance, etc.	11.4	7.2	39.2	20.2	22.0	100
Services	19.1	8.3	35.9	25.2	11.5	100

Source: CSOF 1992c

Table 6.12. Average weekly hours of work of the self-employed in selected OECD countries, by gender, 1987 and 1990

	Total		Average weekly hours worked Men		Women	
	1987	1990[*]	1987	1990[*]	1987	1990[*]
Belgium	51.8	52.0	55.7	54.7	47.5	49.2
Canada	36.1	40.1	40.3	40.8	29.3	30.7
Denmark	48.2	48.7	49.9	50.3	46.3	46.9
Finland	..	46.0	..	47.9	..	41.9
Germany	47.2	47.2	51.5	51.8	42.8	42.5
Italy	47.4	46.6	54.1	53.0	34.9	34.5
Japan	47.4	46.6	54.1	53.0	34.9	34.5
Netherlands	39.4	39.3	49.7	49.5	28.7	28.5
Sweden	46.8	46.4	48.9	49.0	40.1	40.3
United Kingdom	44.2	44.5	51.8	51.0	36.5	37.6
United States	41.0	40.8	44.0	43.8	35.1	35.3

[*] data for countries of the European Community are for 1989.

Sources: OECD 1992; CSOF 1992c

Large differences exist in the average weekly hours worked by the self-employed in different countries. The self-employed reported an average working week of 50 hours or more in twelve countries examined in table 6.12. According to a more detailed analysis of the self-employed – not shown here – that divides into those with employees and those without, the former group (of employers) are more likely to work longer hours than the latter group of own-account workers.

According to OECD statistics, part-time self-employment is particularly common among women in the Netherlands and the United Kingdom, where 71 per cent and 55 per cent respectively work under 30 hours a week (OECD 1992). This pattern is less common in other countries. In Finland, for example, only 16 per cent of self-employed women, including those in agriculture, work less than 29 hours per week while the majority work more than 35 hours per week.

Compared to those in waged work, do the longer working hours of those in self-employment mean more money, then? In general, data on the monetary incomes of the self-employed are both harder to obtain and less reliable than similar data for employees. Few studies contain information on the actual income of the self-employed, and even fewer include information on the earnings of self-employed women. While it is widely accepted that even employees may perhaps understate their incomes to some extent in order to avoid taxation, less attention has been paid to the fact that the self-employed have both more opportunities and greater means with which to engage in tax avoidance.

The results from the OECD analysis (OECD 1986c) of the median earnings of the self-employed, which was based on information up to 1982 covering Finland, the Federal Republic of Germany, Japan, Sweden and the USA, may be condensed into the following three conclusions: First, in all countries except the FRG, the median earnings of the self-employed were lower than for employees. Secondly, the ratio between the median earnings of the self-employed and those in paid employment was lower for women than for men. Thirdly, for both women and men, the ratio had declined over time. *In fact, in countries where information about the earnings of women and men has been available, it appears that the median earnings of self-employed women remain lower than the median earnings of self-employed men.*

Table 6.13. shows the ratio of the median earnings of the self-employed to those in civilian employment in the non-farm sector of the economy. With the exception of Japan, the table compares the median earnings of the self-employed and those in civilian employment as a whole. As the share of self-employment to total employment is relatively small in all countries, the data also indicate trends in the relationship between self-employment earnings and wages and salaries. In recent years, the ratio between the median earnings of the self-employed and of the civilian population has been moving in different directions in different countries. In the United States it has risen sharply. For women, especially, it has increased from one-third to almost two-thirds at a time when the representation of women in self-employment has also been growing rapidly (OECD 1992).

Table 6.13. Ratio of median earnings in self-employment to median earnings in civilian employment, non-farm sector, in selected OECD countries 1979-1989 (%)

| | Percentages Women and men | | | | |
	1979	1983	1985	1987	1989
Canada	72.3	64.7	72.2	71.7	71.2
Finland	98.9	92.3	..	83.8	..
Japan	91.0	84.1*	..	82.9	..
Sweden	..	68.8	56.7	58.8	61.5
United States	88.7	73.5	81.9	111.0	115.5

* = 1982

Source: OECD 1992

It is generally assumed that the distribution of incomes among the self-employed is more polarised than is the case for manual workers and administrative employees, so that self-employment contains a higher proportion of both low and high income levels. Low incomes would be expected as a result of insecurity and also due to a tendency to understate incomes. On the basis of OECD data, it appears that self-employed women are more often found among the upper earnings levels of the self-employed than women employees are with respect to the distribution of wages and salaries. This means that there may be more self-employed women than women waged workers at both ends of the scale. (OECD 1988a) However, the complexity of the distribution of self-employed earnings is illustrated by the Canadian data contained within the same study: the self-employed with employees have much higher incomes, on average, than those without.

According to the Finnish income distribution statistics for 1990, the average disposable income of non-farm *self-employed households* increased in the 1980s by over 12 per cent, while the average increase in *paid employment households* was 11 per cent. Table 6.14. shows the proportion of the self-employed and of the employees with incomes above and below the levels selected from the 1990 income distribution set. The levels are constructed so that the lower level lies between the bottom two deciles of the distribution of earnings of the economically active population, and the upper limits lie between the top two deciles.

Table 6.14. Income distribution in self-employment and in paid employment, 1990 (%)

	Percentages			Total
	Under 65 000 FIM	65 000– 160 000 FIM	Over 160 000 FIM	
Self-employed and assisting family members	7.6	63.3	29.1	100
Employees	3.4	73.0	23.6	100

Note: distinction between employment status on basis of main income source.

Source: CSOF 1992b

As noted earlier, there appears to be little difference between the motives of women and men in choosing self-employment. The usable source of data confirms that *self-employed women earn less than self-employed men* and that their earnings are also lower than those of both women and men in waged work. This unfavourable earnings situation for self-employed women is also found to varying degrees in other industrialised countries (Haber et al. 1987).

The comparison of the total self-employed population with all employees does not reveal large differences in income distribution. When agricultural self-employment is excluded from the analysis and the group of salaried employees (i.e. administrative or clerical workers) is divided into two parts, namely lower and higher level salaried employees, greater differences between groups do show up. Unfortunately, information in respect of gender was not available for the year 1990. However, earnings differences by gender also transcend different types of employment.

Turning to household expenditure, it emerges that the households of upper-level white-collar workers and self-employed persons were the biggest spenders according to the 1990 household survey data, although the structural differences in consumption were in general slight (Income and consumption 1992). This situation has remained more or less the same during the last decade. Occupational status has more of an effect upon income in the case of men than in the case of women. In the case of women, only women employers earn notably more than other occupational groups of women (Salmi 1991, 90) (table 6.15).

Table 6.15. The form of income by gender, 1985 (%)

The form of income	Women	Men	Total
Wage and salary income	47.6	52.4	100
Income from self-employment	36.1	63.9	100
Other income	41.0	59.0	100

Source: CSOF 1988a

When income from self-employment is divided into different income classes, as in figure 6.1.A., we notice that the income of both self-employed women and men assume rather similar patterns. Women receive on average 72 per cent of the entrepreneurial incomes of men. This corresponds to the income distribution of employees, where women's incomes are 71 per cent of men's (1985). The average entrepreneurial income for self-employed women was 39 500 FIM per year (1985), while the corresponding income for self-employed men was 54 500 FIM in the same year (CSOF 1988a).

Many reasons exist as to why self-employed women earn less than self-employed men. Although the part-time self-employed cannot be distinguished from their full-time counterparts in the data concerning income, the larger number of part-timers among self-employed women decreases their earnings in comparison to men. Another plausible explanation for the lower earnings of self-employed women is the relatively lower scale and level of capitalisation of their businesses. A higher proportion of businesses owned by women are home-based and more women than men work as own-account workers. These facts, combined with differences in industrial and occupational distributions, and the scale and capitalisation of businesses owned by women, produce differences in income levels.

6.6. Education and occupations of the self-employed

In general, the low level of basic education combined with a lack of training in specific business skills such as marketing, accounting and financial planning, are thought to be the main reasons for high failure rates among the self-employed, and for the small number of the self-employed in general. The educational level of the self-employed has not been studied on a large scale, and it is usually assumed that self-employment within 'traditional' fields of business, such as retail trade and metal manufacturing industries is associated

Table 6.16. Educational levels in paid employment and in self-employment, by gender, 1990 (%)

Occupational status, percentages

Educational qualification*	Manual workers		Administrative employees		Self-employed		Assisting family members	
	women	men	women	men	women	men	women	men
Basic education	54	46	27	18	47	32	65	69
Lower middle level e.	37	45	26	16	35	32	26	26
Upper middle level e.	8	8	28	33	13	12	8	3
Higher education	1	1	19	5	5	7	1	2
Total	100	100	100	100	100	100	100	100

* Basic education here means education at the first level, 1 to 9 years education (corresponding to the ISCED classification level 1). Lower middle level education means 10 to 11 years education (corresponds to ISCED classification level 3). Upper middle level education means 12 years education (ISCED level 5). Higher education here includes all university degrees or equivalents, postgraduate degrees and equivalents (ISCED levels 6 and 7).

Source: CSOF 1992c

with a low level of educational attainment. However, an examination of the statistical data on educational attainment indicates that the first of the above assumptions does not hold true in the case of the Finnish self-employed. The educational level of the self-employed[17] – both women and men – is higher than that of waged workers (table 6.16). Furthermore, a number of minor changes occurred in the educational levels of all groups during the late 1980s (see table 6.2.A in appendix).

Taking the population as a whole, those with a first-level educational qualification accounted for 50 per cent of the population aged 15 years and over in 1990. Those with a second-level educational qualification accounted for 37 per cent of the population aged 15 years and over, and those with a third-level for 13 per cent (CSOF 1992c). In the case of the employed, the educational level of those in administrative employment is more evenly distributed between different levels than for manual workers and the self-employed.

17. Agriculture included.

However, it might be assumed that it is the lack of various specific skills in business activities, such as marketing, accounting etc., rather than a general lack of basic middle-level education that creates most of the problems found in self-employment. This view has been cited on numerous occasions during interviews I have conducted among self-employed women (see Kovalainen 1990). A lack of knowledge with respect to accounting and financial management were seen to have caused most of the major problems encountered by these women in their business activities. Moreover, my respondents frequently complained that a lack of knowledge made it difficult to contact the 'right' people and reach the 'best' solutions to everyday problems confronted in self-employment.

20 most usual occupations for self-employed women

1. *Farmers*
2. *Retailers*
3. Barbers and hairdressers
4. Waiters in bars and restaurants
5. Child care in families and at home
6. Tailors, salon seamstresses
7. Dentists
8. Beauticians
9. *Motor vehicle drivers*
10. *Business managers*
11. *Horticulturists*
12. Bookkeepers
13. Agents
14. Livestock breeders
15. Masseuses
16. Pharmacy workers
17. Cooks
18. *Fur farmers*
19. Housekeeping and related work
20. Artists

20 most usual occupations for self-employed men

1. *Farmers*
2. *Motor vehicle drivers*
3. *Retailers*
4. *Business managers*
5. Construction machinery operators
6. Machine and engine mechanics
7. *Horticulturists*
8. *Fur farmers*
9. Painters etc.
10. Forestry workers
11. Plumbers
12. Fishermen
13. Salesmen
14. Construction carpenters
15. Service station attendants
16. Sheet metal workers
17. Door-to-door salesmen
18. Civil engineering technicians
19. Electricians
20. Sawyers

Source: CSOF 1988a.

154

In which occupations do women then work as self-employed? *One of the ideas which was raised in parts II and III of this work was that occupational segregation prevails in paid employment, and that segregation might also be expected to be present among the self-employed.* Segregation in the field of education, naturally, is reflected in the segregation found within self-employment. When occupations are arranged into order according to the number of people in each occupation, the 20 most common occupations for self-employed women and men are described above. The differentiation of the occupations also refers to the segregation of self-employment, into male and female spheres of self-employment, in addition to waged and salaried employment. The list of occupations has to a large extent remained the same during the 1980s.

There are six common occupations for women and men in the above listing of the twenty most usual occupations for both genders: farmers, retailers, motor vehicle drivers, business managers, horticulturists and fur farmers. Outside of the agricultural industries (excluding: fur farmers, horticulturists and farmers), the number of common occupations decreases to three, those of business management, retailing and motor vehicle driving. This fact clearly shows the differentiation of the spheres of female and male self-employment. Salmi has examined Finnish home-based work, and while a part of the home-based workers are classified as self-employed and a part as waged employees, her research shows that there is also a clear difference between the occupations of male home-based workers and those of their female counterparts (Salmi 1991).

6.7. Summary

As evidence from many of the OECD countries has shown, there has been a rise in the number of self-employed people. In all Nordic countries, this rise seems to stabilise at the beginning of 1980s. According to the statistics, it seems that the highest growth figures, and also the highest proportion of female self-employment, can be found in countries where the public sector has not followed the lines of the Nordic model, and where general economic development has been positive. In countries where the public sector is large, the figures for female self-employment are less significant.

The discussion around the growth of entrepreneurship in the OECD countries has, however, been partly gender-blind in the sense that the existence of historical and invisible forms of self-employment has been forgotten. By historical and invisible forms of self-employment I mean the various activities of women performed alongside farming, in order to earn a livelihood (knitting, sewing, various forms of needlework and handicrafts, etc.). These activities, at least in Finland, were an important way to earn a living. Other invisible forms of entrepreneurial activities include different forms of ethnic family businesses, especially in the textile and clothing industries and in retailing in various OECD countries.

Regarding women's work in Finland, it may be noted that even in the very early period of industrialisation, women were active in the labour force. The segregated nature of both industrial and occupational structures has not, however, diminished. Finnish researchers refer to this segregation as a part of a modern type of gender contract, the basic characteristic of which is the normalisation of women's paid employment (Rantalaiho 1993).

I also wanted to explore whether the rise in women's self-employment is linked to the changes in employment within or between industries. According to the shift-share analyses presented in this chapter, the changes in female self-employment in Finland during the 1980s are more due to internal changes in industries than to the structural changes in the Finnish economy. It may well be that the changes in self-employment that are taking place at the moment and into the mid-1990s are more structural by nature, but this remains to be seen.

During the inspected time-period, the relative distribution of female self-employment within industries has changed as a consequence of the diversification of the economic structure. However, the two typical features have not changed: there are more women active as own-account workers than as employers, and most of female self-employment has been concentrated in a very limited number of service sector industries.

A general note concerning the long working hours of self-employed women was made in this chapter, but there are some differences between industries, largely depending on the nature of the industry. On the basis of general income inspection there are gendered differences regarding incomes from self-employment. Contrary to the general assumption of a poor educational level amongst the self-employed, it seems that for both women and men the educational level is higher than that of waged workers. An inspection of the most usual occupations for self-employed women and men strengthens the idea of separate spheres of female and male self-employment.

7 Women's business activities in Finland – industrial distribution and trends

In this chapter I shall focus on the development of women's self-employment in various industries and different parts of those industries. I will concentrate on features particular to women's self-employment and its development,[1] using statistical material and interviews as the basic empirical data.

7.1. General development and the main features of manufacturing industry

When indicators such as the gross value of production, value added, and total labour force share are inspected, the structure of the Finnish manufacturing industry in the 1960s is seen to have been heavily concentrated in the manufacture of wood and paper products, and of metal products. According to these indicators there have not been substantial changes; on the contrary, the metal and wood processing industries have increased their share of the gross value of production and value added production during the period 1960-1990. Furthermore, their share of the total labour force in the manufacturing industries also rose in 1960-1985 (table 7.1.). However, when the share of wood processing industries are compared, in 1985 and 1990 there is a slight decrease both in the gross value of production, in the value added, and in the share of labour. The share of the metal industries has risen in all categories.

According to industrial statistics, the different manufacturing industries have to a large extent maintained their pecking order when measured by their share of labour employed in manufacturing industries, gross value of production and value added during the years 1960-1990. The three largest sectors of manufacturing industry are also male dominated when inspecting the division of self-employment into female and male dominated spheres. However, food products and beverages manufacture is an exception to the pattern set by metal

---

1. 1988 saw changes in industrial classification compared to the previous version. These changes are taken into account to the extent it was possible.

Table 7.1. Share of principal manufacturing industries of total manufacturing gross value of production, value added and share of labour, 1960, 1985 and 1990 (%)

Industry	Gross value of production			Value added			Employed		
	1960	1985	1990[*]	1960	1985	1990[*]	1960	1985	1990[*]
Wood and paper	26	26	22	29	25	19	29	28	19
Metal and machinery	21	26	33	24	31	36	27	24	35
Textiles and clothing	8	4	3	11	6	4	18	12	9
Chemical products	6	13	13	7	10	13	5	9	7
Food products	25	16	17	13	11	13	11	13	13
Other	14	15	12	16	17	15	10	14	17
Total	100	100	100	100	100	100	100	100	100

[*] classification has changed between 1985 and 1990. There are slight differences in the classification of some sub-branches in wood products manufacturing.

Source: CSOF 1962, 1988b, 1992d

and wood product manufacturing industries in the sense that the labour force has been and still is female dominated.

One of the most labour intensive sectors in the manufacturing industries has been the textiles and clothing industry[2], which employed a fifth of the total labour in all manufacturing industries in the 1960s, even though the gross value of production and the value added were only one tenth of the total value added across all manufacturing industries. The relationship in terms of labour intensiveness has changed according to industrial statistics, but there has also been a decline in the gross values of production and in the value added.

One important issue, when we inspect the size of the business units, is that until the 1970s the size of industrial enterprises grew in Finland, as measured by the number of employees, but after 1970 in particular, the share of large business units (employing over 500 people) began to decrease (CSOF 1977). However, this decline stopped in the 1980s. The changes are clear across Finnish manufacturing industry during the period 1971-1986 when measured by the size of business unit. The majority of the enterprises are small, employing less than 50 workers (94 per cent in 1984; CSOF 1987). At the same time, during the period 1971-1984, large companies' share of all those

---

2. Clothing industry refers to the statistical group of 'wearing apparel' which includes manufacture of clothes, leather clothes, other wearing apparel and accessories, manufacture of articles of fur, footwear and luggage.

employed in manufacturing grew from 34 per cent to 47 per cent (Ahde et al. 1987, 40).

Furthermore, the large companies' share of total turnover and technological innovations has also grown. In 1987, the ten biggest manufacturing companies, which produced 40 per cent of total manufacturing output, accounted for a clearly larger proportion of R&D activities, that is 55 per cent of the R&D expenditure of the manufacturing sector (Vartia 1990). In this respect we can say that industrial production in Finland has to a large extent concentrated itself in large business units, even if recent research reports have argued that average plant sizes are declining due to the newly emerging techno-economic system (see Carlsson 1988).

This concentration towards larger business units has also been seen as one of the reasons why the number of self-employed women in manufacturing has declined. For example, Riitta Jallinoja (1985) considered the share of employment, and saw this concentration as one reason for the decline in the number of self-employed women. Paavo Okko approached the growth of business units from a different viewpoint: According to Okko there have been changes in the growth of productivity, which are partly dependent on the size of the business units (Okko 1985). For example, in the metal industry the nature of growth has changed from being capital intensive to productivity intensive, due to the size of the businesses (Okko 1985).

Toivonen inspects the labour force in manufacturing industry and notes that the "maleness" of industrial labour has become increasingly more obvious (Toivonen 1988, 69), but he does not specify reasons for this development. One possible reason for the increased "maleness" of manufacturing industry is the structural change within manufacturing. Besides the metal industries and high technology manufacture which require labour with high occupational qualifications, there are so-called 'light consumption goods manufacturing industries', which include industries such as the manufacture of textiles, fabrics and clothes, and home electrical goods. Common to these industries is a female dominated labour force; further, the majority of such labour possesses no specific occupational qualifications, and production is concentrated in consumer goods (Antti Kasvio 1988, 9). The lack of occupational qualifications is often seen as a typical feature of female-dominated industries.

However, it is important to note that the the lack of occupational qualifications may also be simply *a question of how the occupational qualifications are defined, and what are the specific criteria for the classification of occupational qualifications.* It may also be the fact that women are not paid for those parts of their work which are considered to be 'natural' female tasks (for more see e.g. Prandy 1986). Connected to this, there is also a question of

159

the labour unions and their policies. For example, in the manufacture of textiles, 73 per cent of workers are women, in clothing industries the share is 95 per cent, and in the 'light' electrical and electronic goods industry 68.5 per cent (Kasvio 1988).[3] Taken together, the number of women out of all people employed in the manufacture of consumer goods was 62.2 per cent in 1990. In all manufacturing industries the average share of women in the labour force is 33.6 per cent (CSOF 1992c).

The aforementioned industries have been open to foreign competition during the last few years, at which time production development processes have been more or less constant (e.g. for the development in the clothing factories, see Kasvio 1991). Taken together, these two factors decrease the number of workplaces within manufacturing industry. While the labour force has, in general, decreased evenly from the 1970s onwards, there are some pointers to explain the maleness of the labour force in manufacturing industry. Furthermore, the rationalisation of work in different manufacturing industries has, in the 1980s, increasingly addressed work tasks where women have been dominant in the manufacturing industries (e.g. Pertti Koistinen 1984, 230).

One possible explanation for this lies in the interests of the labour unions. Women's work and its maintenance in manufacturing industries has not been, at least to the same extent as men's work, in the interests of the trade unions. *This has meant that in negotiation situations where reductions have been necessary, women's work has become – through e.g. internal changes in work tasks – marginal in relation to men's work, and thus it has been easier to suppress women's jobs than men's jobs.*[4]

The growth of production and labour in manufacturing industries broke down in 1974, when the number of employed started to decrease. The decrease continued until 1978, after which the number of employed rose within a few years back to its 1974 level (CSOF; labour force statistics 1970-1990). After 1980, the number of employed in manufacturing decreased evenly throughout the decade. In 1960-1970, the rate of production growth in manufacturing was much faster than the general rate of production growth, and much of this growth was concentrated in large metal industry business organisations.

The size of the labour force in manufacturing industries decreased absolutely in 1980-1985 by almost 30 000 persons. Further, the share of labour in

---

3. 'Light' electronic goods industry includes here the production of television and radio transmitters and receivers, sound or video apparatuses etc.

4. For example, Cockburn's research results concerning the printing industry and the trade union's way of functioning clearly show that the above-mentioned is the model applied. It has also been stated that the differences in gender pay levels can be partly due to how a trade union functions in the maintenance of the inequality between genders (Cockburn 1983, 1986).

manufacturing relative to other industries decreased by 3 percentage units, from 28.7 per cent in 1980 to 25.7 per cent in 1985. According to different statistics the development in employment differs somewhat, but the differences are not large. Compared to the respective changes in OECD countries, it can be seen that the *saturation* level of the labour force in Finnish manufacturing industry was reached rather late, in fact not until the end of 1970s.

During the period 1980-1985, and also during the latter part of the 1980s, manufacturing industry´s share of the national product and of the labour force decreased in most Western European countries, together with a decrease in the number of workplaces. The background reasons for this development can be crystallised into three main facts: *the changes in the general structural conditions of economic growth,* which can be seen as a general decrease in investments; *technological development*, which can be seen as the importance of capital in industrial production, *and the international division of labour*, which can be seen in a new division of world markets (Rothwell 1986, 1989).

There have been changes in the division of the labour force between different branches in manufacturing industry. Relatively speaking, the fastest loss of labour has taken place in the manufacture of textiles, rubber, plastics and plastic products, leather products, and in the manufacture of non-metallic mineral products (pottery, china, earthenware). In terms of absolute changes the manufacture of textiles industry, the manufacture of paper and paper products, and wood products manufacturing, have all lost a significant part of their labour share. However, the effects of economic fluctuations are considered to be stronger than the effects of structural changes in the core industries, which are the manufacture of wood and of machinery; so these two industries are not usually classified amongst the declining industries (see also Ylä-Anttila – Heikkilä 1980, 64).

Of all the manufacturing industries, during the years 1974–1984, employment development was most positive in the manufacture of metal products, in the printing industry and in certain areas of the manufacture of chemicals and chemical products. There was some decline of employment in the manufacture of wood products, paper and paper products, and in the manufacture of textiles, leather products, and fur goods. This continued during the 1980s. Between 1975–1989, employment declined both in male and female dominated industries, especially in the manufacture of textiles and clothing, but also in the manufacture of wood products, paper and paper products (CSOF; industrial statistics 1970-1990).

To what extent this was due e.g. to an increase in subcontracting remains unexplained here. It is clear, however, that the importance of manufacturing industry as a whole diminished in the economy. The overall change in the

161

economic structure in the 1970s can be seen e.g. in the change of the socio-economic structure of the migrating population: Fewer people who migrated at the end of 1970s "originated" from the agricultural sector or industrial sector, as originated from the service sector (Söderling 1988, 81).

Are these changes in employment visible in the development of self-employment in manufacturing industries? The proportion of the self-employed in all subindustries of manufacturing industry has remained quite stable during the time period inspected. The number of self-employed in the core branches of manufacturing such as the metal industries, the manufacture of paper and pulp, the printing industries or chemicals manufacture has been quite stable. However, in the metal industries in particular the number of small businesses rose from the 1950s till the 1970s. Development took several directions after the 1970s, and different explanations exist for this development.

One view has been presented by Kauppi, that the increase in numbers was especially prevalent in large rather than small scale production, and the number of small businesses did not therefore rise considerably. Kauppi claims that the rise in the number of small businesses is largely produced by statistical error (Kauppi 1982). I have not investigated this dilemma, since women were not in the majority in small business ownership in the core manufacturing industries and thus not at the focus of my research. However, at least according to Riitta Hjerppe, Kauppi's view is accurate in the sense that the rise in production mainly took place in the large units (Hjerppe 1988, 97).

Although the total picture of self-employment in manufacturing industry as a whole has been rather stable during the time period, there have been great internal changes within different industries. The share of the self-employed in subindustries such as the manufacture of fabricated metal products and machinery rose in 1960-1985 from 9 per cent to 16 per cent. A decline has taken place in the number of self-employed in the manufacture of textiles and clothing. The absolute number of self-employed in the manufacture of textiles and clothing decreased during 1970-1980, being in the 1980s half of what it was at the beginning of 1970, although it rose again during 1980-1985, measured both in absolute as well as in relative terms. This rise continued during the latter part of the 1980s.[5] There has also been a rise in the number of self-employed women. How have these changes developed in different subindustries? In the following chapters I shall inspect development in various subindustries in more detail.

---

5. The figures for the self-employed from the year 1990 also include assisting family members. I have calculated the estimated share for assisting family members on the basis of 1985 data. Bearing this in mind, it can be said that the rise continued in years 1985-1990.

7.2. At the core of the manufacturing industries?
Women's self-employment in manufacturing

An inspection of the main class of manufacturing industry as a whole does not necessarily give the right kind of picture of women's self-employment, but it does create some basis for a more detailed study of what kind of development has taken place within different industries. Table 7.2. shows the development of women's self-employment in manufacturing. Women's share of all self-employed in manufacturing was 22 per cent (in 1990), having declined during the latter part of the 1980s (25 per cent in 1985) despite the rise in the number of entrepreneurs in manufacturing in 1985-1990.

Women's self-employment is not evenly divided between different subindustries, but is mostly concentrated into one manufacturing industry, namely textiles and clothing (69 per cent of all self-employed women in manufacturing in 1990). Other manufacturing industries employ less than 10 per cent each: the manufacture of food products and beverages (8 per cent), publishing, printing and the reproduction of recorded media (5 per cent), and the manufacture of pottery, china and earthenware (3.2 per cent). The remainder of women's self-employment is scattered amongst other manufacturing industries in even smaller numbers. The importance of these industries in the development of industrial production as a whole and employment in manufacturing industries in particular has varied considerably during the inspected time period.[6]

In the following inspections I have made the assumption that the share of assisting family members in relation to the total number of self-employed is at the same level in 1990 as it was in the 1985 census. This is a reasonable assumption given that changes in the numbers of assisting family members have been fairly insubstantial during the 1980s. However, since the available data from the 1990 census on categories of assisting family members and the group of unknown persons in self-employment are somewhat problematic, they should be inspected with some caution, since there may be slight changes in the figures in the final census data. The question of assisting family members will be discussed in chapter 7.5.

---

6. In the following chapters I will present data on female self-employment. For interesting comparisons and findings, as is the case in the manufacturing industries, I will also present data on the development of male self-employment. However, since a comparison of female and male self-employment is not a focus of my study, comparisons between men and women are not presented systematically.

163

Table 7.2. Self-employed in manufacturing industry, by employer status, share of self-employed women in percentages, 1960-1990 [7]

Year	1960	1970	1975	1980	1985	1990[*]
All self-employed	31 200	14 000	9 500	11 700	15 700	19 500
Women's share, %	36	36	26	21	25	22
All employers	6 400	4 300	2 900	4 750	9 650	..
women´s share, %	13	14	13	11	32	..
All own-account workers	24 800	9 700	6 600	6 950	6 050	..
women´s share, %	43	46	33	27	13	..

* the data on self-employment from 1990 includes both self-employed and assisting family members. I have made an assumption that the share of assisting family members is the same in the 1990 census data as it was in 1985 census data, and thus the number of self-employed in manufacturing is 19 500, the number of assisting family members 3 300, and women's share of all self-employed 22 %. (The original figures including assisting family members are 22 835 and women´s share of it 26 %.) The information on the division of self-employed into the categories of own-account workers and employers was not available in the data source.

The general picture of self-employment for women in manufacturing can be sketched as following: women's share of all self-employed declined from the 1960s to the 1980s. In mid-1980, women's share of all self-employed rose by 4 per cent. The rise took place mainly in one single manufacturing industry in 1980-1985. *In 1990, women's share of all self-employed declined again, despite the rise in the total number of all self-employed.* This means, that in both relative and absolute terms, such growth was greater for men than for women. The reasons for this development will be discussed later in this chapter.

The majority of self-employed women in manufacturing industries are own-account workers. The changes in the number of self-employed women and of all self-employed in manufacturing during the years 1960-1985 are shown in table 7.3.

---

7. All the following tables in this chapter 7 are calculated from the population censuses for the years 1960 – 1990 unless otherwise mentioned.

Table 7.3. Development of female self-employment in manufacturing industry, 1960-1990 (%)

	1960 –70	1970 –75	1975 –80	Change-% 1980 –85	1985 –90	1960 –75	1975 –85
All self-employed	-55	-33	23	34	25	-70	65
Self-employed women	-56	-50	-4	61	11	-78	54
of them							
own-account workers	-58	-51	-14	66	..	-79	42
employers	26	45	65	42	..	83	134

I have used comparisons from one set of census data to another in order to show changes during shorter periods of time, in tables which describe the trends in different industries. I have also made comparisons between longer time periods, and chosen the comparative years mainly from the point of view of the economic situation. Thus, the year 1960 forms the base year for comparison because my inspection starts from development in 1960. The year 1975 is another year used in comparisons due to the fact that the decline in the number of self-employed, which took place in the 1970s, peaked in 1975. The years 1975 and 1985 are compared in order to be able to show a longer and more recent development, which includes both the stagnation process of the 1970s and the rise in economic development in the 1980s.

The number of self-employed women in all manufacturing industries declined by 55.5 per cent during the ten year period 1960-1970, and also during the following five years, 1970-1975. There was a change in this development in 1975-1980, when the decline slowed. In 1980-1985 the number of self-employed women began to rise again. The rise had already occurred in 1980 in the case of female own-account workers without employees, but the rise in the number of women who were employers was not visible until the 1985 data. Nevertheless, the change percentage during 1975 and 1985 was positive, at 54 per cent. Again, the rise slowed down in the latter part of the 1980s, as presented in table 7.3.

Compared to the development which has taken place in male self-employment, the number of self-employed women has declined more sharply, and over a longer period. This decline took place during the years 1960-1975 and, furthermore, the number of self-employed women rose more slowly in the 1980s than was the case for men. The decline has also been sharper for women than for men.[8]

---

8. The number of self-employed women declined 50.4 per cent during 1970-1975, while the corresponding figure for men was only 22.4 per cent.

Table 7.4. Development of male self-employment in manufacturing industry, 1960-1990 (%)

	1960 –70	1970 –75	1975 –80	Change-% 1980 –85	1985 –90	1960 –75	1975 –85
All self-employed	-55	-33	23	34	25	-70	65
Self-employed men	-54	-22	33	27	45	-65	68
of them							
own-account workers	-63	-16	14	28	..	-69	46
employers	-33	-32	66	25	..	-54	108

Furthermore, when female self-employment was still clearly in decline in 1975-1980, the development in male self-employment was already on the upturn. The growing difference in the absolute numbers of female and male self-employed is clearly visible in the 1985-1990 trend: the number of self-employed men rose 45 per cent, while the number of self-employed women rose by only 11 per cent.

Male self-employment, measured in absolute numbers, also fell from the 1960s up until 1975 (table 7.4.). However, at the same time, the nature of business activities has changed: subcontracting, considered to be an important area of self-employment, has grown in most of the OECD countries where the number of self-employed has grown (see e.g. Toivonen 1989).[9] These changes are naturally in part due to differing trends in various manufacturing industries. Generally speaking, the growth of self-employment in manufacturing that began after 1975 has taken place partly in the 'old' industries which were previously in decline, and partly in the 'new' growth industries. What then are these 'old' and 'new' industries?

Taken from the viewpoint of research literature, the question of the division between old and new industries is at least two-dimensional. On the one hand, the division between old and new is not so much dependent on the industry´s end-product as the potential to utilise new production technologies in the production process, and thus diminish production costs (Kasvio 1988). On the other hand, the division between old and new is related to the restructuring of the economy: for example, textile and clothing industries, a traditional part of the Finnish production structure in manufacturing industries, have faced decreasing output volume and employment even where new technologies have been quite rapidly adopted in manufacturing processes (Vuori – Ylä-Anttila

9. The problematic position of subcontracting is quite clear when the subcontracting agreement ends for some reason. Most problems are connected to the dependent position of the subcontractor, which was discussed earlier in chapter 5.

1989).

Simultaneously, one of the industries which may be considered to be 'old', namely the metal manufacturing industry, has grown in importance measured both by the number of firms and share of employees in manufacturing industries in general (Ripatti et al. 1989). This refers to a complex set of factors such as the potential to utilise new production technologies, demand and foreign competition, all of which effect the development of manufacturing industries. Those industries such as chemical products manufacture may be considered to be 'new', when compared to textile and clothing manufacture, and to metal product manufacture. The entire industry was established only a few decades ago. In this sense, measured by the 'age' of an industry, the division between old and new is clear, even though it does not reveal the whole picture.

The decline in the number of self-employed in the 1970s was greatest in industries where female self-employment was dominant, that is mainly in the manufacture of textiles and clothing. A more detailed analysis shows that the majority of female self-employment was in the manufacture of textiles and clothing, and in the manufacture of leather products, whereas other industries – as mentioned earlier – are male dominated. Furthermore, typical female manufacturing industries are those of food products and beverages, the manufacture and finishing of textiles, clothing and leather products, and non-metallic mineral products. In these branches women's share of all self-employed grew during the 1980s, whereas during in 1960-1975 the typical growth industries were mostly textile manufacturing and clothing, and the manufacture of leather products.

The periods of time which are chosen for comparison in the tables here become more significant when the fact that *women's self-employment is to a large extent situated in the 'open' part of the economy* is taken into account (most branches in manufacturing industry).[10] This is due to the changes in production and also to the increasing competition in various industries, e.g. in the textile manufacturing industry. The division between the open and closed sectors of an economy is rather problematic, in the sense that in a small country almost all industrial production could be classified as the open sector (this is proposed by Ylä-Anttila – Heikkilä, for instance 1980, 38).

Textile and clothing manufacture have, in particular, been open to fluctuations in demand, also through foreign competition in Finland; the effect

---

10. Researchers usually classify the manufacture of food products, printing and publishing, production and distribution of electricity and gas in the closed sector of economy. Other subindustries are classified in the open sector of the economy (e.g. Ylä-Anttila - Heikkilä 1980).

of both is clearly visible in the declining figures of the 1970s. In addition to the industries' 'openness', we have to take into account the general development of the different industries, whether they are growing or declining.[11] Textile, clothing and leather products are all declining industries in terms of the number of business units and their share of the total labour force.

7.2.1. Manufacture of textiles and clothing

The fluctuation in the profitability of textile, clothing, leather and footwear manufacturing[12] has, in general, been greater than the average of manufacturing industries. In addition to the wider changes in profitability, footwear manufacturing and especially clothing and accessories have shown a clearly declining trend in productivity from the early 1970s onwards (Ylä-Anttila – Heikkilä 1980, 62). This is visible as a decline in the number of self-employed women in industry (table 7.5.). Powerful economic fluctuations were particularly clearly reflected in the functioning of the small business sector as general profitability declined. The relative changes in profitability were the strongest, in the 1970s, in the manufacture of textiles and less so in other manufacturing industries (Ylä-Anttila - Heikkilä 1980).

The large *number* of self-employed women in the 1960s census data is in reality a result of a much longer trend that is based on a rapid rise in textile and clothing manufacturing and a change in the production systems. This rise took place mainly in 1948-1963. During this early period, the production of textiles and clothing, accessories and footwear doubled in terms of the gross value of production (Pipping – Bärlund 1966). Such growth was, during these years, based mainly on the growth of *industrial* production, which displaced the previously dominant 'agrarian' home-based production mode. This growth in production capacity and the number of self-employed was strongly supported by the growth in demand, especially the growth in trade with the East (Hiilamo 1971). However, this development did not continue in such a positive fashion during the 1970s; measured by the share of total employment, the textile and clothing manufacturing industries employed 4.0 per cent in 1970, and 2.9 per cent in 1975, of all employed.

---

11. One previously mentioned reason for the growth in the number of self-employed was a general restructuring of production in the sense that part of industrial production was shifted into countries where labour and production costs are lower. Thus, new possibilities are opening up for flexible, small-scale production.

12. I use the terms "textile and clothing manufacture" and "textile and clothing" in referring to industrial classes 12 and 13 in the 1988 classification, and 32 in the 1979 classification (corresponding ISIC rev. 3 classes are 17, 18 and 19). They include all textiles, clothing, wearing apparel and leather industries.

Table 7.5. Self-employment in the manufacture of textiles and clothing, by employer status, share of women in percentages, 1960-1990

	1960	1970	1975	1980	1985	1990	Change-% 1960 –75	1975 –85
All self-employed	14 680	5 510	2 750	2 520	3 600	3 660	-81	31
Women´s share, %	67	80	65	65	74	75	-82	28
All employers	1 380	830	460	660	780	..	-67	70
Women´s share, %	36	39	39	37	44	..	-64	89
All own-account workers	13 300	4 680	2 290	1 860	2 820	..	-79	23
Women´s share, %	76	87	80	65	83	..	-81	34

Home production had already given way to industrial production in Finnish textile and clothing manufacture before World War II. The scale of production was, however, very modest before the 1940s: there were less than ten registered employers in the textile industries in the mid-1920s. The growth in production took place after World War II. The manufacture of textiles, clothing and leather products, and the various occupations related to these manufacturing processes like sewing and cutting, have traditionally been considered to be female work, and the labour force has been very female dominated: almost the entire labour force has been made up of women.

Women's share of the employed in textile and clothing manufacturing has developed as follows: in 1960 it was 78 per cent, in 1970 77 per cent and in 1975 it was 79 per cent. At the same time as the importance of textiles and clothing manufacture declined in the economy as a whole, women's share of all employed in textiles and clothing grew slightly.

This development implies to some extent the 'feminisation' of waged workers in textile and clothing manufacture during the 1970s. Between the years 1980 and 1985, the industry became to some extent even more feminised. In 1990, the proportion of women sank back to the 1975 level at 79 per cent. At the same time, the share held by textile and clothing manufacturing of the total labour force developed as follows: in 1980 it was 2 per cent, rising slightly in 1985 to 3 per cent. In 1990, the proportion of textile and clothing manufacturing labour of the total labour force declined to 1.6 per cent according to 1990 census data.

Economic fluctuations have resulted in a decline in self-employment, especially in 1970-1975, but there is little research literature on how small and medium-sized businesses have behaved during this fluctuation. According to Riitta Hjerppe, the share of the smallest fell at the economic upturn in the beginning of the 1970s; this decline is explained by the delay in the effects of fluctuations. In addition, the changes in statistical classification systems help to explain some of the decline (Hjerppe 1972). While we know that textile, clothing, leather and shoe manufacturing are all strongly concentrated in small business units – even given the marginal growth in the number of medium-sized firms in 1972-1985 – it is even simpler to understand the sharp decline in the number of firms in the market place during recession. The most important reasons for this decline lie in the fast changing picture of trade with Eastern Europe, in addition to the effect of ageing production machinery (Hiilamo 1971; Kasvio 1991).

The volume of textile and clothing manufacture industries grew during the 1970s and at the beginning of the 1980s. Since the year of highest volume, in which the number of employees in this sector stood at 33 500 employed in 1979, some 6 per cent of all those employed in manufacturing industries (CSOF 1982), the decline has been relatively fast even though, according to the most recent statistics, the number of firms seems to have risen over 5 per cent each year in 1985-1988 (Company register 1990).[13]

As a whole, the decline of self-employment in the textile and clothing industries is not solely a special feature of the Finnish economy, since *the declining share of textile and clothing industries out of total industrial production and the whole labour force follows the general pattern of Western European development* (see e.g. Hjerppe 1988, 74). One reason for the general decline in textile and clothing manufacturing in most OECD countries can be seen in *the transfer of production* into the third world countries, and into countries in Europe where labour and production costs are not so high.[14] During the 1970s, the pattern of international trade in clothing changed rapidly: export and subcontracting from the developing countries and – to a lesser extent – from Eastern European countries increased rapidly (Vuori – Ylä-Anttila 1989). In spite of this change, the shifts are not necessarily similar in different countries: For example, in Great Britain textile and clothing manufacturing units have been transferred to developing areas of the country and to those sectors of employment that are marginal by nature and thus offer cheaper labour (migrants, older women, home-based working women, and the grey sector of the economy) (see e.g. Rainnie 1989, 89-91).

---

13. Unfortunately it is impossible to get information concerning the owner structure from these statistics.

14. The NIC-countries, in particular, compete with low priced labour costs.

The textile and clothing industries have traditionally been characterised by low capital intensity and a slow rate of technical change. The basic technology has remained relatively simple and unchanged for a long period of time. This has meant that *entry barriers into self-employment in the industry have traditionally been very low.* Partly because of this, the share of women among the self-employed has been relatively large, especially among own-account workers without employees: *in 1985, 83 per cent of all own-account workers in the textile and clothing industries were women.*

The changes in different countries have also been important because of the *indirect impact of technological changes,* which seem to alter the industry´s life-cycle, even to the extent that the decline phase shortens or turns upward; this has been predicted in textile manufacturing which takes advantage of CAD/CAM production methods (Vuori − Ylä-Anttila 1989). The major technological changes to date have been in the use of computers in cutting and sewing. However, it should be remembered that these high-tech applications are diffused mainly to large firms with long production runs and stable lines, due to high capital costs involved.

In addition to these factors, which are more 'international' by nature, the changes in the former Eastern European markets were reflected quite directly in the Finnish textile manufacturing industry. The rapid decline in demand in the Eastern markets at the end of the 1970s and beginning of the 1980s made it impossible to redirect textile and clothing production to entirely different kinds of markets in the West. Changes in production strategies are needed instead of long product runs, such as flexible production systems and shorter product runs (Kasvio 1991).

I have so far described the broad lines of change in the manufacture of textiles and clothing. As shown in table 7.5, most women are own-account workers without employees. This means that their businesses are small and the work is not so much the manufacture of textiles as that of clothing, the dressing and dyeing of fur, tanning and dressing of leather, manufacture of luggage etc. In addition to the manufacture of clothing, manufacturers of knitted and crocheted fabrics and articles are also to be found amongst self-employed women in textile and clothing industries. How these general features were reflected into the lives of self-employed women will be discussed in more detail in chapter 7.2.4.

7.2.2. *Manufacture of food products and beverages*

The narrowness in the division of women's self-employment is visible in the share of female self-employment in the manufacture of food products and beverages of all female self-employment in manufacturing industry. This share is set at 8 per cent. However, the number of women who are classified as assisting family members in the manufacture of food products and beverages is relatively large in this industry. I will come back to this question later in my work.

The manufacture of food products is – unlike the textile and clothing industries – part of the closed sector of the economy in Finland in other countries; according to the value added, 60 per cent of the companies are located in industries where the import of food products and raw materials is restricted by tolls etc.[15] According to industrial statistics the manufacture of food is, in terms of both the gross value of production and the labour employed, the third largest manufacturing industry in Finland (see table 7.1.).

From the viewpoint of female self-employment, the most important area in the manufacture of food products is that of the manufacture of bakery products. The majority of such businesses are small, local affairs. This is contrary to Finland's food manufacturing industry in general: the average size of business in the manufacture of food products is even larger than in manufacturing in general (CSOF 1988b). According to industrial statistics, the manufacture of food products employs 10.5 per cent of all employed in manufacturing industries. Compared to gross production the number of people employed is rather small, at 1.8 per FIM 1m of goods produced, while the industry average is set at 4.2 persons per FIM 1m (CSOF 1985).

The food production industry is rather centralised. In Finland, 18 industrial food companies contribute over half of the industry's gross production (Ala-Peijari 1987, 41). At the 5-digit level we can specify the manufacture of bakery and dairy products, and the meat processing industries as the most important when measured by the number of employed; of these subindustries the manufacture of bakery products employs most women and contains the most self-employed women.

The proportion of all self-employed in the industry who were active in the manufacture of food products in 1985 stood at 7.5 per cent, whereas in 1960 the corresponding figure was 9.4 per cent. There has been a slight decline, and the bottom rate in the number of self-employed was reached in 1975. One of the factors sharpening the decline may be that productivity in the manufacture of food products has not risen in the 1980s and the importation of non-restricted trade consumer goods has simultaneously grown. These factors, perhaps together with the increased interest in 'home production' (baking machines, rising prices of industrial food products in comparison to home

15. Different kinds of import surcharges, tolls and licences protect agricultural production and self-sufficiency in agricultural products.

Table 7.6. **Self-employment in the food products industry, by employer status, share of women in percentages, 1960-1990**

	1960	1970	1975	1980	1985	1990	Change-% 1960 –75	1975 –85
All self-employed	1 940	1 170	870	930	1 180	1100	-55	36
Women´s share, %	21	23	22	30	27	25	-52	65
All employers	990	690	410	580	690	..	-59	68
Women´s share, %	22	24	20	28	23	..	-61	86
All own-account workers	950	480	460	350	490	..	-52	8
Women´s share, %	19	20	24	34	33	..	-42	49

baking etc.), have decreased demand for those domestic agricultural products that are competing with foreign ones. The development of all self-employed people in the manufacture of food products industry is described in table 7.6.

The development of the number of self-employed women in the food product industry (table 7.6.) follows the development of the industry as a whole, but the period of decline between the years 1960-1975 was especially regressive for women employers, whose business activities – mostly bakeries – were rather small in scale and employing only a few people[16], although the total number of self-employed men in the industry declined even further.

There was a relatively long period of reorganisation in the food product industry through a series of company mergers in the 1970s. The general level of productivity was at its lowest in 1976-1978, despite the company mergers and the closed nature of the industry (Ylä-Anttila – Heikkilä 1980). There was some increase in the number of self-employed women in the industry in 1975-1985, but it does not seem to be continuing into the 1990s. Women's share of own-account workers rose during the 1980s.

The manufacture of food products is usually considered to be a declining industry in the 1990s, where protective duties, regulated import controls and licensing are being discharged. The EC in particular, as well as the GATT agreements, have suggested that food product trade has to be deregulated in countries where protective duties exist (Ala-Peijari 1987, 124). In this respect the Finnish food product manufacturing industry follows – in a similar vein to the textile and clothing industries – the reorganisation model of industrial production in the Western European countries: its share of employed labour and total production in industry has been declining for years.

16. For more productivity comparisons see Kallinen 1986.

7.2.3. Female self-employment in other manufacturing industries

In addition to small-scale textile and clothing production and the bakeries, there are few self-employed women in other manufacturing industries. The next largest manufacturing industries – measured by the number of self-employed women – are publishing, printing and reproduction of recorded media (in 1985, 5.2 per cent of all female self-employment in manufacturing industries), and the manufacture of pottery, china and earthenware (in 1985 3.2 per cent of all female self-employment in manufacturing industries).

Even though the number of self-employed women is not by any means large in these industries, it has grown during the inspected time period. In publishing, printing and the reproduction of recorded media there has been an 86 per cent growth in the number of female self-employed in 1975-1985. This growth is possibly due to the growth in the various forms of subcontracting. The production of pottery, china and earthenware grew in the 1980s. Reasons for the growth are varied, and a large part of the growth has taken place in handicraft production, e.g. small scale arts and crafts production.

How have women been represented in other manufacturing industries, such as wood and wooden products, basic metals, machinery and related products, and others? Generally, it may be said that there have been very few or even no self-employed women in industries such as the manufacture of wood products, of chemical products, fabricated metal products (e.g. machines) and in the metal industries. There are three facts that link these industries: First, the dominant large business unit size for companies within these industries; secondly, the industries are highly capital intensive, and require far greater investment in production machinery than any of the industries where women are actively self-employed, and thirdly, the employed labour force is male-dominated, which also means that recruitment to self-employment is male-dominated.

7.2.4. Concluding remarks: experiences of self-employed women

In 1985, 11.2 per cent of all self-employed women were active in manufacturing industries, whereas the corresponding figure for 1960 stood at 36 per cent. *This reflects the relatively large shift from manufacturing industries into other areas of the economy, mainly into the service industries.* In 1985, the majority of the self-employed women in manufacturing industries (77 %) were active in two areas only, in the manufacture of food products and of textiles and clothing. The larger number of women worked in the latter sector (69.4 % of all self-employed women active in manufacturing industries

174

in 1985); neither did this internal division within the manufacturing sector change to any great extent in 1990.

Both of the two major industries for self-employed women in manufacturing have undergone major changes since the 1960s, and both are classified as being among the declining manufacturing industries. The extent to which these general conditions are reflected in individual work experiences and everyday business activities will now be discussed.

It is clear that individual experiences seldom provide a wide perspective on developmental factors, but they do inject a variety of such experiences into the generally known picture. In the following, I will illuminate the broad sweep outlined in earlier chapters with some interview material from the 'typical' female industries described above. These short extracts from interview reports are not intended to be exhaustive in nature; some parts of the interviews and completed questionnaires are used here to bring out additional aspects of the problems of self-employed women in manufacturing.

As mentioned before, one of the typical features of the manufacture of textiles and clothing is the domination of own-account workers in the group of self-employed. Own-account working is in many cases combined with retailing the final product, and thus the business works at two levels: manufacturing and retailing. This usually means that long periods of time are taken up by the production process, and short intervening customer visits. One of the own-account working women I interviewed, who designs, sews and sells her own products – clothes and various handicrafts – in her shop, commented:

> "There are days when I wish that nobody would pop into the shop during the day, so I could have some time just for sewing and perhaps also planning some new models and looking through the fabrics I've bought ...hmm ... but then, of course, the customers are essential to the business, and you have to serve them really well so that they feel welcome and might return and become regular customers. Both the whole production process from planning to sewing, and then finally selling the product are really hard work, harder than I ever expected." (C.[17], interview 1990).

Another one of the women I interviewed, A., aged 35 years, said that in her area of business – the manufacture of clothing, and the dressing and dyeing of fur, in addition to selling the final products – one of the major difficulties in small-scale production is that the production process itself usually takes so

---

17. The names of the women interviewed are omitted in this report, and detailed information about the business is not reported as was the requirement of most of the respondents. The questionnaire used, in addition to the short description of all interviewed women and their businesses, can be found in the appendix.

much time. For her, finding the right balance (time) for the various business activities such as accounting, marketing, and planning, in addition to production and retailing, is the most difficult facet of self-employment. The fact that there is 'too much to do and too little time' seems to be a complaint of many of the self-employed women interviewed, especially for own-account workers without paid employees, such as A. Having always dreamed of having a small shop, and making clothes and selling them, she bought her business in 1986 without a great deal of forethought. The firm she bought was established in the 1970s and had a rather stable clientele. Gradually she has widened the range of business into fur products and hats, which she makes herself.

During the interview, A. mentioned that she has had major problems in only one business function, namely financing the business. She did not see that her gender had anything to do with this, since her husband (with a small firm of his own in the construction business) had similar problems with finance at the beginning of his 'entrepreneurial career'. A. was very satisfied with her business and her own way of running it and did not see the manufacture of clothing as a problematic area.

> But, as she put it herself: "my production and all the functions of my business are on a really small scale, and perhaps I would not manage a larger firm by myself. And when everything is taking place on a small scale, both production and retailing, the general problems of the industry are not truly reflected in your business operations and activities" (A., interview 1990).

Another of my interviewees also works in manufacturing. Her area of operation is another female dominated one, namely a bakery. This she runs together with her husband. Her expertise lies in knowledge of the production process, as she has occupational training in food processing and supervising large-scale food production. B., aged 46 years, owns a relatively large bakery and a small cafe jointly with her husband employing a total of 34 people. Her entrepreneurial career started together with her husband, and with a background in both food production and managerial tasks in catering, she did not find it too difficult to start a business of her own. The bakery was established in the 1950s, and B. and her husband bought it in 1980.

> "The labour intensive nature of the industry together with the costs associated with employment represent the most difficult problems for the company"; at the time of interview, in 1990, she was considering selling the company because of increasing labour costs and marginally falling sales. (B., interview 1990)

The general historical trend is that women's self-employment has shifted from manufacturing into service industries during the inspected time period. This development reflects the general trend in society away from manufacturing industries as the main employers towards the service sector. In a similar vein, the importance of manufacturing as the main sector for self-employed women has also declined. The reasons for the decline are many and varied, but may be summarised in three main points.

First, the industrial structure of the Finnish economy has diversified: service industries have grown and new service industries have arisen. Manufacturing has lost its position as the dominant employer although export industries present exceptions. However, the largest increase in employment has taken place in the service industries. For a variety of reasons, which cannot be discussed in more detail here, most of the service jobs have been traditionally viewed as women's work. Firstly, they require many of those qualifications associated with women's domestic responsibilities: caring, supporting, serving others. Secondly, since wages, rather than equipment (machines, etc.) have constituted the main costs in the service sector, the work has been typically low-paid.

The concentration of the population of Finland in the south of the country and especially in the province of Uusimaa in the 1960s and 1970s is a result of *the restructuring and diversification of the economy*: it wasn't until 1975 that the migration started to slow. In 1970-1975, the service sector in particular grew in these areas. Manufacturing industries grew relatively more in development area 1 (a so-called fringe area) than in Uusimaa.[18] This regional change was partly supported by the regional and employment policies of the government (Valkonen 1985, 231). The fact that the economy diversified in the 1970s also caused the change rate to slow in all three main sectors of the economy, a fact that is further visible in the change in the number of entrepreneurs in manufacturing industries after 1975.

Secondly, the oil crisis in the 1970s is considered to have been a general factor in the development in the number of entrepreneurs. The oil crisis caused an overall economic depression and was manifested in the diminishing number of new businesses established (see e.g. Stanworth – Curran 1986, 109). Other examples include diminished productivity growth due to a decrease in industrial investments and export demand and the decrease of regional mobility in

---

18. This development is clearly visible in the statistics published by Valkonen (1985), where jobs in the primary sector have diminished by 67 per cent in Uusimaa in 1950-1975, and 65 per cent in development area 1, (D.A.1., a fringe area). The number of jobs in the secondary sector grew by 37 per cent in Uusimaa and 67 per cent in D.A.1. The greatest change took place in tertiary sector jobs which grew by 120 per cent in Uusimaa and 115 per cent in D.A.1. (Valkonen 1985, 228-229).

Southern Finland (Valkonen 1985, 230). The development and diversification in the economic structure had already, by the 1970s, resulted in the growth of employment of women in the service sector, so the reduction in the secondary sector did not particularly influence women's employment, even though the effects were seen in tertiary sector employment a little later. The effects of depression in the open sector of the economy were especially pertinent in decreasing women's self-employment (e.g. through the changes in export demand in the manufacture of clothing and textiles).

Thirdly, the extension of women's labour force participation, and the increase in the number of industries where women were employed in the 1960s, undoubtedly affected the diminishing importance of manufacturing industry as the principal sector of women's self-employment. Some general features of the structure of women's employment have been dealt with earlier. In comparison to women's self-employment, women's labour force participation followed a similar kind of model; economic activity – in terms of official paid employment – was not general for married women in the 1960s, partly because welfare benefits such as the communal day-care system were not yet enacted. The share of married women in employment of all married women between the ages of 15 - 64 was 45 per cent in 1960 in the country as a whole, but it rose to 53 per cent in 1970, 63 per cent in 1975, and 70 per cent in 1980.

The growth in the range of work opportunities offered better possibilities for women, in the sense that the decline in manufacturing work did not directly diminish women's potential for labour activities. However, the gendered division of labour has gathered strength even with the growth of women's labour force participation: many tasks which were typical to women's housework in the pre-industrial age and later (baking, knitting, etc.) were men´s jobs when first entering the waged arena. As labour force participation grew and the value of the work decreased, they became women's jobs again.[19]

In summing up the general developmental features of women's self-employment in manufacturing industry, it may be said that there have been both production and size-related changes, especially in those industries where women's self-employment has been important, i.e. in the manufacture of textiles, clothing, leather products, shoes and food products. In textiles, clothing, leather products and shoe manufacturing growth has been particularly notable in medium-sized businesses.

However, it should be kept in mind that e.g. industrial statistics exclude small firms employing less than five persons from their scope. As a consequence we can only see changes in the number of own-account workers

---

19. The manufacture of food products and the bakeries are mentioned as examples of this (Jallinoja 1985, 260; Grint 1991).

and small-scale employers in the population statistics. According to such statistics, the number of self-employed women as employers decreased in the manufacturing of textiles, clothing, leather products and shoes from the 1960s to 1975, and the number of women who work as own-account workers declined up to 1980. Changes in the manufacture of food products, such as the reorganisation of the whole production process and company mergers have decreased not only the number of self-employed women, but the number of small employers and own-account workers as a whole.

7.3. Development in the service sector – the re-emergence of self-employment

According to the shift-share analysis presented earlier, at least some part of the growth in small firms and self-employment can be attributed to the shift in economic activities from manufacturing to services. The service sector, measured by the number and also share of the labour force has grown quite strongly in Finland during the 1970s and 1980s. In spite of this development, the share of the service sector of GNP and of employment has been relatively low in Finland, when compared to respective figures in the US, UK, or in Japan (Lastikka 1984, 15).

When production is inspected, the share of the wholesale and retail trade, restaurants and hotel industry has been slightly over 20 per cent of the total production in services, and this has remained relatively stable from the 1960s up to the 1980s. The share of the so-called 'new' services, such as business related activities, e.g. financial intermediation, insurance, real estate, renting and business services, grew from 25 per cent to 28 per cent during the years 1964-1981. The share of transport, storage and information communications remained quite stable at 15 per cent, as was also the case in the share of social and personal service activities, at around 7 per cent of all production in the service sector (Lastikka 1984, 20-21).

Which industries are included in the service sector, then? The concept itself, 'services', is rather problematic in the sense that it consists of 'non-material' goods, which cannot be transferred to another person, nor can they be stored up, or acquired to be used later. Still, the demand for services is derived demand in the economic sense and based on the existence of goods. In fact, the interdependency of services and material goods can also be inverted: the production of service activities creates material goods production.

Service occupations, instead of directly producing goods, offer services to others. However, the statistical concept of service is to some extent imperfect and does not register all related services, but only the main activity of the statistical unit. This means that e.g. in the case of one of the women I interviewed, the classification of the main activity can be problematic. She both designs and manufactures her models, and sells the designed and produced clothes in her own shop: is she a manufacturer, or is she mainly 'producing retail services', which occasionally seems to take most of her time?

Wholesale and retail trade, and hotels and restaurants are both industries which are classified as being that part of the service sector, which has grown relatively fast during the inspected time period. Other industries classified as growing services, are transport, storage and communication, financial intermediation, insurance, real estate business and business service activities, and community, social and personal service activities. Self-employment activities are most essential in the service sector – in addition to public, private, non-profit and home-based activities – when measured as a share of value added (70 per cent of all the aforementioned activities).[20] It could be said that small businesses and the services are inextricably linked. Even if the demand for services is 'indirect' in the sense that its development depends on the development of other areas in the economy, it can be said that the services also smooth fluctuations in the economy.

The share of all services of GNP has grown and represented over half of total GNP in the 1980s (Hjerppe 1988, 75). The fastest growing of all industries have been the wholesale and retail trade, hotel and restaurant services, transport and information communications and different kinds of social and personal service activities, when measured by the number of people employed.

Table 7.7. Employed in various service sector industries as percentage of EAP, 1960-1985

	1960	1970	1975	1980	1985[*]
Wholesale/retail trade	11.8	15.5	14.6	13.8	14.5
Transport	6.3	7.1	7.6	7.9	7.6
Financing, etc.	1.9	3.4	4.7	5.3	6.8
Personal, etc. services	14.0	13.4	21.0	24.8	28.5
Total	34.0	39.4	47.9	51.8	57.4

* the information concerning the year 1990 was available only at 2-digit level, so precise calculations due to changes in the classification between 1985 and 1990 censuses were impossible to make. Thus, information from the year 1990 is excluded here.

20. Even though I discuss the whole service sector here, and consequently use the name of that sector, it does not necessarily mean that each industry is as important as another in the observed development, nor does it mean that they developed at the same rate.

Inspection of the shares of different industries of all service industries and the development within each one, in 1960-1985, yields a division as shown in table 7.7. *The share of the labour force in the service sector as a whole grew from 34 per cent (1960) to 57,3 per cent (1985) up to 60 per cent in 1990.* In terms of the employed labour force, the emphasis between different branches within the services has changed primarily towards social and personal service activities, and also towards financial intermediation, insurance activities, real estate and renting services, and business related service activities.

Although the service sector has grown, as measured by its share of the total labour force, there have been additional changes in the internal structure of the industries, and also in the regional distribution of their services. The regional emphasis in the growth of services had already shifted in the 1970s, but was especially pronounced during the 1980s: it seems that since 1975 the growth of the service industries has shifted from Uusimaa and industrial Southern Finland to the development areas, the North and East of the country. In Uusimaa and industrial Southern Finland, the rate of growth of the service industries – measured by the employed labour force – slowed and later stagnated (for further information, see Valkonen 1985, 231).

The number of employed decreased between 1970 and 1980 in the wholesale and retail trade, hotels and restaurant services. After 1980 the number of employed started to rise again slightly (the change percentage was 7.1 per cent in 1980-1985). The greatest changes have taken place in the internal structure of the industry, a point to which I shall return in the next chapter. The transport, storage and communication services have remained rather stable; their share of all employed remained almost static between 1975 and 1985.

However, there has been a growth of self-employment in the service sector as a whole, but women's share of all self-employed has not grown to any great degree. The share of those employed in financial intermediation, insurance activities, real estate and renting services, and business related service activities has risen evenly (the change percentage between 1980-1985 was 30 per cent). In the social and personal service activities the growth in the employed has taken place mostly in the public sector. In the service sector as a whole the growth percentage of the employed was 13 per cent between 1980 and 1985.

The growth in the number of employed in the service industries has been based on the growth in the number of women employed in services in a similar way as the growth of the labour force as a whole is based on the growth of the female labour force. This has also meant that the contents of work have changed and become more demanding in nature. The development in work content has to some extent been controversial e.g. in retail trade occupations. It

181

has been suggested that the nature of retailing changed at the beginning of the First World War in the UK – this change took place later on in Finland – as many traditional craft skills were passed over to wholesalers and manufacturers and retailing concentrated on the sale of finished goods only (Broadbridge 1991). This transformation helped to undermine the skilled nature of the work. The expanding market resulted in an increasing need for shop assistants who, as Holcombe argues, did little more than keep the stock tidy, show merchandise, and receive payment (Holcombe in Broadbridge 1991, 44). Similar changes were also visible in other service industries.

7.3.1. Female self-employment in traditional services — the wholesale and retail trade, hotels and restaurant services

The traditional image of a self-employed woman is claimed to be that of running a small grocer's shop, perhaps together with her husband, where she serves the neighbourhood and takes care of everybody's business as well. This image may well have been – and still is, to some extent – reality, since the wholesale and retail trade, and restaurants and hotel businesses have been and still are the most usual industries for self-employed women: they have been previously referred to as the traditional area for women entrepreneurs.

It is claimed that the base for the growth of trade, hotel and restaurant businesses was created by three factors: industrialisation, the growth of foreign trade and general economic growth (Pipping – Bärlund 1966, 233). *Part of the growth can be claimed to be due to the invisible work of women in family businesses.* The family business enterprise unit was once a very important form, and still is e.g. in retail and the restaurant business: in 1985 there were almost as many women registered as assisting family members as there were own-account working women in the retail business. In theory, this could mean that almost all men registered as own-account workers in retailing have their wives working in the business. Whether this represents the true picture is naturally impossible to say on the basis of statistics, but assuming the contractual nature of many marriages (see chapter 7.5) this could bear some resemblance with reality.

The growth in private expenditure and changes in consumption patterns have meant that the whole service sector grew quickly and specialised further. This development has, in particular, taken place in both trading and restaurants and hotel businesses. Production in this area has been closely followed by changes in the volume of private consumption (Hjerppe 1988), and also in the widening scale of the consumed services. In this chapter I will mainly inspect the quantitative development in the number of self-employed women and reflect some of the interviews conducted. Several structural changes have taken place both in the trade and hotel and restaurant businesses during the time period inspected.

Female self-employment occupies half of all self-employment in trade, restaurants and hotel businesses (table 7.8).[21] Most of these businesses are small, and the own-account working women thus represent the majority of all female self-employment therein. In practice, this means small 'one-woman' shops, long working days, no holidays other than short periods during which the shop is closed. The 'family business' is still very common, especially in food retailing, but less so in business areas such as clothing retail.

The number of self-employed women grew steadily from 1960 to 1970, but in the 1970s started to decline slightly: there was some decline in both the number of own-account workers and the number of employers between the years 1970 and 1975. This decline turned, however, swung upwards again, and continued to rise from 1975 to 1985 and on into the 1990s. *According to preliminary information from the 1990 census, the absolute growth in female self-employment (assisting family members included) stood at 13.5 per cent in 1985-1990.*

The number of self-employed women as employers fell altogether by 20.6 per cent in 1960-1975 in the trade, restaurant and hotel industries. In 1975 female self-employment was at its lowest. However, in relation to male self-employment it was relatively higher than before, 1975 actually representing the peak during the period under inspection (44 per cent of all entrepreneurs were women).

Table 7.8. **Women´s share of self-employment in wholesale and retail trade, restaurant and hotel industries, by employer status, 1960-1990 (%)**

	1960	1970	1975	1980	1985	1990	Change-% 1960 -75	1975 -85
Women´s share of								
all self-employed	51	43	44	43	42	41	-13	37
all employers	46	42	40	38	37	..	-21	42
all own-account workers	54	45	47	47	47	..	-7	33

---

21. The industry includes the following main areas: wholesale and retail trade, commission trade, hotels and restaurants, bars and canteens.

If we inspect the development that has taken place in male self-employment, it can be seen that during 1960-1975 there was a sharp decrease in the absolute number of male self-employed, and that almost half of this decrease took place in the number of own-account workers. In the trade, hotels and restaurants industry as a whole, male self-employment grew relatively more quickly than female self-employment after the period of recession in the mid-1970s: the change was measured at 50.7 per cent for men in 1975-1985.[22] This growth mostly took place not in the number of own-account workers, which had previously been in decline, but in the number of *employers*: the change was 64.2 per cent for male employers, and 37.5 per cent for male own-account workers between 1975-1985.

This rise in male self-employment (assisting family members included) also seems to have continued in the late 1980s, the figure standing at 53 per cent for 1985 to 1990. This represented a relatively faster rise than in female self-employment (13.5 per cent).[23]

All in all, the rise in self-employment that started in the 1980s continued to the 1990s. Furthermore, the available data reveals that the rise occurred differently for men than for women. Further elaboration reveals that the growth industries for men have been different than those for women. The reasons for the growth may be sought both in general economic growth and especially in the specific features of the industry in question. The recession at the beginning of 1970s, and consequent rationalisation of wholesale and retail trade led to a decrease in the number of small businesses, and affected both the *regional distribution* of retail trade and *average business size.* Furthermore, the structure of retail trade has changed, partly because of internal migration and partly because of various factors such as e.g. the spread of cars in society, the latter leading to a change in shopping behaviour, and more or less directly to the closing of the small businesses such as local grocer's shops.

The majority of female self-employment in the trade, restaurant and hotel services is still in the retail trade, even though the number of self-employed women grew more in restaurant and hotel businesses during 1980-1985, and again in 1985-1990. When assisting family members are included, the rise in the wholesale and retail trade stood at 10.7 per cent in 1985-1990, while the rise in restaurant and hotel businesses was 23.8 per cent.

---

22. It is interesting to notice that a similar pattern took place in manufacturing industry after the 1970s recession.

23. The absolute number in 1985 of self-employed men and men who were assisting family members was 18 670; in 1990 the corresponding figure was 28 580. The absolute numbers for self-employed women and women who were assisting family members were 18 340 and 20 810 respectively.

When the development in the number of waged workers in the branch is inspected, it can be seen that the number of employed women grew by 1.5 per cent and employed men by 8.4 per cent in 1975-1985. The relative share of men of all employed in the branch has grown further than the women's share, the latter standing at 62 per cent in 1975 and 60.5 per cent in 1985 (CSOF 1978a, 1988a). In 1990 the share of female employed declined further to 58 per cent.

The growing 'maleness' of employment creates an interesting question regarding possible connections between the strong growth of the industry and the high number of male self-employed. The change in the number of employers and data on the structure of restaurant and hotel businesses refer to the general development that had already begun in the 1960s. This development meant that the overall number of small retail trade shops had not grown, but instead growth took place in the number of larger shops e.g. department stores, and in the number of new restaurants, bars, cafes, canteens and hotel businesses. I will now move on to inspect development *within* the industry in greater detail.

In the wholesale trade and agency business, female self-employment has been marginal, at 5 per cent of all self-employed in 1960. However, the share of women grew so that in 1985 12 per cent of all self-employed in the wholesale trade were women. The growth occurred relatively evenly during the inspected time period; an exception to this is the period 1980-1985, during which time the number of self-employed women doubled (change percentage 87.6 per cent). This rise continued to the end of 1980s; the change percentage for 1985-1990 was 26 per cent[24].

Measured as absolute numbers, these changes do not mean very much, since there are only a few hundred women in the wholesale trade. However, it is of interest and also refers to a 'new kind of self-employment' that the growth has taken place in the number of own-account working women. This means self-employed women who run small 'one-woman' based agency businesses or import businesses, which are perhaps based on their specific knowledge of areas such as retail or catering businesses and usually also require a high degree of knowledge and skills regarding foreign languages and cultures. The growth has been stronger in the number of self-employed women than men in this industry.

In the retail trade, the share of self-employed women has varied a lot (table 7.9). Of all self-employed in the retail trade, the share of women stood at 38.2 per cent in 1960. The number of women then started to decline slightly in the 1960s, but less so than did the number of men, so there was in fact a slight rise

24. Assisting family members included.

185

in the share of female self-employment (41,6 per cent in 1970). Between 1970 and 1975 the number of women in retail trade decreased almost 30 per cent, and their share of all self-employed in the retail trade also declined by one percentage unit, resting at 40.6 per cent in 1975. The number of self-employed men declined as well in 1970-1975, though the decline for men was smaller than for women, at 25 per cent.

The general trend for self-employed women in the retail trade (table 7.9.) could be summarised as following: *Women have increased their share of own-account workers; however, their share of employers has declined in spite of the growth in the absolute number of all employers.* In 1980-1985, the number of own-account working women – i.e. small shopkeepers who do not have employees – grew considerably more than the number of women employers.

There are several factors to be considered in the development of self-employment in the retail trade. First, there is *internal migration,* which gradually 'shifted' small shops, such as grocer's shops, from the countryside into population centres. Simultaneously, the number of people employed in relation to retail capacity declined sharply, indicating intensive (based on technology) rather than extensive (based on employment) growth (Hjerppe 1988).

Secondly, *the influence of supermarket chains* on small retail shop density and size is crucial, since almost all retail traders belong to a retail chain. Development in the 1960s and 1970s may be termed as 'near distance services' in the retail trade, since the number of small shops at this time was high both in rural areas and urban population centres (Hjerppe 1988, 77). In the case of the wholesale trade, rationalisation and the influence of the supermarket chains have been more important factors in the development of the number of self-employed than migration. It has been forecast that the employment structure in retail trade will shift towards part-time employment, and this does indeed seem to be the future trend, according to employment statistics. Another factor which gains increasing influence is the use of 'new' technology.

All the factors mentioned add to the need for concentration and integration of activities with the central retail companies. This development is likely to trim down the number of entrepreneurs in the future (Lastikka 1984, 60), and especially the number of own account workers, i.e. small shop keepers without employees. According to the census data from 1970, 1975 and 1980, the most important forms of retail trade are "general" (i.e. retail in non-specialised stores) and food retail.[25] Both represent areas where the share of self-employed women grew in 1970-1980.

---

25. It was not possible to get a more detailed division of retail trade at 3-digit level for the years 1960, 1985 and 1990.

Table 7.9. **Women's share of self-employment in retail trade, by employer status, 1960-1990 (%)**

Women's share of	1960	1970	1975	1980	1985	1990	Change-% 1960 –75	1975 –85
all self-employed	38	42	41	41	41	..	-30	35
all employers	38	38	35	34	34	..	-43	39
all own-account workers	38	46	46	48	49	..	-18	33

The traditional female industry, the retail of textiles, clothing, leather products and shoes is dominated by women; women's share of all self-employed in those areas has grown evenly, and stood at 68 per cent of all self-employed according to the census data of 1980. The retail trade in motor vehicles, mainly cars, is male dominated; women's share has remained under 10 per cent of all self-employed in the area in 1970-1980. By including assisting family members, the percentage of women of all self-employed in motor vehicle retail business rose to only 10 per cent in the 1990 census. One of the women I interviewed is a motor vehicle retailer, running the business jointly with her colleagues. Her experiences of being a self-employed woman in a very male dominated area are discussed in the next chapter.

If, as has been suggested, the small independent retail business is somewhat obsolete, such shops possibly have no part in a modern, efficient distribution system. However, the efficient ones do fulfil an important social and economic function in society. The independent model can be changed into franchising, or participation in a large retail chain (Statens offentliga utredningar 1987). On the other hand, changes in consumption patterns, such as recycling, ecological products, etc., require perhaps more independent shops and the small-scale organisation of business functions.

There was a strong growth of self-employment in *hotel and restaurant businesses* during the five year period 1980-1985, and in the following period 1985-1990. This growth was mainly seen in male self-employment, especially that of male employers. *The growth in female self-employment was at its greatest in 1975-1980* (table 5.11). The fastest growth in the output of restaurant and hotel businesses took place during 1960-1973 according to Lastikka, but productivity fell during the 1980s (Lastikka 1984, 33) as a result of overcapacity in the industry. Various factors influenced the growth in the number of entrepreneurs: urbanisation, 'city-culture', an increase in canteen facilities, growth of tourism, etc. The changes in the alcohol legislation offered restaurant keepers more options: the 1968 legislative change led to a rise in the number of restaurant owners as seen in the 1970 statistics.

Table 7.10. Women's share of self-employment in restaurant and hotel services, by employer status, 1960-1990 (%)

	1960	1970	1975	1980	1985	1990	Change-% 1970 –75	Change-% 1975 –85
Restaurant services								
women's share of employers	86	81	74	72	64	59	-30	42
women's share of own-account workers	*	87	86	87	75	*	15	15
Hotel services								
women's share of employers	74	56	51	50	40	33	-46	24
women's share of own-account workers	*	78	69	65	57	*	-28	41

* included in the figure above.

We have to take into account when inspecting the figures in table 7.10. that on international comparison the trade and service industries have not become as important in the structure of the service sector in Finland as they have done elsewhere. Trade, restaurant and hotel businesses are all considered to be sensitive to economic fluctuations. Changes in the volume of private consumption are viewed as changes in the volume of output (Lastikka 1984). General factors influencing a growth in business include the deregulation of foreign trade that has, together with a growth in the level of income, increased the potential for private consumption, and thus also diversified production. The strong dependency of the services on the development of goods' production and diversification can be seen in the development of the service sector after World War II (Lastikka 1984, 27).

7.3.2. Concluding remarks: experiences of self-employed women

Even though the service industries and not e.g. the manufacturing or construction industries are the major domain of female self-employment, the variety of divisions in the services make it difficult to find as clear a pattern as exists for self-employed women in manufacturing industries. The diversity of subindustries occupied by the interviewed women (also borne out by statistics) indicate, however, the traditional work areas of women, and thus a pattern similar to manufacturing industries; that is, *the small size of the business activities and traditional areas of business.*

There was one striking feature, however, related to the segregation of business areas into male/female spheres. If an industry was male dominated, it became obvious from the interviews that many of the difficulties were related to the fact that:

> "...As a woman one is acting in a male sphere of the economy where one does not belong, not at least as an entrepreneur who knows her line of business well", as one of the interviewed commented (E., interview 1990).

The problems in the male dominated industries were clearly more related to men's difficulties in accepting the credibility of women than to the actual business-related factors, even if the latter were also mentioned. One of the most common comments made in the questionnaires, and also in some of the interviews, concerned the prejudices met in different situations with business interest groups, e.g. financial institutions, customers etc.

The women interviewed had developed various strategies to tackle these situations where their credibility in business activities was questioned. The second youngest of the interviewees, D., 24 years old, had established her business jointly with her two male friends only six months before the interview. Since the line of the business was very male-dominated – motor-vehicle retailing – she had already faced situations where her credibility was called into question. Hence, in taking care of the company´s financial operations, her strategy was either to send her male colleagues alone, or ask them to join her in business meetings where her credibility would otherwise have been low. This was not because of her lack of self-confidence, but she saw it more as a strategic solution:

> "It is quicker to use a male colleague as a kind of mouthpiece, than to try to convince the other side in a negotiation that, yes, in spite of my youth and my being a woman, they can rely on my skills." (D., interview, questionnaire 1990).

It was, however, obvious that the older women I interviewed did not have such positive ideas as D., especially where the line of business or industry was male dominated. For these women, credibility had come to a large extent through the husband and his actions in the family business. Their husbands had either been present at meetings where financial matters were discussed or the division of work tasks within the business was clearly a traditional one, so that the husband took care of e.g. financial negotiations with the bank, while the wife looked after office routines. This was the case regarding H.'s way of organising her work, she owned a construction business jointly with her husband. This division of work tasks was also used by L., who owned an interior decoration company jointly with her husband. This 'avoidance' strategy also seemed to be the easiest solution for most women who had faced credibility problems, even though it restricted the division of labour to the traditional mode.

The credibility problems were only faced in the male dominated industries, a picture which is also borne out by research literature (see chapter 4.4.). It became apparent in the interviews that women who were self-employed – either as own-account workers or employers – in traditional female-dominated areas, faced fewer problems regarding their credibility in various business activities.[26] Despite this, however, the large-scale operation of female dominated lines of business tends to combine elements of the operational problems present for women in male or female dominated areas. As one interviewee, G., who owns and runs her own business jointly with her husband, commented:

> "Even if the 'selling of flowers' is very feminine work, the cultivation of flowers as a large-scale business is still very male work". Her problems have been related to large-scale business activities, not the everyday business of selling flowers. (G., interview 1990).

The credibility problem many of the interviewed women had faced, relates to a larger question of rigid boundaries for women's economic activities, gender relations, and patriarchal bargains or contracts. A patriarchal bargain or contract refers to the existence of set rules and scripts which regulate gender relations, to which both genders accommodate and acquiesce, yet which may nonetheless be contested, redefined and renegotiated. (For the use of the concept, see e.g. Kandiyoti 1991.) The interviews revealed some of the coping mechanisms and strategies the self-employed women used in dealing with these problems. A systematic analysis of these coping mechanisms would expose the nature of patriarchal practices both in public and private patriarchy. Further analysis, which cannot be done in this study, would also reveal some of the cultural and temporal concreteness of the patriarchal practices, which do not arise in theoretical discussions of patriarchy.

---

26. This was also reinforced in the questionnaires.

7.4. The growth sector of the economy – the modern entrepreneurs?

Economic restructuring – understood here as the process of change involving a set of closely articulated causal powers – has taken place in various fields of society, such as in the structure of manufacturing industry, trends in employment patterns, the nature of consumption and the organisation of production.[27] Similar patterns to the changes in industrial structure undergone e.g. in the UK cannot be seen in the Finnish economy. Neither has the growth in the small business sector in Finland been substantively as large as in some other OECD countries. The growth in the 'high-tech' sector and in producer services partly reflect this restructuring. The various service activities such as financial intermediation, insurance related activities, real estate activities, business related services and social and personal services, are all classified as being part of the 'new' service economy, part of the restructuring.

Whether or not the rise of the 'new' services and increased restructuring of the economy should be addressed together, there is a tendency in research literature to discuss the rise of service sector entrepreneurism together with growing privatisation and restructuring of the economy. It is beyond the scope of this study to debate this question in detail. However, common to all these 'new' services is their being seen as the principal growth areas of the service society, either because of the intensive growth in production (communication services, financial services and insurance services), or because of the growth of employment (business related services). In addition, a growth in self-employment is common to the aforementioned industries.

I shall first inspect some of the features in the development of the transport, storage and communication industries, in financial intermediation, insurance, real estate and business service activities, and in community, social and personal service activities. I will then move on to inspect the quantitative development of self-employed women in some of these service industries.

The size of the employed labour force in all the aforementioned industries grew to some extent in 1960-1985. Women's share of the labour force grew slightly in 1980-1985, this growth taking place in transportation activities (e.g. supporting and auxiliary transport activities, travel agencies). However, women's share of all employed labour in the communication services has decreased slightly. The growth of the employed labour force has been greater in financial intermediation, insurance, real estate and in business services than in transport services.

---

27. The notion of 'flexibility' has been the subject of extended debates (see e.g. Burrows – Curran 1989; Burrows 1991).

Measured by the number of employed, growth has been fastest in the category of social and personal services. *The feminisation of the service sector continued in the 1980s. The strong growth in women's share of employment in the services reflects on the one hand the high proportion of women in the labour force, and on the other the segregated labour markets.* The number of women in paid employment in 1980-1985 grew to 21 per cent, while the corresponding growth in the case of men was 12 per cent. According to preliminary data from the 1990 census, this development also continued up to the 1990's.

In Finland, both the output and employment shares of service sector activities are still rather low compared to other countries and, furthermore, they are differently emphasised in comparison with other OECD countries aside from some similarity with Sweden (see e.g. Lastikka 1984). The derived nature of demand can be seen in all service industries: changes in the volumes of trade, transport and business related services correlate especially well with the volumes of manufacturing and private consumption, according to ETLA's calculations (Ripatti et al. 1989).

7.4.1. Female self-employment in transport, storage and communication services

For a long time, business activities in the transport, storage and communication services were concentrated mainly in personnel and goods transportation (1960-1975). This meant that the majority of the self-employed were male truck owners working for themselves, even though some of them did have employees. Of all self-employed outside agriculture, 21.2 per cent were active in these areas in 1960. In 1985 their share had risen slightly (23.7 per cent of all self-employed outside of agriculture).

Table 7.11. Women's share of self-employment and of paid employment in transport and communication activities, 1960-1990 (%)

	1960	1970	1975	1980	1985	1990[a]
Women's share of						
all self-employment	1	2	3	4	4	3
paid employment	21	23	26	25	27	31
transport	21	14	17	18	19	25
communication	*	49	47	45	45	44

a The share of assisting family members is estimated to be at the same level as 1985.
* included in the figure above.

Female self-employment has been low in the transport, storage and communication industries, but grew steadily during the time period inspected. The largest increase in the number of self-employed women took place during the years 1960-1975, with an 83 per cent rise. Growth also occurred during the following ten years at 27 per cent for 1975-1985. However in 1985, the share of self-employed women stood at only 3.9 per cent of all self-employed in the transport, storage and communication industry. Compared to male self-employment, female self-employment was thus quantitatively small.

The share of female self-employment remained more or less static in 1985-1990 in the transport, storage and communication services. The slight decrease in the number of own-account workers was compensated for by the growth in the number of women active as employers in transportation or storage services in 1980-1985. Unfortunately, the 1990 census data did not reveal separate figures for own-account workers and employers (table 7.11.).

There was a slight decrease in the number of men: during 1970-1985 male self-employment declined 16 per cent. In practice this meant to a great extent that e.g. the number of men who worked as professional drivers decreased. Women's share of the employed in the industry has grown, especially in the transport services, from 13.5 per cent (1970) to 19.4 per cent (9185) and 25 per cent (1990). However, this was not the case in information communications, where women's share of all employed decreased (49 per cent in 1970; 44 per cent in 1990).

Own-account workers make up the largest proportion of self-employed women who are active either in the transport services or in storage services. The number of own-account working women increased sharply in 1960-1975 (change percentage 179 per cent). Growth then shifted to employers. (The growth percentage for female employers is not as large as previously: 57 per cent in 1975-1985.)

7.4.2. New possibilities in new services?

In his book "After Industrial Society?" Jonathan Gershuny stated that far from becoming service economies, Western societies are on the way to becoming self-service economies that are increasingly reliant upon material production. In 1978, Gershuny even saw signs of decline in the service industries. The Gershunian idea, however, does not seem to hold true in most Western countries, at least not when the number of those employed in services is inspected. This is also the case for Finland. The industrial classification used here does, of course, focus on the product and not on the contents of the job itself. Thus, according to Gershuny (Gershuny 1978), it does not really tell us much about job content. The industrial classification of, say, 'new' services includes various occupations which are not directly connected to the 'product', while an occupational classification looks only at the nature of the job and not the product, and thus excludes from the classification such occupations which are not directly related to 'service product'. But while my interest here lies partly in the development of the economic structure, and thus the product is the important result rather than the occupational structure *per se*, and while the focus of my study lies in self-employed women's share of the development of the economic structure, my use of the industrial classification speaks for itself.

Most of the employed labour force in the so-called 'new' expanding services, i.e. financial intermediation, insurance services, real estate and business related service activities, are women (Table 7.12.). Of these different branches, women's share of the labour force in *financial services* grew rapidly in 1960-1970. Since then, their share has remained relatively stable, at 80 per cent in 1975-1985 and 78 per cent in 1990, while the absolute number of women in employment in the industry has grown. In *insurance services*, women's share of the labour force is a bit lower, but has also grown slightly, standing at 70 per cent of all employed in insurance services in 1990. Of the new service industries, women's share of all employed had been lowest in *real estate services* and in *business related services* (45 per cent of all employed). Keeping this in mind, it does not seem so strange that women's employment has grown most in these two areas. The main part of this growth took place in 1960-1970. Business related services is a term that can be used to cover a wide range of various activities providing expertise and services to businesses. These services include tangible products and intangible expertise.

When the growth of all the industries mentioned is measured by the changes in paid employment, it appears to have been relatively rapid: the strongest growth took place in 1960-1975. The number of employed women in the branch grew by over 200 per cent. After 1975, the growth slowed somewhat during the following five years, but picked up again in 1980-1985. The number of employed has grown slightly over 50 per cent during 1975-1985, although women's share has grown rather more slowly than men's (table 7.12.).

Even though the number of women who worked as employees in these industries had already grown strongly in the 1960s, *this growth has been rather slow and insignificant when compared with the growth in male self-employment.*

Of the industries mentioned, self-employment has been concentrated in the *real estate services* and *business related services.* These two industries represent the actual growth area of the whole sector: the number of self-employed persons in the real estate services and business related services grew by 113 per cent in 1960-1985. The nature of the derived demand for services became clear in the 1970s, when the number of self-employed had declined by 25 per cent in a ten year period. The decline continued up to 1975, after which a sharp upswing set in: the change percentage between 1975 and 1980 was 71 per cent.

Even though female self-employment activities in business related services are still rather minor, consisting of only one third of all entrepreneurs, the growth for women in 1985-1990 was positive, the number of self-employed women in business related services increasing by 33 per cent. For male self-employment, the growth in 1985-1990 stood at 40 per cent.

In 1980-1985 the number of self-employed women more than doubled and the growth in women's entrepreneurship exceeded the growth in women's employed labour.[28] The growth in the number of employed women in 1980-1985 was rather less, however, standing at only 24 per cent. In spite of the swift development in 1980-1985, the share of female self-employment of all self-employed is only 25 % (table 7.13.).

Table 7.12. Women's share of paid employment in financial, insurance and in real estate services, 1960-1990 (%)

							Change-%		
	1960	1970	1975	1980	1985	1990	60-75	75-85	85-90
Women's share of									
paid employment	57	62	62	60	59	58	211	54	23
in finance	73	77	80	80	80	78	173	27	10
in insurance	54	59	63	63	64	70	60	31	35
in real estate	36	50	48	46	45	48	487	73	29

Table 7.13. Women's share of self-employment in business related services and real estate services, 1980-1990 (%)

				Change-%	
	1980	1985	1990[a]	1980–85	1985–90
Women's share of total					
self-employment	23	27	25	134	34
in real estate service	*	16	15		49
in business related s.	*	28	27		33

a the share of assisting family members is estimated to be at the same level as 1985
* included in the figure above.

---

28. Unfortunately, 3-digit figures from 1990 census were not available.

Both female and male self-employment have been concentrated in business related services (especially e.g. accounting, consulting, educational services and the renting of machinery and equipment) to a somewhat larger extent than in real estate services. Many of the services arose for the first time in the 1970s, and some as recently as the 1980s. The number of self-employed in business related services has grown much faster than in real estate services. If this growth is compared to that in the number of waged workers in both industries, it can be seen that the number of waged workers has also grown much faster in business related services than in real estate services.

The growth of the real estate business and business related services has also been extensive in the Finnish economy when compared to other services: both output and employment have clearly grown faster than in other service industries, and manufacturing industries as well (Lastikka 1984). At the 3-digit level the most important areas in real estate and business related services are: home management business, real estate business, ADP and computer related activities, technical business services, marketing services and leasing.

Both the structural features and the importance of economic fluctuations in the development of self-employment are different in each of the three subindustries under observation. Financial intermediation, insurance services, real estate and business related services are clearly more labour dominated than estate ownership and renting activities, which is a very capital intensive activity. The capital intensity of the activity institutionalises the ownership structure and thus lessens the potential for smaller companies to stay in business (e.g. Rothwell 1989). Both capital intensity and the level of risk investment are noted to lessen women's willingness to enter a business activity (e.g. Carsrud et al. 1986a).

Whether it is merely a question of 'willingness', or more of the degree of difficulty in, for instance, arranging finance for the business has not to date been unambiguously settled. This difference, however, is essential in the sense that the former refers more to gendered socialisation, whereas the latter refers to institutionalised barriers. This also came up in the interviews discussed in earlier chapters. According to Sundin and Holmqvist, the barriers are more institutional by nature, and not related to the personality or the nature of self-employed women (Sundin – Holmqvist 1989, 137).

Above all, business related services have been considered to be 'the ones for women', i.e. with heightened education and potential to start one's own business that is centred on specific know-how (e.g. architectural and engineering planning and consulting, legal and accounting consulting, book-keeping and auditing activities, market research), or based on a network of business activities (business and management consultancy) (Goffee – Scase

1985; Rita Mae Kelly 1991). Professionalism, together with careerism, have become important factors in the debate about the 'new' entrepreneurship of women, since there is a body of evidence that some women have fared better by starting their own companies than by working their way up existing corporate ladders (Goffee – Scase 1985; Kelly 1991). There has been no research into this phenomenon in Finland or the other Nordic countries. A characteristic of these businesses is that they often develop from simple product lines by correctly timing their start-up.

As one of the women I interviewed, (F), mentioned, the start-up time for her business (1988) was the best possible, since the demand for business related services had risen notably at the time she established her company jointly with a colleague. After one year's business activity, the turnover of the firm had risen more quickly than expected. Typically for women who work in a specialised field of business and who base their business idea on the possibilities offered them by their high educational qualifications, she comments as follows:

> "I've had no inspirational models for my self-employment, nor have I had any contact with self-employment before starting on my own ... for me this is really the way to serve clients, to make my own living ... if there are things that are difficult for them, and that I can handle well." She continues: "I have not really faced any difficulties with my business plan or financial plans, since my bank has believed in my chances and my knowledge, and we have good contacts." (F. interview 1990).

This a very typical comment, the type of which is also to be found in other research reports. Typical, in this case, means a comment from women who establish their company in a business related service, and are interviewed concerning the difficulties they may have faced (Goffee – Scase 1985).

The figures for the rapid growth of women's businesses in these 'new' services, mostly in business related services, which are given in country reports from the US and UK, do not hold true in the case of Finland, and some doubts must be cast over other Nordic countries as well. Even though the glass ceilings in large corporations are still difficult to break, in Finland as well, the number of self-employed women has not – when the whole group of self-employed women in the Finnish economy is considered – risen to the same extent, or in the same way as in the US and UK. *This suggests that self-employment in Finland is not an option for women, not at least to the same extent as has been reported in other countries* (e.g., see DeCarlo – Lyons 1979; Sexton – Kent 1981; Watkins – Watkins 1984, 1986).

Why should this be so? First, self-employment is not treated in this study as if it were automatically a better option for women than wage employment; the interviews did not often reveal this to be the case. From the individual woman's viewpoint, self-employment may offer more possibilities than wage employment (Kovalainen 1990). However, when the rise of self-employment is viewed from a structural point of view, at least two factors can be sketched out. First, the effect of the welfare society and its growth, which in countries such as the UK and US has never reached the breadth of that found in Nordic countries. Secondly, related to the development of the welfare state, the position of women in Nordic countries has been different in the labour markets than in countries such as the UK and US, as noted in chapter 4.

All in all, self-employment within the new services seems to differ somewhat from within traditional manufacturing enterprise, or some other service sector branches, e.g. catering and hotel activities. The narrow line of business combined with the high level of skills (education), commitment to profit-making and relatively high independence from customers (in terms of e.g. subcontracting) are characteristic of business activities in the new services.

According to statistical information, *the new services have not opened up new possibilities for self-employed women to any great extent, even though female self-employment has grown in some industries.* The growth percentage in male self-employment in 1985-1990 exceeds that in female self-employment, as it does in areas such as business related services.

There is no unambiguous explanation for this phenomenon. The high educational level linked to the new services does not seem to 'help' women into self-employment. Is this because self-employment is no better option than waged work, or is it because of the difficulties faced in self-employment in these industries? Explaining women's absence from self-employment strictly in terms of individual factors or in terms of their early socialisation, provides a static view of people's lives and their interrelations within dynamic social processes. The explanation most probably lies in a more complex set of structural factors and e.g. in the everyday practices of women's personal lives and business life. In reality, as the interviews also revealed, many women's decisions about work and time consumed at work are not premised on a notion of individual choice, but rather they reflect their family responsibilities, the structure of the economy and the child care system. The everyday practices of business life include, according to some interview comments, practices which resemble the patriarchal structures discussed earlier in the work. All these factors together contribute to the lack of women in self-employment in the new services.

7.4.3. *The traditional women's sphere – social and personal services*

Traditionally, female self-employment has been associated either with the work of a small retailer or of a hairdresser, or perhaps that of a beautician, who works by herself and may have an apprentice or occasional helping hand with her. The cultural product of femininity does not arise from nowhere: the helping hands of hairdressers, beauticians and maybe even other professionals in the beauty parlour are needed. New service activities such as solarium clubs, massage treatments and slimming care facilities are attached to the older ones, traditional beauty salon's and hairdresser's services.

One of the main ideas that I took up earlier in this study is that *occupational segregation is reflected even more directly in the distribution of self-employed women than women's waged labour among different industries.* An inspection of the general division of female self-employment between different industries, measured either by absolute numbers or relative share, supports this notion. This was further reinforced by the occupational ranking given earlier in chapter 6.5. Outside the agricultural occupations, retailing and hairdressing are the two most usual occupations for self-employed women.

In the following, I shall briefly inspect the composition of waged labour in these more traditional services as against those discussed earlier, and then move on to inspect self-employment within social and personal services.

Various *domestic services*[29] is one of the most important employment areas in social and personal services, even though the number of employed has declined steadily. The years 1960-1970 saw a slight growth, but this turned in 1970-1980 into a decline of over 30 000 persons (42.5 per cent). The decline was particularly prevalent in the number of employed women who worked in the domestic services. At the 3-digit level in the domestic services, the reparation of various kinds of motor vehicles and household appliances grew most up to the 1980s, as measured by the number of employed. However, according to the statistics, domestic service activities such as the number of domestic helps have decreased steadily from the 1960s onwards. One of the reasons for this decline has been the implementation of the municipal day-care law passed in 1973. As the municipal day-care system expanded its span of operation, it began to include a wider range of families. This diminished the need for domestic help, and the number of women classified as self-employed within domestic services declined.

Male self-employment declined further in 1970-1975 than female self-employment. This was largely because men were in branches where the number of small businesses declined sharply in the 1970s (e.g. various repair

29. I have here used the 1979 ISIC classification division here as a basis for the inspection.

services), whereas women were in branches which are very traditional and able to stay in business on even a marginal income, such as hair-dressing salons or barbers' shops, the number of which grew, even in the 1980s.

The most important employer in the social and personal services is in various teaching and research services, as well as different kinds of medical services, private services in the social service sector, other services with educational aims etc. In addition, organisational, community, and cultural activities are to be found among the labour intensive industries.

Women make up the majority of the labour force in the personal and social services. Women's share has grown since the 1970s, and it stood at 69 per cent of all employed in social and personal services in 1985. The growth in the number of employed women was strongest in 1975-1980: as mentioned earlier, the growth of waged labour in services is based on the growth in women's employment. *The feminisation of waged labour between 1960 and 1985 had already started in the 1960s: the number of women already exceeded 60 per cent of all employed in the industry in 1970, to stand at over 70 per cent in 1990* (Table 7.14.).

Between the years 1980 and 1985 waged labour continued to grow; the number of women grew by 21 per cent, while the number of men rose by 12 per cent. But, there are also other reasons for the growth being timed at the turn of the decade in 1970: changes in the economic structure were also visible as changes in the occupational structure and, furthermore, the growth of the public sector was visible as the growth of employment possibilities created by the state and local authorities. The largest growth in the number of women in the cleaning services, refreshment and cultural services, and activities attached to international organisations took place in the 1980s. Of these, the largest growth percentage for women (47 per cent) was to be found in the cleaning services, whereas for men this was located in activities attached to international organisations (growth percentage 119 per cent), even though the growth in absolute numbers was not very great.

Table 7.14. Women's share of self-employment and employment in social and personal services, 1960-1990 (%)

	1960	1970	1975	1980	1985	1990[*]
Women's share of						
all self-employed	47	54	52	53	54	60
all employed	57	63	66	68	69	71

* the share of assisting family members is estimated to be at the same level as 1985.

Women's share of all self-employed in the whole category of social and personal services was already, in 1960, almost half of all self-employment in the industry, and it remained at more or less the same level during the 1980s (Table 7.14.). However, the *nature* of women's self-employment seems – according to the statistics – to have changed relatively little during the time period inspected.

The total development of female self-employment in various branches of social and personal services from 1960 to 1985 is shown in table 7.15. Female self-employment exceeded male self-employment in 1970; percentage changes for women were greater than for men in 1960-1985. In 1960-1970, the growth percentage of self-employed women was 57.4 per cent, whereas for men it stood at 32 per cent.

The largest growth of self-employed women took place in domestic services. The general decline in the economy in the 1970s also affected the number of self-employed in personal and social services. In 1970-1975 there was a 9.5 per cent decline in the number of self-employed women, whereas in the case of men the decline was less than 8 per cent. The largest decline in the number of women took place in'other social services', which means that the decline occurred mostly in private medical services and private child-care services. For men, the largest decline took place in services such as repairs, barbers shops etc.

Table 7.15. The relative distribution of self-employed women and men in health services, personal private services and other services, 1970-1990 (%)

| | 1970 | 1975 | 1980 | 1985 | 1990 | Change% | | |
						75-80	80-85	85-90
Health services								
women	59	57	67	68	62	52	60	5
men	41	43	33	32	38	-3	54	54
Total	100	100	100	100	100			
Personal private services								
women	59	61	58	58	66	5	32	45
men	41	39	42	42	34	17	34	2
Total	100	100	100	100	100			
Other services*								
women	28	24	27	38	45	..	..	..
men	72	76	74	62	55	..	..	..
Total	100	100	100	100	100			

* includes the category 'unknown services'. Since the category 'unknown' varies considerably depending on how well the data collection has succeeded, the comparisons between years were left out.

Most own-account working women – those who do not have employees – are active in services such as teaching, consulting, research activities, medical and dental services and veterinary activities. The greatest number of employers can be found in various domestic service activities, such as shoe repair, goldsmiths, laundry services, and personal services like barbers, hairdressers and photographers. In other words, employers can be found in those business activities where it is not possible to run a 'one woman business' as easily as in occupational groups such as lawyers, dentists, physicians, consulting professionals etc. However, the occupational division in self-employment is clear even though the development has been different for women and men.

When women's self-employment in social and personal services is inspected in more detail, it can be observed to be concentrated in a few specific branches that closely follow the gendered segregation of the labour force. In the following I shall inspect the development of these industries in more detail.

Personal services – all for women's beauty?

The total growth of self-employment in social and personal services is largely concentrated in personal services, where women's self-employment has traditionally been high. Growth took place in 1980-1985 and 1985-1990. Even though the activities of male entrepreneurs were concentrated in the declining parts of the industry, the growth of female entrepreneurs has not exceeded the growth in the number of male entrepreneurs: *the growth in women's entrepreneurship in 1980-1985 was 30 per cent, and men's 32 per cent.*

One typical form of self-employment is franchising, where the independence of the entrepreneur is rather limited, and does not fulfil the definition of the traditional entrepreneur in terms of independence, risk-taking and freedom. The internal growth in this area is concentrated on hair- dressing and barber service activities, and beauty salons – to which new services such as solarium, massage, gym and health club services are attached. The majority of both self-employed and employees are women (see table 7.14.).

J. represents a typical – if such a word may be used – entrepreneur in the personal services in the sense that her business has widened from the original business plan – a fitness club – to cover both fitness and health club services, solarium, massage and beauty salon services. The major reason for her start-up was her own hobbies: after being at home with four children for many years, she did not want to go back to work as an employee in a totally different area (she had previously worked in an electrical engineering office as a technical draughtswoman for 10 years). Instead, she decided to make her hobby into her business. At the time of the interview she was not receiving any support from her husband; in fact she was the only one of my interviewees whose husband openly opposed his wife's business. Finding a balance between home and business was the biggest problem for the interviewee (J., interview 1990).

What J. seems to be doing, in terms of her business and family, closely resembles the choices faced by 'conventional' female entrepreneurs in the typology suggested by Goffee and Scase (1985, 55). Confronting the conflicting pressures which emanate from business and marital conflict at home, she seems unable to find a solution to her situation. At the time of the interview, her business was doing very well but her husband was complaining of her being away from home: "the better the business goes, the worse my husband's behaviour gets" (J., interview 1990). Still, she does not seem to fit the typology mentioned, since her commitment to the business was very positive and based on a search for self-fulfilment, rather than on those motives which Goffee and Scase take up for 'conventional' businesswomen (Goffee – Scase 1985, 83). This example reveals, for its part, the difficulties with universal typologies, a point which was discussed in chapter 4.4.

Not all for beauty but some for health as well

The next largest area of women's self-employment, after personal service activities, are various health services and social work services such as private medical and dental activities, veterinary activities and nursing. These professions are usually seen as essentially open to both genders. However, Harriet Bradley divides, for example, the practice of medicine into two functions: 'curing' and 'caring' (Bradley 1989). She thus reveals the historically gendered structure of social service professions. In Finland, women are not so clearly excluded from the 'curing' tasks as in the modern British health service or in American health service systems, even though e.g. the medical professions are still marked by both horizontal and vertical segregation.

In addition to the growth which has taken place in self-employment, there has also been growth in the waged labour of women in these industries. The growth in women's wage work persisted throughout the total time period inspected. It was strongest in 1975-1980 (at 38 per cent). This is due to the growth in public sector employment. Privately produced social services account for only 8 percent of the total expenditure of social service volume (Simonen 1993). *Female self-employment has grown since 'the bottom of the wave' in 1975 to a larger extent than male self-employment,* and the change in the number of self-employed women during 1980-1985 was larger at 59 per cent than the change in the number of women in waged labour (22 per cent).

The sharp rise may in part be due to the fact that some of the women who run children's day-care activities in their private family homes are classified as own-account workers in the statistics. Naturally this does not explain all of the growth, which has been strong from 1975 onwards (change percentage 63 in 1975-1980). Changes in the structure of the economy may also be influential here. What are the various activities for self-employed women in this industry then? One of the activities, nursing, has already been mentioned. Other activities, such as private medical and dental services and veterinary services, grew considerably during the 1980s, but the business model also changed: from the own-account worker model to something more closely resembling the waged worker than self-employment. This was because the size of business units grew and were most often joint stock companies owned by other companies, rather than by workers.

Some for cleanliness as well

It is not possible to discover the entrepreneurial division of the subindustries[30] in cleaning, but based on occupational statistics the largest divisions are cleaning and other sanitation activities. Women's share of waged labour here grew in 1960-1970 and 1980-1985, quite sharply in the latter period, by 47 per cent. *However, women's self-employment is rather minor in absolute numbers, when compared to men's self-employment and the major development which has taken place among male self-employed.* Male self-employment grew fastest in 1970-1975, but also grew in 1975-1980. The growth of women's self-employment did not take off until 1980-1985: relatively, entrepreneurial growth was greater for women (167 per cent) than for men (17 per cent), but measured as an absolute change the figures for women and men are almost the same.

It is not easy to find reasons for the scarcity of women's businesses in e.g. the cleaning activities, when this scarcity is compared with the number of women in waged work. One possible cause is that those who start up the businesses have, in fact, never been cleaners themselves: the owners of the businesses are not the same people as those who do the actual work. *The sharp rise in the relative share of self-employed women in 1980-1985 is related, however, to the beginning of such growth during the 1980s.* Factors such as the growth in subcontracting undoubtedly contributed to the rise of the cleaning business in the 1980s. This rise continued up to 1990s, according to 1990 census data.

---

30. Including e.g. cleaning, waste management, chimney sweeping etc.

Employment in the various cultural service activities has risen as a whole, but the number of entrepreneurs in the area remains low. However, there was a slight rise in the number of women involved in 1980-1985, amongst artists who are classified as own-account workers. The change in 1980-1985 was 105 per cent for female entrepreneurs and 55 per cent for male entrepreneurs.

The variety of service industries is illustrated by one of my interviewee's, K.'s, business area. K. owns a puppet theatre which she runs alone, selling her puppet theatre performances to schools and various other institutions around her county, and occasionally in other parts of the country. She also manufactures puppets and sells them to other theatres, as well as acts as a trainer on puppet theatre courses. K. started her business in 1987, being bored with her work in a kindergarten, though she liked children very much. Her waged work gave her the inspiration, and while attending a theatre course she got an idea which within 4-5 years led to her business. The production of the plays and puppet manufacturing takes up most of K.'s time, and she sees it as her greatest problem:

> "The service business – being available and present in case somebody calls to ask for my services – takes my whole time ...so I haven't had enough time for planning the future. My business sort of lives from hand to mouth, I'm afraid, and that is not a very happy situation." (K., interview 1990).

All in all, the number of self-employed in social and personal services grew in 1960-1985 and up to 1990. The economic fluctuations of the 1970s were not particularly visible in a decline in the number of male entrepreneurs, but were so in the decline in the number of female entrepreneurs. Growth was visible in 1975-1980, at a time when women's share of waged labour was almost 70 per cent. It is somewhat surprising that the number of self-employed did not grow more during the last part of the 1980s.

State-governed care work is linked to the growth of the entire social service sector, especially in the 1970s' Finland. Many of the tasks previously taken care of by women at home have been shifted to waged labour employed either by the state or municipal sector – women have moved from the home to waged labour, and the waged labour model is now the 'normal' one for women today, as discussed in chapters 4 and 5. This is seen as one of the general diminishing factors in women's self-employment (especially in the social and personal services). This fact is also supported by many observations concerning the growth in women's self-employment, in those countries where the employing effects of the public sector are small and the public sector's share of care and nursing work is minor compared to the Scandinavian countries (e.g. Baker 1985). The change in the quality of work is also linked to the growth of the service sector: women's work in the service sector has mostly been the so-called 'pink-collar' work, not manual labour.

7.5. Invisible women entrepreneurs – assisting family members

So far, to some extent, I have deliberately avoided describing one group of women which could, at least according to some criteria, be included in the group of self-employed women. This group of women is not just one group, in the sense that the women work in the same branch and possibly have similar kinds of business problems, or would resemble each other in terms of other criteria. There are aspects which do combine these women, however, in spite of the variety of fields of activity and the fact that they could be drawn into the group of self-employed. However, this group of women rarely has the similar kind of autonomous position that other self-employed women (i.e. own-account workers or employers) usually have.

The group of women in question, who are classified as 'assisting family members' in statistics, consists of family members who work or help in a business run by some other member of the family. They assist the business without monetary payment or any other form of compensation, and usually own no legal share of the business or receive any kind of monetary reward. Statistical classifications hide the variety of the positions these women have variety in terms of economic dependence, workload, and social and familial situation (for Finnish research, see e.g. Salmi 1991). The question of classifications and their fairness from a gender perspective has not yet been addressed in this study. The social status and hierarchies which are implicitly written into the statistical classifications also include patriarchal relations (Kinnunen 1989), a fact which is particularly reflected in the category of assisting family members.

It is interesting to note that the concept of 'assisting family member' is constructed around the concept of 'housewife', and around a patriarchal view of women's role within a family. The assisting family member is in practice an extension of the role of housewife, imbued in addition with qualities that are sometimes assumed to be 'natural' for women, such as competence and skills in the 'care' work of the office, i.e. various clerical tasks. The basis of the work situation of the assisting family member lies in the marriage contract. This is, of course, the case for male assisting family members as well: the marital contract creates a basis for the work contract, "for better, for worse". But can the marriage contract be considered as an employment contract in which labour or services are contracted out for use by another?

Carole Pateman rejects the idea that the marriage contract should closely resemble the employment contract. The problem is – according to Pateman – that the sexual contract is forgotten: women cannot become 'workers' in the same sense as men[31], rather the employment contract *presupposes* a marriage contract (Pateman 1988, 131). While the public and private spheres of civil society are both separate and yet inseparable, they are also incapable of being understood in isolation from each other. Pateman's critique focuses on the idea of the equivalence between wives and workers, the classical idea based on Engels' work.[32]

While there is a difference between the marriage contract and other social contracts, the practice of assisting family members in entrepreneurial families is built on the 'use' of the other person's labour in the conjugal relationship. In general, however, any contract that is conventionally believed to defeat the patriarchal order, may in fact "usher in a new form of paternal right" (Pateman 1988, 218), which means that the basis of modern patriarchy is unchanged. This seems to be the case for family businesses.

The work of women and children within the family 'business' is not by any means a new phenomenon, but is based on work tradition in the pre-industrial societies. In pre-industrial society men and women were, in the main, working side by side within the family or household enterprise, usually a farm. The growth of waged work and capitalism changed the family-based production system into one of market-based production, and thus it also changed the role of women and the family in production. It has been severely questioned, however, whether the growth of capitalism and industrialisation did in reality lead to a sharp split between the private sphere of the home and the public sphere of work and politics (see. e.g. Allen and Wolkowitz 1987; Bradley 1989). A large number of women has always been employed as outworkers or homeworkers, and this poses a challenge to the thesis presented as does the persistent category of 'assisting family members'. It also raises the question of the definition of work. All in all, a large number of people has continued to work from home: farmers, small retailers and self-employed people. The reality of women who work at home as assisting family members seems to be,

---

31. The original construction of a 'worker' presupposes that he is a man who has a woman - a wife - to take care of his daily needs (Pateman 1988, 131).

32. 'The Origin of the Family, Private Property and the State' in which the higher servant, the slave and the worker (all men in the contract theory) are compared to women (Pateman 1988).

according to Salmi's study (1991), different to those who are homeworkers in their own right.

In industrial societies where farming has become more mechanised the role of women has usually changed. However, where small-scale peasant-style farming is still the practice, women are likely to be more involved in working in the fields, though in a subsidiary role to men, and often on a seasonal basis.[33] Family members have an important role in production: not only in agriculture but also in services such as the retail trade and artisan bakeries, where the family-based work system has persisted.

The vital role of wives in the family business is clearly shown in Daniel Bertaux's and Isabelle Bertaux-Wiame's (1981) study of artisan bakeries in France. The wives of the small artisan bakeries keep the shop open 10 to 12 hours per day, six days a week. In addition to that, they usually have the work of any housewife and mother. What is very interesting in Bertaux and Bertaux-Wiame's study, is that it reveals the key role of the wife for the success of the business: to become self-employed, the bakery worker needs two things: money and wife. "In the competition between small bakeries, the appeal of the baker's wife plays a greater role than the quality of the bread, which does not vary very much from one shop to the other." (Bertaux – Bertaux-Wiame 1981, 163).

The hidden social mechanism of the successful business lies in the hands – or actually in the *social capacity* – of the wife: how can she keep customers, and keep them satisfied with the service, since the bread is alike everywhere. As Bertaux and Bertaux-Wiame conclude: "the sociological truth about bakers' marriages seems to be that the relationship between husband and wife becomes at once a relation between an artisan and a shopkeeper who got together as business partners." (1981, 169). If the wife refuses to take the shop, it usually means that her husband is never able to set up his own business.

Bertaux and Bertaux-Wiame do not discuss the contractual nature of the bakery business and marriage any further, but refer to the work of the husband and wife as the 'collaboration of two business partners', as shown above. While using Pateman's frame of reference as an interpretation model, Bertaux and Bertaux-Wiame seem to fail in bringing out the real nature of the business relationship, that is, *the unequal relationship between spouses in the bakery business*. According to Pateman's theory, the relationship between husband and wife does not become that of business partners, but something else. This could be named as a *'patriarchal domestic production mode'* that has its roots not in the resemblance between wife and worker, or wife and business partner

---

33. For example, in France and Italy, see Bradley 1989; in Finnish agriculture, for more, see Pirjo Markkola 1989.

as Bertaux and Bertaux-Wiame suggest, but more in the conjugal relation between spouses, which creates the basis for the patriarchal relationship.

Family work has historically had an important role within farming, artisan production and in service industries (restaurants, hotels, small retail outlets). To some extent this is still the case, even though family labour has been the 'hidden' element in the labour market: women, the overwhelming majority of assisting family members, are neither waged workers nor self-employed. The work and the situation of the assisting women in the family business varies from full-time work (retail trading businesses, hotels) to part-time office duties which can be taken care of when time is available (e.g. small construction businesses, where the wife takes care of office and administrative work at home).

Industrial classification first defined assisting wives as married women who help their husbands in the business, which is considered to be equivalent to marriage, a family business. However, not necessarily all assisting family members are women (although most), and we have to remember that not necessarily all women helping in the family business are classified into this group (Mønsted 1982, 45). It is rather difficult, if not impossible, to assess how exact the figures for the assisting family members are in Finland. It should be remembered that the variations in the statistical category 'unknown' have tended to be considerable[34], and it can be assumed that the 'unknown' category also includes, to some extent, assisting family members. Historically, the largest group of assisting family members has consisted of wives in farming: in the statistics the wives of farmers are classified as assisting family members, and the husbands (male farmers) as own-account workers, or employers if they have paid employees such as temporarily hired (male) farm-hands.

However, the majority of women as assisting family members in farming is not only historical fact. Even in 1985 in Finland, 81 per cent of all assisting family members in agriculture were women, and this seems to be changing very slowly. Also, the majority of the assisting family members outside agriculture are women, and *women's share of assisting family members has grown more than men's share in 1975-1985*. In table 7.16., the development of the number of assisting family members is shown for 1960-1985, both the absolute number of all assisting family members and women's share of them.

---

34. In the 1990 census data available four times more persons were included in the category 'unknown' than in the 1985 census data. This means that there were almost 10 000 persons in the category 'unknown self-employed and assisting family members', as opposed to respective figures from 1985 which were 1 000 'unknown assisting family members' and 2 300 'unknown self-employed'.

Table 7.16. Assisting family members outside agriculture, women's share in percentages, 1960-1985

	1960	1970	1975	1980	1985	Change% 1960	1975
All assisting						–75	–85
family members	14 950	16 730	14 810	11 730	17 070	-1	15
Women´s share, %	69	71	71	82	76	2	23

Quantitatively measured, the majority, (46 per cent), of all assisting family members who are women and working outside agriculture are active in the wholesale and retail trade and restaurant and hotel businesses, while 15 per cent of them are active in various manufacturing industries, and 13 per cent in financing, insurance, real estate and business related services. The rest of the assisting family members are evenly divided between other industries. There have been some changes during the inspected time period, especially in the retail trade, which has lost assisting women both in absolute and relative terms.

A more detailed inspection of the different industries reveals the large share of various retail trade businesses in wholesale and retail trade and restaurants and hotels. The number of women who are assisting family members in the retail trade fell by 31 per cent in 1960-1985. This reflects the changes that have taken place in the organisation of retail trade, especially the sharp decline of small businesses in rural areas in the 1970s, which was discussed earlier. In 1960, 69 per cent of all women classified as assisting family members were active in the wholesale and retail trade, and restaurants and hotel businesses, whereas the corresponding figure for 1975 was only 56 per cent.

However, the absolute number of women active as assisting family members in manufacturing has risen even more than the number of men. *In addition to manufacturing industry, the feminisation of the assisting family members category is also visible in other industries in 1960-1985* (table 7.17). Financing, insurance, real estate and business services are exceptions to this pattern. Taking into account both the number of male and female entrepreneurs and their development, and the nature of the businesses in these categories, it is, however, natural that the number and share of assisting family members should be rather low here.

The absolute number of women assisting in manufacturing rose slightly in 1960-1985, by 19.2 per cent. The change that has taken place in manufacturing is also reflected in the division of assisting family members: in the food manufacturing industry the relationship between the shares of men and women as assisting family members has changed. The number of assisting women in the food manufacturing industries grew by 183 per cent in 1975-1985, whereas the number of assisting men declined by 84 per cent.

Table 7.17. Women's share of assisting family members, by industry, 1960-1985 (%)

	1960	1970	1975	1980	1985
All industries	54	63	70	83	75
Manufacturing	30	42	52	77	54
Construction	82	83	83	84	83
Wholesale, retail	12	29	36	69	67
Transport	12	29	36	69	67
Finance	..	89	89	94	80
Services	88	72	75	86	80

Growth in the number of women as assisting family members in textile and clothing manufacturing was even sharper. The growth percentage for assisting women was 533 per cent, whereas the number of assisting men declined by 70 per cent.[35] The change figures refer to the previously mentioned growth trend in textile and clothing industries, which can only be seen in the industrial statistics of the last few years.

Two of the women I interviewed were assisting family members, in the sense that they did not legally own any part of the family company and one of them was occasionally occupied in waged work outside the family business. It became quite clear that they were both thoroughly involved in the work of the family business, and self-employment held a very strong appeal for them. Family and business were the two enterprises of the family, as they saw it. They had not faced any particular problems within entrepreneurial activities, which they both thought to be due to the active role of their husbands in negotiations with the bank and customers.

The position of an assisting family member in the business most often comes without any legal form or strict definition of legal position. Where wives are concerned, they usually work with clerical matters and the various tasks necessary to keep the business running; these tasks could be termed "reproduction within the business", which is an essential area of small business operation. *In family businesses this means that work and family activities are combined into partly "invisible" work, which becomes an internal rather than external obligation: "for better, for worse".* For women who work as assisting family members in the family business it is not so much a question of waged

---

35. Here I would like to comment on the large group 'unknown' in the 1975 statistics. It can be assumed, and it also seems very probable, that this class includes a large number of assisting family members. It thus biases the statistical categories of 'assisting family members' and 'unknown'. However, it was not possible to trace down the real statistical status for these groups. The absolute changes in the textile industry for women are 70 (1975) -> 443 (1985) and men 351 (1975) -> 103 (1985).

work, or even of being an independent entrepreneur, but more a *question of widening the household responsibility rationality into business activities.* Business is seen as one of the joint projects, like family and the children's upbringing (see e.g. Mønsted 1982).

The widening of responsibility from household to business activity also takes place – in addition to women who work as assisting family members – in the case of self-employed women who have a family. It seems, however, that women who work as assisting family members differ from self-employed women in at least one crucial respect. Self-employed women seem to lend their business activities extra meaning, which is independent and self-sufficient from their family context and home lives (see e.g. Sundin – Holmqvist 1989; Kovalainen 1992). This was also the case for one of the women I interviewed: she saw her business as being the good thing in her life, while her marriage was deteriorating (J., interview 1990). It seems that independence and self-sufficiency in a marital relationship do not necessarily follow for women who assist in the family business and are not economically independent of their husbands.

7.6. Concluding remarks: a more complete picture

The image of the small shopkeeper or hairdresser has been the persistent one for self-employed woman, while I would argue that the image of self-employed man is more multifaceted. The focus of inspection in this chapter has been the development of women's self-employment. This part of the study has addressed, more specifically, the development of Finnish women's self-employment within various industries, and the changes within those industries. In addition, I have raised some issues which came up in the interview material gathered for this study. For women, the most usual entrepreneurial model is small-scale activity and own-account working, rather than employing others.

Women's self-employment in manufacturing grew positively during the 1980s, mainly concentrated in the manufacture of textiles and clothing, as has been the case for the last 30 years. Most of the own-account workers in textile and clothing manufacture are women, and women's share of all employers has risen, being now close to 50 per cent. *The food product industry is another 'feminine' area, meaning in this case mostly small bakeries run by women.* Less than 10 per cent of all self-employed women in manufacturing are active in other manufacturing industries such as publishing, and the manufacture of pottery, china and earthenware. There are practically no self-employed women in industries such as metal or fabricated metal products i.e. the manufacture of

212

machines, etc. *The general historical trend has been that women's self-employment has shifted away from manufacturing industries into service industries, and the importance of manufacturing as the main sector for self-employed women has declined.*

From an historical perspective, an additional research task would be to relate the information regarding women's self-employment to the logic of development the different industries have followed. According to Harriet Bradley, the gendered division of labour in industries such as the manufacture of textiles and clothing, and food products and beverages has been highly dependent upon relationships and work practices in the preindustrial age. In the so-called new industries – e.g. in the production of new types of products, or producing them in a form only made possible by recent technological advance – no such traditional practices have yet been established.

It would thus seem easy to come to the conclusion that relationships of a more equal nature would be possible between male and female workers, and also that the structure of self-employment would be different – more equal – in these new industries. However, this is not the case. With a remarkable rapidity, these industries seem to have produced a structure of gender-typed jobs, and, according to Bradley's study, they have shown "a more rigid sexual segregation than the old industries"(Bradley 1989, 159)[36]. As I see it, this means that these rapidly developing, exclusive mechanisms can hinder women from becoming self-employed in sectors such as the new business related services, or in branches where the overwhelming majority of employed consists of women and where self-employment has risen quite recently, as in the cleaning industry.

What are these exclusive mechanisms? Although I am not referring to openly and actively exclusive mechanisms, such as laws, statutes, etc., I assume them to be a part of those patriarchal structures discussed in chapter 3.2.2., which are not necessarily visible, but which are the emergent properties of patriarchal practices occurring at a more concrete level of analysis. Patriarchal structures such as patriarchal relations at work have changed over time, both in form and degree. If we examine at the number of men and women doing cleaning work and the structure of self-employment in the newly risen cleaning businesses[37], there are differences in the development of self-employment in this industry and older industries, even though the composition

---

36. Bradley has studied the development in three industries: tobacco, confectionery and electrical goods, which I discussed in the section 'light consumer goods industry' in chapter 7.1.

37. The cleaning business in the form of small, private cleaning companies did not really arise before the economic boom of the 1980s.

of the labour force is female dominated. How is this to be explained?

In many service subindustries the aforementioned picture does, to a large extent, hold true. Traditional and 'old' service activities such as retailing and restaurant businesses are 'the one's for women', even if there have been great changes in the number of women working e.g. in the retail trade.[38]

The so-called new services, such as communication services, financial and various business related services, have been seen as the main growth service industries in society, partly because of the growth in the number of self-employed persons. *However, according to statistics, these new services have not opened up new possibilities for self-employed women to any great extent,* even though a higher educational background is often required. Thus, they differ from the older, more established industries such as retailing or restaurant businesses. It seems that the association of self-employed women either with the retail grocer or hairdresser holds true: *various personal service and health service activities are important branches for women's self-employment in Finland.* It remains to be seen what the future of privatised social services are, as offered by women who perhaps become unemployed as a result of the declining welfare state.

Most of the changes in the number of self-employed women have taken place within a variety of industries, even though the changes have not been very great. However, there is a group of women who are classified in the statistics as assisting family members, which has maintained its position when measured in numbers. As such, the group of assisting family members reflects the contractual nature of the family business, be it in agriculture or other industries. According to Carole Pateman, the nature of the contract is sexual, even though the models for arranging work activities may vary greatly depending on the line of business and the intertwining of family and business activities.

One of the questions posed earlier, in the theoretical analysis in chapters 3. and 4., was how to 'measure' the gendering processes and patriarchal structures? My discussion has focused on a number of historical and sociological factors; the dynamics of industrial development and various forms of power within the household. In addition I have taken up socialisation processes as well as the role of the state in fostering certain social definitions of

---

38. Boserup (1970) pointed out that, especially in Europe, retailing did become something of a woman's preserve; and with the advent of capitalist systems in industry, retailing remained an area of business from which women were excluded, and this was visible even in statistics. Bradley mentions that according to the 1851 Census there were more female than male shopkeepers in England and Wales (Bradley 1989, 176).

male and female.[39] The aforementioned discussions raise many questions. Can the gendered division of labour be satisfactorily explained in terms of the capitalist economy, or can patriarchy, gendering and socialisation processes be said to be at the core of the explanations concerning the rigidity of economic structures.

My argument has been that self-employment does not offer liberation from patriarchal relations in paid work, or from gendered labour structures. This notion is also strengthened by data for the primary development in Finnish women's self-employment over the last 30 years. The development of women's self-employment in general seems rigid: the old structures of the 'industrial branches for women' seem to remain the same, although there are some slight changes within them.

---

39. Although important, the role of institutions like the educational system and media in fostering certain social definitions of male and female, were not discussed here.

Part IV

Part IV

8 Discussion

The analysis of self-employment and entrepreneurship as concepts, as well as the analysis of women's self-employment and its development in Finland during the last 30 years, have both revealed that self-employment is gendered, much as is waged work. Thus self-employment – as a conceptual category as well as an empirical reality – is not an isolated phenomenon, in spite of the fact that it has usually been inspected as 'untouched by the gendered nature of society'. Both the interviews with self-employed women and the study of the industrial division and development of female self-employment presented here have lent support to the idea that *self-employment is in some respects even more gendered than waged work*. Self-employment is regulated by different kinds of gendered conditions than waged work. The diversity of various forms of self-employment and, above all, the invisibility of female self-employment, make the gendering and patriarchal processes less noticeable than is the case for waged work.

The idea of overcoming gender-based forms of subordination within the labour market through self-employment received much attention in the research literature in the 1980s. This notion of self-employment as a route for women to escape the subordination of paid work rests upon the assumption that self-employment provides better opportunities than waged work, be they in terms of independence, perhaps of working hours, autonomy or economic rewards. However, little has been done to investigate how women's self-employment has changed in various countries and whether gendered patterns are visible; or whether it is really so that self-employment in practice is an escape route for women from a subordinate position in the labour market, or in the economy and society as a whole.

* * *

The main criteria for the definition of self-employment in research literature have mostly been attached to the ownership of means, and to a relatively large degree of autonomy. I have argued in my work that the historical notion of an entrepreneur as a shapeless, faceless and mythical heroic figure, has in reality garbed the entrepreneur in a masculine cape which, in turn excludes any feminine manifestations from the concept of entrepreneurship. More detailed discussion indicates that the traditional concept of the entrepreneur is not sufficient when dealing with women's entrepreneurship, for two principal reasons. The majority of the research concerning women's entrepreneurship discusses it from classical premises which date all the way back to the conceptual ideas of Weber and Schumpeter. Hence, first and foremost, the classical image of the heroic, masculine entrepreneur has remained more or less unaltered, and this masculinity has implicitly been rewritten into texts and studies that deal with entrepreneurship. Secondly, discussion in the bulk of research that I have discussed in my work is not in any way related to the concept of gender as a social structure.

How, then, have self-employed women previously been studied? Before discussing the studies dealing with women's self-employment, I found it necessary to present an analysis of the concept of entrepreneurship. Why should this be? Would it not have been sufficient to present an analysis of the existing studies of self-employed women? An additional aspect attached to the studies of women in self-employment, is that in much of the research literature women are compared with men in self-employment either within various socio-economic sets of variables, or within various sets of psychological traits and characteristics. Usually this type of research has taken a consideration of socio-demographic variables and personality traits as its starting point. This has most often meant that men constitute the standard and women are deviations, fitting the mould of 'standard self-employment' neither in rhetoric nor in real life. Also, results from these studies have often been quite contradictory, as I have discussed here.

While it has been noted that it is precisely waged work experiences that are the essential factors for many women in the business start-up process, less attention is given to the possibility that overall gender divisions within waged work are connected with the segregated divisions of female self-employment. As I see it, this merely reflects the restricted scope of the existing studies in women's self-employment. In chapter 4, I have provided a general picture of those theories which seek to explain women's labour force participation, as well as a picture of the growth in occupational segregation. I explored the issue of economic and sociological theories used in explaining entrepreneurship, and their relevance in explanations of women's self-employment, and labour market theories and their implication for nascent women's self-employment.

In my study I have understood gender to be structured within social, cultural, and ideological systems; it is defined as an asymmetrical relationship and a social category which is recreated continuously in the aforementioned structures. The social construction of gender, and its usage as an analytical category, means that the concept of gender is different here from its 'everyday' meaning. Gender relations enter into and are present as constituent elements of every aspect of human experience, also in the structuring and development of self-employment.

* * *

The traditional image of a self-employed woman – running a small grocer's shop, being a hairdresser or beautician – remains close to the real picture, since the retail trade and hair/beauty salons have been for 30 years and still are the most common industries for self-employed women. However, traditionalism does not necessarily mean traditionalism in any other sense than the field of business. The number of self-employed women seems to be growing steadily, but relatively slowly, compared to the growth in men's self-employment in business related services, for example.

As the statistical material and interviews show, women's self-employment is restricted in only in a few specific areas of the economy. Where women's entrepreneurial activities are located in male dominated industries, women quickly seem to encounter credibility problems. The idea that the relative stability of the structure of women's self-employment is due to patriarchal processes and practices affecting everyday business activities, gained some support from the interview material. While subordinate positions in the labour market and in the economy, as well as positions of self-employment in the economy, are created and reproduced in everyday practices, it means that they are best analysed as a set of institutionally rooted discourses. A detailed analysis of women's self-employment in one or two industries, in terms of patriarchal structures and practices, would constitute one of my future research tasks. An analysis of various patriarchal structures, processes and practices would entail the narrowing of the perspective of development into a more detailed analysis of one or two of the industries under examination, to illustrate in detail those structures and practices that mould women's possibilities in self-employment and waged work.

Another piece of evidence to support the idea presented above is offered in my study by the invisible group of self-employed women, namely the assisting family members. The existence of such a group, of which over 75 per cent are women, speaks volumes of a patriarchal structure based on sexual contract, since the assisting family member is in reality an extension of the role of

221

housewife, imbued with those qualities which are sometimes assumed to be 'natural' for women, such as competence in the various clerical tasks to be found in the office. The basis of this labour lies in the marriage contract; the practice of assisting family members in entrepreneurial families is built on the 'use' of the spouse in the conjugal relationship, and in this sense one patriarchal structure remains unchanged.

* * *

Even though the patterns of gender relations have to some extent changed in Finland during the inspected time-period, this has not necessarily meant that women's position has become 'better', even by many objective criteria. According to several researchers the Finnish welfare state is built on a gender contract, which expresses the subordinate position of women in the labour market (Acker 1989; Silius 1992; Julkunen 1992; Rantalaiho 1993). The concept of a gender contract "implies an invisible, unconscious and tacit contract between women as a group and patriarchal structures such as state and the labour market" (Silius 1992, 312). Grasping the contract and its different forms in the structures of the economy and women's self-employment over time, and analysing their impact on the potential for women's self-employment is, however, another research task, and is thus left for a future instance.

According to the statistics, the new services have not yet opened fresh potential for self-employed women, and on inspection of personal and social services it seems that one of the main ideas taken up earlier in the study holds true: occupational segregation is reflected even more directly in the distribution of self-employed women, in their division between different industries, than it is in the waged work. The shift-share analysis of the changes within women's self-employment in Finland during 1980-1990 supports the idea of rigid structures within self-employment: women do stay within a few industrial classes, rather than of being able to widen their area.

In addition to revealing the gendered structures in self-employment in the Finnish economy, this study discusses how these gendered structures arise. Patriarchy and gender contract as conceptual tools proved useful here, since the rigid segregation of self-employment into female and male spheres is not to be explained with the help of economic concepts alone.

* * *

In conclusion, the majority of self-employed women are active in industries where the tradition of women's entrepreneurship is long. This means that most women in manufacturing industries are based in textiles and clothing, and food products (small bakeries). Less than 10 per cent of all self-employed women in manufacturing are active in other manufacturing industries. While the general historical trend has been that female self-employment has shifted from manufacturing industries into service industries, it would seem simple to suppose that relationships of a more equal nature would be possible between male and female workers in the new areas. Thus, the structure of self-employment should be more equal in the new industries such as business related services.

However, this is not the case. The rise in the demand for the new services is not visible within the structure of women's self-employment; it seems that this sector has not opened up possibilities for women in self-employment to any larger extent. 'Traditional' activities such as retailing and restaurant businesses are dominant in the structure of female business activities in the services. As an example of the new businesses and how the gendering process seems to work in this sector, let us take an activity where the business idea is based on women's 'traditional' work, and where almost all the work is done by women. This subindustry, namely the cleaning business, is a fine example of how quickly a new area of business becomes occupied by men. Male self-employment in cleaning activities has risen considerably, starting out in practice from zero, even though it could be assumed that women know the field and the work activities much better than men, occupying the majority of waged positions.

I posed myself a question at the end of chapter 7, page 213, regarding the explanation of gendered patterns such as the one described above. Can the gendered division of labour and gendered patterns be satisfactorily explained in terms of the capitalist economy, or might some other processes (e.g. socialisation processes) be at the core of explanations concerning the rigidity of such economic structures? As I see it, the potential to find one all-encompassing explanation for the processes taking place in new business activities, such as the one described above, is not to be found in the focus of conceptual categories such as gender system theories, patriarchy or gender contract theories. Instead, each of these conceptual approaches illuminate and explain different aspects in the processes previously described. However, seeing the gendered patterns in the processes is crucial.

I have discussed a number of historical and sociological factors, in order to illustrate at least some of those factors that represent the gendered processes in the economy. I do not wish, however, to promote the idea that the economy is the one and only determinant of women's position, since no single factor can explain e.g. various policies towards women. To be able to describe the 'big picture' of Finnish society and its development, I should also have to include a study of the impact of the women's movement in Finland, and perhaps of other political and societal actors and the impact of the state, in addition to the discussion of structural factors presented here. That is, however, beyond the scope of my present work.

Because I have emphasised the way in which gendered structures in self-employment have pushed women into a few certain places in the industrial division of self-employment, that does not mean that men, too, do not suffer from the pressures of having to live up to "ideas of masculine behaviour, which may be alien to them as individuals" (Bradley 1989, 239).

The question of the shifts between publicly produced social services and the growth of self-employment, though an important one, remains open for my future studies. What will happen to women who are now employed in the public services, providing health care, child care, and care for the elderly funded by public finance? The decline in the number of publicly produced services means a decline in women's paid employment, but not necessarily, it is claimed here, a rise in women's self-employment. Self-employment as an employment option is not a vacuum phenomenon situated outside the waged labour market and gendered economic structures. Before self-employment in the social services – that is privately produced social services – were to rise considerably, we would have to totally rethink the role of the welfare state. This means, also, changes in the present gender contract. Another question then is whether the aforementioned development will increase the inequality in society, and to what extent such inequality might be allowed to grow.

* * *

Contrary to many studies concerned with women's self-employment, my argument here has been that, at least for women as a group, self-employment does not equal liberation from patriarchal relations in paid work, or from gendered labour structures. Instead, I have argued that society's patriarchal and gendered relations remain powerful, no matter what form of economic activity we examine. However, in their own personal lives women seem to be able to fulfil some part of the concept of independence that is so often attached to self-employment, by taking that route even though individual solutions do not seem to be able to change any of the persistent patterns of gendered and rigid structures in self-employment. It has become clear from the theoretical discussion – backed by empirical evidence of the relatively rigid structures within self-employment – that the patriarchal or gendered relations of society remain powerful, no matter what form of economic activity is in question.

Appendices

Computing formulas for the shift-share analysis

$$(1) \qquad \frac{\sum e_i^0}{\sum t_i^0} * \sum t_i^1 = \text{hypothetical number of self-employed (H)}$$

$$(2) \qquad \sum e_i^1 - H = \text{net change (N)}$$

$$(3) \qquad \sum \frac{e_i^0}{t_i^0} * t_i^1 - H = \text{structural shift (S)}$$

$$(4) \qquad \sum \frac{e_i^t}{t_i^t} * t_i^0 * \frac{\sum e_i^1}{\sum t_i^0} - H = \text{internal shift (I)}$$

$$(5) \qquad N - S - I = \text{interaction shift (Ia) (residual term)}$$

where e_i = self-employed women in industry i

t_i = employed women in industry i

$0, 1$ = the years under consideration

The calculated formulas between 1980-1985 were as follows in the number of self-employed women: structural shift 570,52 internal shift 12344,04, interactive shift -5647,4, net change 7 267.

The calculated formulas between 1985-1990 were as follows in the number of self-employed women: structural shift 4785,61, internal shift 13715,22, interactive shift -2266,88, net change 16 233.

The interview material and the questionnaire

The information gathered from the women interviewed:

Personal information
Turnover of the company, when the company or business form is established, how many paid employees (family members not included), area or line of business. Some additional information: difficulties in various areas of business (finance, marketing, balancing between home and work, etc.).

The interviewed women, short presentation:

A., aged 35 years. Married, two children, born 1978 and 1979.
Works as own-account worker, no paid employees, husband helps occasionally (helps with fixing places, small repair jobs etc. but does not participate in production or retailing processes). The turnover of the business stood at c. 500.000 FIM in 1990.
Line of business: manufacture of clothes, and the dressing and dyeing of fur. In addition to production, A. also sells the final products herself in her shop. Both businesses under the same business name.

B., aged 46 years. Married, two children, born 1966 and 1969.
Co-owner of a bakery, jointly with her husband; both work actively in the business, though not directly in the production process, participating in e.g. retailing and delivery activities. The turnover of the business stood at c. 9 million FIM in 1990.
Line of business: bakery, and selling the bakery's products in a small café attached to the bakery. Owns the café.

C., aged 42 years. Married, two children, born 1972 and 1975.
Sharp decline due to the fact that the family had moved when her husband changed workplace. She was compelled to change the location of the business. Own-account worker, no paid employees. The turnover of the business stood at c. 100.000 FIM in 1992.
Line of business: designing, manufacturing and retailing own models, mainly women's clothes.

D., aged 24 years. Single, no children.
Car retailing business established in 1990 jointly with two male colleagues. All three work actively in the business. Turnover not yet available.

E., aged 38. Married, one child, born in 1976.
Established the business herself in 1981, husband joined in later and now works full-time as co-owner with E. In addition, the firm employs 2 people. The turnover of the business stood at c. 1 million FIM in 1990.
Line of business: retailing and rental of various kinds of machinery.

F., aged 26 years. Single, no children.
Established her business in 1988 jointly with a female colleague. No other workers. The turnover of the business stood at c. 350.000 FIM in 1990.
Line of business: accounting firm and real estate activities on a contract basis, subcontracting of office services to other businesses.

G., aged 28 years. Co-habiting, no children.
Bought the company jointly with her partner in 1989. Occasional help, one to two people, no permanent workers. The turnover of the business stood at c. 1.2 million FIM in 1990.
Line of business: market gardening, horticulture, selling of flowers and gardening products.

H. aged 42 years. Married, two children, born 1978 and 1981.
Established construction business jointly with her husband in 1976, employs 3 people in addition to herself and her husband. The turnover of the business stood at over 3.7 million FIM in 1990.
Line of business: all kinds of construction work, subcontracting in the construction industry.

I., aged 42 years, Married, two children, born 1968 and 1977.
Joined the business her husband had established in 1983. Company employs 2 people in addition to herself and her husband.
Line of business: retail sale of hardware, construction goods, paint etc.

J., aged 40 years. Married, four children, born 1970, 1978, 1980 and 1984.
Established her business in 1987. Employs one person. The turnover of the business stood at c. 350 000 FIM in 1990.
Line of business: fitness club, solarium services and beauty salon included.

K., aged 48 years. Married, two children, born 1967 and 1971.

Established her business in 1987. Own-account worker. The turnover of the business stood at c. 90 000 FIM in 1990.

Line of business: puppet theatre, various other cultural activities, manufacture of puppets, consulting in puppet theatre training.

L., aged 42 years. Married, one child, born 1967.

Works in her husband's business, established by husband in 1972. In addition, two paid employees. Turnover 2 million FIM in 1990.

Line of business: interior decoration, retail trade.

M., aged 40 years. Married, two children, born 1981 and 1982.

Jointly established company in 1981 with husband. Employs 2 people. Turnover 3 million FIM in 1990.

Line of business: importing, marketing, selling and installation of window shades and Venetian blinds.

N., aged 41 years. Married, three children, born 1976, 1978 and 1980.

Bought company jointly in 1982 with husband. Employs 8 people.

Line of business: renovation of buildings, apartments, etc.

O., aged 49 years. Married, three children, born 1965, 1970 and 1976.

Bought her first company in 1970. Presently owns a company with her husband. Employs 3 people. The turnover of the business stood at c. 1.4 million FIM in 1990.

Line of business: hamburger restaurant.

P., aged 21 years. Married, one child born in 1991 (carrying child at the time of interview).

Works in her parents' company, expects to take over within a few years. The company was established in 1980 by both parents. Employs 1 person (in addition to her and her parents).

R., aged 36 years. Married, one child, born 1974.

Established her company in 1990. Own account worker, turnover varies considerably.

Line of business: various business related services.

<u>S</u>., aged 41 years. Married, no children.

Established her business in 1990. Own account worker, turnover varies considerably.

Line of business: production of radio programmes, freelance based activity.

The questionnaire included the following questions:

Personal information:

Age, marital status, occupational status of husband/co-habitee, employment status of husband/co-habitee, number of children, their years of birth, interviewee's basic education, occupational training, continuing education.

Family background:

Parent's socioeconomic position, number of siblings, entrepreneurial background, own estimate of the importance of home/family/ siblings/family wealth to self-employment.

Life situation at the time of company or business formation/decision to start up on one's own. Support of husband/co-habitee/family/relatives. Importance of education.

Work experience:

Work history, importance of various work-related factors to the decision to become self-employed.

Time when business started, where located, which line of business/sector of industry.

Number of people employed, turnover, future prospects, changes which have taken place in business activities, time for the incubation of the business idea, time budget for various activities in business.

Difficulties faced in business activities at the beginning of entrepreneurial career, present difficulties, any changes in the nature of difficulties.

Situation of women as entrepreneurs, combining family and business, difficulties attached to that, own experiences of the difficulties related to gender.

Table 1.1.A   The share of non-farm self-employment of the total labour force in selected OECD countries, 1970-1990

Country	Year							
	1970	1973	1976	1979	1982	1985	1988	1990
Belgium	12.6	11.8	11.2	11.1	11.2	11.8	12.5	14.3
Canada	6.7	6.2	6.0	6.9	6.6	7.2	7.2	7.5
Denmark	10.6	9.5	9.1	9.0	..	6.6	6.0	6.8
Finland	..	6.3	7.4	5.6	5.4	6.1	6.9	8.8
France	12.9	11.7	10.9	10.4	10.1	9.9	10.0	9.1
Germany	8.0	7.6	7.5	7.6	7.4	7.6	..	8.0
Italy	..	23.2	23.1	18.4	19.9	21.0	21.4	22.2
Japan	14.3	14.7	14.2	14.7	14.1	13.5	13.1	11.6
Norway	8.6	7.6	6.8	..	6.4	6.6	6.3	6.1
Sweden	3.9	4.8	4.6	4.6	4.9	4.5	7.1	7.1
Great Britain	6.8	7.4	6.9	6.6	7.7	9.3	10.8	12.4
United States	6.8	7.2	6.9	7.4	7.4	7.5	7.7	7.7

.. = information missing

Source: OECD 1986a, 1992

Table 6.1.A   Distribution of wage employees, salary employees, and self-employed by weekly hours actually worked, by gender, 1986–1990

		Under 29 hours	30-34 hours	Percentages 34-50 hours	41-50 hours	Over 50 hours
Wage employed						
Men	1986	3.2	1.4	91.5	2.6	1.2
	1987	3.4	1.7	90.7	2.8	1.3
	1988	2.8	1.8	91.4	5.1	1.8
	1989	3.2	1.9	91.5	2.5	0.9
	1990	3.1	2.4	90.7	2.4	1.4
Women	1986	12.7	4.2	81.3	1.3	0.5
	1987	13.3	3.8	81.2	1.2	0.5
	1988	11.7	4.1	82.6	1.0	0.6
	1989	11.8	4.1	82.5	1.0	0.6
	1990	11.1	3.8	83.3	1.2	0.6
Salary employed						
Men	1986	4.0	2.0	83.0	7.7	3.3
	1987	4.2	4.0	83.0	6.0	2.8
	1988	4.2	4.3	83.1	5.9	2.5
	1989	4.4	4.3	82.8	6.2	2.3
	1990	4.1	3.7	83.1	6.3	2.7
Women	1986	8.9	7.2	78.7	4.2	0.5
	1987	8.9	7.3	79.0	3.9	0.5
	1988	8.1	7.1	80.0	3.9	0.9
	1989	8.4	7.5	79.2	3.9	1.0
	1990	8.6	7.6	78.9	3.8	1.1
Self-employed						
Men	1986	9.6	4.6	20.8	20.7	44.4
	1987	8.6	3.8	21.8	21.8	44.0
	1988	7.6	3.3	21.2	23.8	44.1
	1989	7.8	3.7	21.5	22.8	44.1
	1990	7.1	4.0	23.2	23.7	42.0
Women	1986	20.3	5.6	21.0	25.3	27.6
	1987	18.7	5.6	21.8	24.8	29.0
	1988	18.0	5.6	21.5	26.4	28.4
	1989	16.6	4.5	21.7	26.0	31.2
	1990	16.0	4.5	22.3	26.2	30.9

233

Table 6.1.A   continues

		Under 29 hours	30-34 hours	Percentages 34-50 hours	41-50 hours	Over 50 hours
Assisting family members						
Men	1986	32.4	7.7	16.5	15.4	27.4
	1987	31.3	9.0	15.7	17.5	26.5
	1988	37.0	8.0	13.8	18.8	22.4
	1989	37.0	6.9	19.2	19.2	17.7
	1990	36.2	8.6	19.0	14.7	22.4
Women	1986	42.2	6.5	13.0	17.9	20.3
	1987	48.5	6.7	18.1	14.3	11.4
	1988	39.8	8.0	15.6	14.4	11.2
	1989	50.0	3.7	18.8	16.2	11.3
	1990	52.6	4.0	18.0	15.4	10.0

Sources: Labour Force Surveys 1986-1990, tables 148.

Table 6.2.A.   The educational levels of wage and salary employed and self-employed, by gender, percentages, 1986 – 1990.

Occupational status, percentages

	Waged workers		Salaried employees		Self-employed		Assisting family members	
Year 1986	women	men	women	men	women	men	women	men
Educational level								
Basic education	59	53	31	19	59	58	68	62
Lower middle level e.	35	42	27	17	29	28	23	30
Upper middle level e.	6	5	24	34	8	6	7	7
High education	0	0	18	30	4	8	2	1
Total	100	100	100	100	100	100	100	100
Year 1987	women	men	women	men	women	men	women	men
Educational level								
Basic education	54	51	27	19	47	57	65	60
Lower middle level e.	38	43	26	15	35	28	65	29
Upper middle level e.	8	6	28	32	13	9	8	8
High education	1	0	19	34	5	6	1	3
Total	100	100	100	100	100	100	100	100
Year 1988	women	men	women	men	women	men	women	men
Educational level								
Basic education	56	49	28	18	52	54	68	65
Lower middle level e.	38	44	25	16	34	30	26	29
Upper middle level e.	6	6	28	33	10	9	4	5
High education	0	1	19	33	4	7	2	1
Total	100	100	100	100	100	100	100	100
Year 1989	women	men	women	men	women	men	women	men
Educational level								
Basic education	54	48	24	17	49	50	67	70
Lower middle level e.	38	45	23	16	35	32	24	13
Upper middle level e.	7	7	36	33	11	10	6	13
High education	1	0	17	34	5	8	3	4
Total	100	100	100	100	100	100	100	100
Year 1990	women	men	women	men	women	men	women	men
Educational level								
Basic education	54	46	27	17	47	50	65	70
Lower middle level e.	38	45	26	16	35	33	25	13
Upper middle level e.	8	8	28	33	13	9	8	13
High education	1	1	19	34	5	8	1	4
Total	100	100	100	100	100	100	100	100

Source: CSOF Labour Force Surveys 1987-1991, tables 07.

Figure 1.1.A.   Number of self-employed women in selected OECD countries, 1970–1988

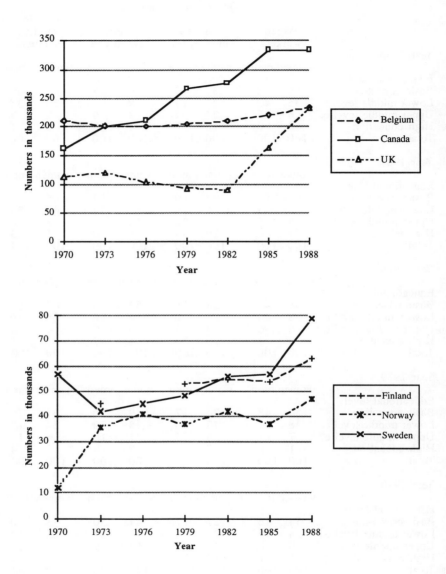

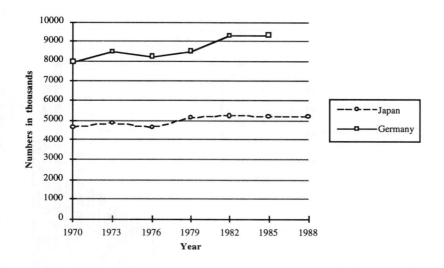

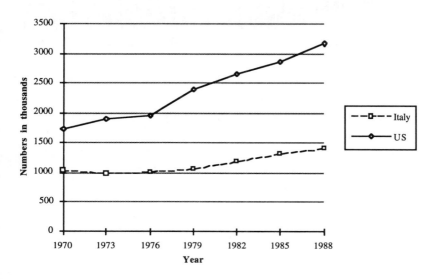

Figure 1.2.A.   New registered companies in Finland, 1960–1991

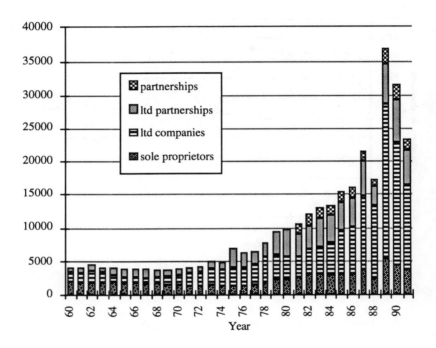

Figure 4.1.A.   Typology of female entrepreneurs by Goffee – Scase

		Attachment to Conventional Gender Roles	
		High	Low
Attachment to Entrepreneurial Ideals	High	Conventionals	Innovators
	Low	Domestics	Radicals

Source: Goffee - Scase, 1980

Figure 4.2.A.   Typology of self-employed women by Sundin – Holmqvist

Connection to gender roles		Means and ends in the lifeforms		Attitude towards self-employment and business type in different lifeforms	
		Traditional	Modern	Traditional	Modern
LIFEFORM	STATUS				
Independent lifeform	married / co-habiting	family and work/ self employment	well being for both family and work/ self-employment	assisting family member	family business
	single	work/ self-employment	work/ self-employment	typical business within female branch	typical business within female branch
Waged worker lifeform	married / co-habiting	family and husband´s work	family, husband´s and own work	business for bread only	part-time business for bread only
	single	own work and future family	own work and future family	business for bread	business for bread
Careerist lifeform	married / co-habiting	own well-being and husband´s career	own career and husband´s career	assisting family member/hobby	professional business
	single	own career	own career	professional business	professional business

Figure 6.1.A.   Income by gender and employment status in Finland, 1985

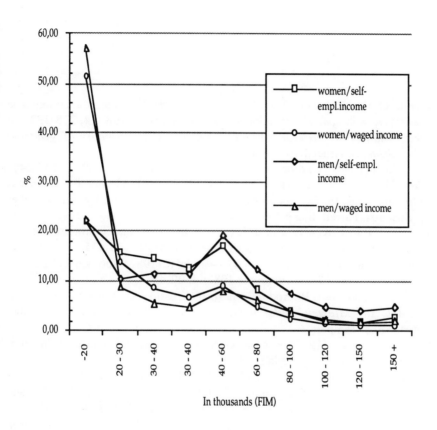

Bibliography

Aarnio, Outi – Eriksson, Tor (1987) Onko naisten palkkatuloilla tulonjakoa tasoittava vaikutus? *Kansantaloudellinen aikakauskirja* 1987: 4, 378-393.

Acker, Joan (1987) *Hierarchies and jobs: Notes for a theory of gendered organizations.* Arbetslivscentrum: Stockholm.

Acker, Joan (1989) The problem with patriarchy. *Sociology* 1989: 2, 235-240.

Acker, Joan (1991) Hierarchies, Jobs, Bodies: A Theory of Gendered Organizations. In: *The Social Construction of Gender*, ed. by Judith Lorber – Susan A. Farrell. Sage: Newbury Park.

Acker, J. – Barry, K. – Esseveld, J. (1983) Objectivity and Truth: Problems in Doing Feminist Research. *Women's Studies* 1983: 4, 423-435.

Ahde, P. – Karko, J. – Vuori, S. – Ylä-Anttila, P. (1987) Suomen teollisuuden rakennemuutos. *ETLA, Suhdanne* 1987: 4, 22-45.

Alanen, Leena (1986) Reproduktio ja sosiaalisaatio - käsitteiden ja toiminnan kentät. In: *Miesten tiede, naisten puuhat*, ed. by Liisa Rantalaiho. Vastapaino: Tampere.

Ala-Peijari, Jukka (1987) *Elintarviketeollisuus kansantaloudessa.* Elinkeino-elämän tutkimuslaitos. Sarja B 53. Helsinki.

Aldrich, H. – Reece, P. R. – Dubini, P. (1989) Women on the verge of a breakthrough: networking among entrepreneurs in the United States and Italy. *Entrepreneurship & Regional Development* 1989: 4, 339-356.

Alestalo, Matti (1985) Yhteiskuntaluokat ja sosiaaliset kerrostumat toisen maailmansodan jälkeen. In: *Suomalaiset. Yhteiskunnan rakenne teollistumisen aikana*, ed. by T. Valkonen, – R. Alapuro, – M. Alestalo, – R. Jallinoja, – T. Sandlund, WSOY: Juva.

Alic, J. A. (1986) Employment and Job Creation Impacts of High Technology. *Futures* 1980: 4, 508-513.

Allen, Sheila (1983) Production and reproduction: the lives of women home-workers. *Sociological Review* 1983: 2, 146-157.

Allen, Sheila (1989a) The analysis of all forms of women´s labour. Paper presented in European Workshop on the Social History of European

Women. Athens. March 16-19, 1989.

Allen, Sheila (1989b) Economic recession and gender divisions. In: *Industrial Societies*, ed. by Richard Scase. Hyman: London.

Allen, Sheila – Truman, Carole (1991) Prospects for women´s businesses and self-employment in the year 2000. In: *Paths of Enterprise. The Future of the Small Business*, ed. by James Curran – Robert A. Blackburn. Routledge: London

Allen, Sheila – Wolkowitz, Carol (1987) *Homeworking. Myths and Realities.* MacMillan: London.

Amsden, Alice (1980) Introduction. In: *The Economics of Women and Work*, ed. by Alice Amsden. St. Martins Press: New York.

Ansoff, Igor (1979) *Strategic Management.* Macmillan Press: London.

Anttalainen, Marja-Liisa (1986) *Sukupuolen mukaan kahtiajakautuneet työmarkkinat Pohjoismaissa.* Tasa-arvoasiain neuvottelukunta. Valtioneuvoston kanslia. Naistutkimusmonisteita 1986: 1. Helsinki.

Anttonen, Anneli (1989) *Valtiollisesta yhteisölliseen sosiaalipolitiikkaan.* Sosiaaliturvan keskusliitto: Helsinki.

Aronson, Robert L. (1991) *Self-employment. A labour market perspective.* ILR Press: New York.

Arrow, Kenneth (1976) Economic Dimensions of Occupational Segregation. A Comment. In: *Women and the Workplace*, ed. by M. Blaxall – B. Reagan. The University of Chicago Press: Chicago.

Bade, F.-J. (1987) The Economic Importance of Small and Medium-Sized Firms in the Federal Republic of Germany. In: *New Firms and Regional Development in Europe*, ed. by D. Keeble – E. Wever. Croom Helm: London.

Bagguley, Paul – Mark-Lawson, Jane – Shapiro, Dan – Urry, John – Walby, Sylvia – Warde, Alan (1990) *Restructuring: Place, Class & Gender.* Sage: London.

Bagguley, Paul (1991) Post-Fordism and enterprise culture. In: *Enterprise culture*, ed. by R. Keat – N. Abercrombie. Routledge: London.

Baker, A. (1985) *The Pathway to Proprietorship: the Process of Becoming a Small Businessman.* School of Business and Management. Occasional Paper Series No. 1. Ealing College of Higher Education: London.

Bannock, Graham (1981) *The Economics of Small Firms: Return from the Wilderness.* Blackwell: Oxford.

Barrett, Michele (1985) *Nykyajan alistettu nainen.* Vastapaino: Tampere.

Barron, R. D. – Norris, G. M. (1977) Sexual divisions and the dual labour market. In: *Dependence and Exploitation in Work and Family*, ed. by O. C. Barker – S. Allen. Allen & Unwin: London.

Baude, A. et al. (1987) *Kvinnoarbetsliv*. Arbetslivscentrum: Stockholm.

Bechhofer, Frank – Elliott, Brian (1974) The petite bourgeoisie in the class structure: the case of small shopkeepers. In: *The Social Analysis of Class Structure*, ed. by Frank Bechhofer – Brian Elliott. Tavistock: London.

Bechhofer, Frank – Elliott, Brian (1981) Petty Property: the Survival of a Moral Economy. In: *The Petite Bourgeoisie. Comparative Studies of the Uneasy Stratum*, ed. by Frank Bechhofer – Brian Elliott. Macmillan: London.

Bechhofer, Frank – Elliott, Brian (1986) Persistence and Change: The Petite Bourgeoisie in Industrial Society. In: *The Survival of the Small Firm. Vol. 1. The Economics of Survival and Entrepreneurship*, ed. by J. Curran – J. Stanworth – D. Watkins. Gower: Aldershot.

Becker, Gary (1965/1980) A Theory of the Allocation of Time. In: *The Economics of Women and Work*, ed. by Alice H. Amsden. St. Martins Press: New York.

Becker, Gary (1973) A Theory of Marriage: Part I. *Journal of Political Economy* 1973: 2, 211-216.

Beechey, Veronica (1987) *Unequal work*. Verso: London.

Beechey, Veronica – Perkins, Tessa (1987) *A Matter of Hours. Women, Part-time Work and the Labour Market*. Polity Press: Cambridge.

Benhabib, Sheila (1987) The Generalized and the Concrete Other. The Kohlberg-Gilligan Controversy and Feminist Theory. In: *Feminism as Critique*, ed. by Sheila Benhabib – Drucilla Cornell. Polity Press: Oxford.

Benhabib, Sheila (1990) Epistemologies of Postmodernism. In: *Feminism/Postmodernism*, ed. by Linda J. Nicholson. Routlegde: London.

Benhabib, Sheila – Cornell, Drucilla (1987) Introduction. In: *Feminism as Critique*, ed. by Sheila Benhabib – Drucilla Cornell. Polity Press: Oxford.

Berger, Suzanne (1981) The Uses of the Traditional Sector in Italy: Why Declining Classes Survive. In: *The Petite Bourgeoisie. Comparative Studies of the Uneasy Stratum*, ed. by Frank Bechhofer – Brian Elliott. Macmillan: London.

Bergmann, Barbara R. (1974/1980) Occupational Segregation, Wages and Profits When Employers Discriminate by Race and Sex. In: *The Economics of Women and Work*, ed. by Alice H Amsden. St. Martins Press: New York.

Bergmann, Barbara R. (1986) *The Economic Emergence of Women*. Basic Books: New York.

Bertaux, Daniel – Bertaux-Wiame, Isabelle (1981) Artisanal Bakery in France: how it lives and and why it survives. In: *The Petite Bourgeoisie. Comparative Studies of the Uneasy Stratum*, ed. by Frank Bechhofer –

Brian Elliott. Macmillan: London.

Binks, Martin – Jennings, Andrew (1987) Small Firms as a Source of Economic Rejuvenation. In: *The Survival of the Small Firm. Vol 1. The Economics of Survival and Entrepreneurship*, ed. by J. Curran – J. Stanworth – D. Watkins. Gower: Aldershot.

Birley, Sue (1989) Female Entrepreneurs: Are They Really Any Different? *Journal of Small Business Management* 1989: 1, 32-37.

Blau, F. D. – Jusenius, C. L. (1981) Economists' Approaches to Sex Segregation in the Labor Market: An Appraisal. In: *Women and Workplace*, ed. by Martha Blaxall – Barbra Reagan. University of Chicago Press: Chicago.

Boissevain, Jeremy (1981) *Small Entrepreneurs in Changing Europe: Towards a Research Agenda*. European Centre for Work and Society: Maastricht.

Bolton Report (1971) *Report of the Committee of Inquiry on Small Firms*. HMSO: London.

Boserup, Ester (1970) *Women´s Role in Economic Development*. St. Martin´s Press: New York.

Boswell, John (1973) *The Rise and Decline of Small Firms*. Allen & Unwin: London.

Bowen, D. D. – Hisrich, R. D. (1986) The Female Entrepreneur: A Career Development Perspective. *Academy of Management Review* 1986: 2, 393-407.

Bowman-Upton, N. – Carsrud, A. L. – Olm, K. W. (1987) New Venture Funding for the Female Entrepreneur: A Preliminary Analysis. Working paper 4. University of Southern California: California.

Bradley, Harriet (1989) *Men´s Work, Women´s Work. A Sociological History of the Sexual Division of Labour in Employment*. Polity Press: Cambridge.

Brekke, L. – Haukaa, R. (1980) Teorin som inte finns. *Kvinnovetenskaplig Tidskrift* 1980: 1, 30-44.

Broadbridge, Adelina (1991) Images and goods: women in retailing. In: *Working Women. International Perspectives on Labour and Gender Ideology*, ed. by Nanneke Redclift – M. Thea Sinclair. Routledge: London.

Brockhaus, R. H. (1980) Risk taking propensity of entrepreneurs. *Academy of Management Journal* 1980: 3, 509-520.

Bryt Nytt (1988) *Nyt fra det nordiske Bryt-projekt*. Marts: København.

Burrows, Roger (1991) The discourse of the enterprise culture and the restructuring of Britain: a polemical contribution. In: *Paths of Enterprise: The Future of Small Business*, ed. by James Curran – Robert A. Blackburn. Routledge: London.

Burrows, Roger – Curran, James (1989) Sociological Research on Service

Sector Small Businesses: Some Conceptual Considerations. *Work, Employment & Society* 1989: 4, 527-539.

Bögenhold, David (1988) Niedergang und Renessaince der Selbständigen! *Zeitschrift für Soziologie* 1988: 2, 390-395.

Calás, Marta B. – Smirich, Linda (1992) Re-writing Gender into Organizational Theorizing: Directions from Feminist Perspectives. In: *Rethinking Organization. New Directions in Organization Theory and Analysis*, ed. by M. Reed – M. Hughes. Sage: London.

Carland, J. W. – Hoy, F. – Boulton, W. R. – Carland, J. A. C. (1984) Differentiating Entrepreneurs from Small Business Owners: A Conceptualization. *Academy of Management Review* 1984: 2, 354-359.

Carlsson, B. (1988) The evolution of manufacturing technology and its impact on industrial structure: an international study. IUI Working paper No. 203.

Carsrud, A. L. – Olm, K. W. – Ahlgreen, R. D. (1986a) Comparison of Female entrepreneurs and M.B.A. students: groomed for success or doomed to failure? Working paper 4-19. Department of Management. University of Texas: Austin.

Carsrud, A. L.– Gaglio, C. M. – Olm, K. W. (1986b) Entrepreneurs – Mentors, Networks, and Successful New Venture Development: an Exploratory Study. Working paper. School of Business Administration. University of Southern California.

Carsrud, A. L. – Sapienza, H. J. (1989) Entrepreneurship in the Social Context. Department of Management. Unpublished manuscript. University of Texas: Austin.

Carter, S. – Cannon, T. (1988) Women in Business. *Employment Gazette* 1988: 2, 565-571.

Casey, B. – Creigh, S. (1988) Self-employment in Great Britain: its Definition in the Labour Force Survey, in Tax and Social Security Law and in Labour Law. *Work, Employment and Society* 1988: 3, 381-391.

Chell, Elisabeth (1986) The Entrepreneurial Personality: A Review and Some Theoretical Developments. In: *The Survival of the Small Firm. Vol. 1. The Economics of Survival and Entrepreneurship*, ed. by J. Curran – J. Stanworth – D. Watkins. Gower: Aldershot.

Cockburn, Cynthia (1983) *Brothers - Male Dominance and Technological Change*. Pluto Press: London.

Cockburn, Cynthia (1986) The Relations of Technology. What Implications for Theories of Sex and Class? In: *Gender and Stratification*, ed. by R. Crompton – M. Mann. Polity Press: Cambridge.

Company Registration Office. Yearly statistics 1960–1991. Unpublished information, Anna-Liisa Viinikka, 25.5.1989 and 17.5.1993.

Connell, R. W. (1985) Theorising gender. *Sociology* 1985: 2, 260-272.

Connell, R. W. (1987) *Gender and Power*. Polity Press: Cambridge.

Cooper, C. – Davidson, M. (1982) *High Pressure*. Fontana: London.

Cornell, Drucilla – Thruschwell, Adam (1987) Feminism, Negativity, Intersubjectivity. In: *Feminism as Critique*, ed. by Sheila Benhabib – Drucilla Cornell. Polity Press: Cambridge.

Craig, C. – Garnsey, E. – Rubery, J. (1985) Labour Market Segmentation and Women's Employment: A Case Study from the United Kingdom. *International Labour Review* 1985: 3, 267-280.

Creigh, S. – Roberts, C. – Gorman, A. – Sawyer, P. (1986) Self-employment in Britain: Results from the Labour Force Surveys 1981-1984. *Employment Gazette* 1986: 2, 193-194.

Cromie, Stanley (1985) Towards a typology of female entrepreneurs. Unpublished manuscript.

Cromie, Stanley (1987a) Similarities and Differences between Women and Men Who Choose Business Proprietorship. *International Small Business Journal* 1987: 3, 43-60.

Cromie, Stanley (1987b) Motivations of aspiring male and female entrepreneurs. *Journal of Occupational Behaviour* 1987: 2, 251-261.

Cromie, Stanley. (1988) The Aptitudes of Aspiring Male and Female Entrepreneurs. In: *Small Business Research: Some Current Issues*, ed. by K. O'Neill – R. Bhanburg. Gower: Aldershot.

Cromie, S. – Ayling, S. (1989) *The Post-Launch Problems and Experiences of Small Business Propietors*. Report to the Economic and Social Research Council. London.

Crompton, Rosemary (1990) Class Theory and Gender. *The British Journal of Sociology* 1990: 4, 565-587.

Crompton, Rosemary – Jones, Gareth (1984) *White-Collar Proletariat. Deskilling and Gender in Clerical Work*. MacMillan Press: London.

Crompton, Rosemary – Sanderson, Kay (1989) *Gendered jobs and social change*. Unwin & Hyman: London.

CSOF (1956) VI C:102. Population census 1950. Central Statistical Office of Finland: Helsinki.

CSOF (1962) 18 A:76. Industrial statistics of Finland 1960. Central Statistical Office of Finland: Helsinki.

CSOF (1963) VI C:103. General census of population 1960. Central Statistical Office of Finland: Helsinki.

CSOF (1973a) VI C:104. Population census 1970. Central Statistical Office of Finland: Helsinki.

CSOF (1973b) 18 A:90. Industrial statistics 1970. Central Statistical Office of

Finland: Helsinki.

CSOF (1977) 18 A:96. Industrial statistics 1975. Central Statistical Office of Finland: Helsinki.

CSOF (1978a) VI C:105. Population and housing census 1975. Central Statistical Office of Finland: Helsinki.

CSOF (1978b) Statistical surveys 71. Labour force survey: results of the labour force survey from the years 1959-1975. Central Statistical Office of Finland: Helsinki.

CSOF (1981) XL:5. Labour force survey 1980. Central Statistical Office of Finland: Helsinki.

CSOF (1982) 18 A:101. Industrial statistics 1980. Central Statistical Office of Finland: Helsinki.CSOF (1983) VI C:106. Population and housing census 1980. Central Statistical Office of Finland: Helsinki.

CSOF (1984a) 41:4. Income distribution statistics 1980. Central Statistical Office of Finland: Helsinki.

CSOF (1984b) Statistical surveys 71. Household survey 1981. Central Statistical Office of Finland: Helsinki.

CSOF (1984c) Statistical surveys 75. National accounts 1981: timeseries for 1960-1981. Central Statistical Office of Finland: Helsinki.

CSOF (1985) Statistical reports 1985:4 National accounts: input-output study 1982. Central Statistical Office of Finland: Helsinki.

CSOF (1986) XL:11. Labour force survey 1985. Central Statistical Office of Finland: Helsinki.

CSOF (1987) 18 A: 106. Industrial statistics 1985. Central Statistical Office of Finland: Helsinki.

CSOF (1988a) VI C:107.Population census 1985. Central Statistical Office of Finland: Helsinki.

CSOF (1988b) Manufacturing 1988: 16. Yearbook of industrial statistics 1985. Central Statistical Office of Finland: Helsinki.

CSOF (1990a) Preliminary data on census 1990. Central Statistical Office of Finland: Helsinki.

CSOF (1990b) Services 1990: 1. Business services 1990. Central Statistical Office of Finland: Helsinki.

CSOF (1992a) Enterprises 1992: 9. Corporate enterprises and personal businesses in Finland. Central Statistical Office of Finland: Helsinki.

CSOF (1992b) Income and consumption 1992: 15. Income distribution statistics. Central Statistical Office of Finland: Helsinki.

CSOF (1992c) Labour market 1991: 30. Labour force statistics 1990. Central Statistical Office of Finland: Helsinki.

CSOF (1992d) Manufacturing 1992: 7. Yearbook of industrial statistics 1990.

Central Statistical Office of Finland: Helsinki.

Curran, James (1982) Starting and Surviving: Some Small Firms in the 1980s. Tenth National Small Firms Policy and Research Conference. Cranfield School of Management. Unpublished paper.

Curran, James (1986a) *Small Firms and Their Environment.* A Report. Kingston Polytechnic. Small Business Research Unit: Kingston.

Curran, James (1986b) *Bolton Fifteen Years on: A Review and analysis of Small Business Research in Britain 1971-1986.* Small Business Reseach Trust: London.

Curran, James – Blackburn Robert A. (1991) Introduction. In: *Paths of Enterprise. The Future of Small Business*, ed. by James Curran – Robert A. Blackburn. Routledge: London.

Curran, James – Burrows, Roger (1986) The Social Analysis of Small Business: Some Emerging Themes. In: *Entreprepreurship in Europe*, ed. by R. Goffee – R. Scase. Croom Helm: London.

Curran, James – Burrows, Roger (1988) *Enterprise in Britain: A National Profile of Small Business Owners and the Self-Employed.* Small Business Research Trust: London.

Curran, James – Stanworth, John (1986) Small firms, large firms: theoretical and research strategies for the comparative analysis of small and large firms in the wider environment. In: *Small Firms Growth and Development*, ed. by M. Scott – A. Gibb – J. Lewis – T. Faulkner. Gower: Aldershot.

Dale, Angela (1986) Social Class and the Self-Employed. *Sociology* 1986: 3, 430-434.

Dale, Angela (1991) Self-employment and entrepreneurship: notes on two problematic concepts. In: *Deciphering the Enterprise Culture*, ed. by Roger Burrows. Routledge: London.

Daune-Richard, Anne-Marie (1988) Gender Relations and Female Labour. In: *Feminization of the Labour Force*, ed. by Jane Jenson – Elisabeth Hagen – Cealleigh Reddy. Polity Press: London.

Davies, Karen (1989) *Women and Time. Weaving Strands of Everyday Life.* University of Lund: Lund.

DeCarlo, J. F. – Lyons, P. R. (1979) A Comparison of Selected Personal Characteristics of Minority and Non-minority Female Entrepreneurs. *Journal of Small Business Management* 1979: 1, 22-29.

Delphy, Christine (1981) Women in Stratification Studies. In: *Doing Feminist Research*, ed. by H. Roberts. Routledge & Kegan: London.

Department of Employment (UK) (1990). Labour Force Survey. Statistical Office: London.

Dex, Shirley (1985) *The Sexual Division of Work.* Wheatsheaf: Brighton.

Dex, Shirley (1987) *Women's Occupational Mobility. A Lifetime Perspective.* Macmillan Press: London.

Doeringer, P. B. – Piore, M. J. (1971) *Internal Markets and Manpower Analysis.* Heath Lexington: Lexington.

Edwards, R. C. (1979) *Contested Terrain: The Transformation of the Workplace in the Twentieth Century.* Basic Books: New York.

Eichler, M. – Lapointe, J. (1985) *On the Treatment of the Sexes in Research.* Social Sciences and Humanities Research Council of Canada: Ottawa.

Erikson, R. – Golthorpe, J. H. (1988) Women at Class Crossroads: a Critical Note. *Sociology* 1988: 4, 545-553.

Felstead, Alan (1991) Facing up to the fragility of 'minding your own business' as a franchise. In: *Paths of Enterprise. The Future of the Small Business*, ed. by James Curran – Robert A. Blackburn. Routledge: London.

Ferguson, Kate E. (1984) *The Feminist Case Against Bureaucracy.* Temple University Press: Philadelphia.

Fernald, L. W. – Solomon, G. T. (1987) Value Profiles of Male and Female Entrepreneurs. *Journal of Creative Behavior* 1987: 3, 234-247.

Finnegan, R. (1985) Working outside formal employment. In: *Work, culture and society*, ed. by R. Deem – G. Salaman. Open University Press: Milton Keynes.

Flax, Jane (1983) Political Philosophy and the Patriarchal Unconscious: A Psychoanalytic Perspective on Epistemology and Metaphysics. In: *Discovering Reality: Feminist Perspectives on Epistemology, Metaphysics, Methodology and Philosophy of Science*, ed. by Sandra Harding – Merrill B. Hintikka. Reidel: Boston.

Flax, Jane (1987) Postmodernism and gender relations in feminist theory. *Signs*, 1987: 4, 621-643.

Flax, Jane (1990) Postmodernism and Gender Relations. In: *Feminism/Postmodernism*, ed. by Linda J. Nicholson. Routledge: London.

Fraser, Nancy (1987) What's Critical about Critical Theory? The Case of Habermas and Gender. In: *Feminism as Critique*, ed. by Sheila Benhabib – Drucilla Cornell. Polity Press: Oxford.

Fraser, Nancy – Nicholson, Linda J. (1990) Social Criticism Without Philosophy: An Encounter Between Feminism and Postmodernism. In: *Feminism/Postmodernism*, ed. by Linda. J. Nicholson. Routledge: New York.

Fuchs, V. R. (1982) Self-Employment and Labor Force Participation of Older Males. *The Journal of Human Resources* 1982: 3, 339-357.

Fuchs Epstein, Cynthia (1988) *Deceptive Distinctions: Sex, Gender and the Social Order.* RSF: New York.

Galbraith, J. K. (1957) *American Capitalism*. Hamilton: London.

Gershuny, Jonathan I. (1978) *After Industrial Society?* Macmillan: London

Gibb, Allan A. – Ritchie, John (1982) Understanding the Process of Starting Small Businesses. *International Small Business Journal* 1982: 1, 26-46.

Gilligan, Carol (1979) *In a Different Voice: Psychological Theory and Women's Development*. Harward University Press: Cambridge.

Goffee, Robert – Scase, Richard (1983) Business ownership and women's subordination: a preliminary study of female proprietors. *Sociological Review* 1983: 10, 625-647.

Goffee, Robert – Scase, Richard (1985) *Women in Charge. The Experiences of Female Entrepreneurs*. Allen & Unwin: London.

Goffee, Robert – Scase, Richard (1987a) Patterns of Female Entrepreneurship in Britain. Paper for Second International Seminar on Women - Local Initiatives - Job Creation. Oslo.

Goffee, Robert – Scase, Richard (1987b) Patterns of Business Proprietorship among Women in Britain. In: *Entrepreneurship in Europe*, ed. by R. Goffee – R. Scase. Croom Helm: London.

Goldthorpe, J. H. (1983) Women and class analysis: in defence of the conventional view. *Sociology* 1983: 4, 465-488.

Goldthorpe, J. H. – Llewellyn, C. – Payne, C. (1987) *Social Mobility and Class Structure in Modern Britain*. Clarendon Press: Oxford.

Granovetter, Mark (1984) Small is Bountiful: labour markets and establishment size. *American Sociological Review* 1984: 2, 323-334.

Grant, Judith (1987) I Feel Therefore I Am: A Critique of Female Experience as the Basis for a Feminist Epistemology. In: *Feminism and Epistemology*, ed. by Maria J. Falco. The Haworth Press: New York.

Green, Robert T. – Allaway, Arthur W. (1985) Identification of Export Opportunities: A Shift-Share Approach. *Journal of Marketing* 1985: 1, 83-88.

Grimshaw, Jean (1986) *Philosophy of Feminist Thinking*. University of Minnesota Press: Minneapolis.

Grint, Keith (1991) *The Sociology of Work*. Polity Press: Cambridge.

Gustafsson, Siv – Lantz, Petra (1985) *Arbete och löner*. Industriens Utredningsinstitut. Arbetslivscentrum: Stockholm.

Haahti, Antti (1989) *Entrepreneurs' Strategic Orientation: Modeling Strategic Behavior In Small Industrial Owner-managed Firms*. Acta Academiae Oeconomicae. Series A:64. Helsinki School of Economics: Helsinki.

Haber, S. E. – Lamas, E. J. – Lichtenstein, J. H. (1987) On their own: the self-employed and others in private business. *Monthly Labor Review* 1987: 5, 17-23.

Habermas, Jürgen (1987) *The Theory of Communicative Action. Vol. 2. Lifeworld and System: A Critique of Functionalist Reason.* Polity Press: Cambridge.

Habermas, Jürgen (1988) *The Logic of Social Sciences.* The MIT Press: Cambridge.

Hagen, Elisabeth – Jenson, Jane (1988) Paradoxes and Promises. In: *Feminization of the Labour Force,* ed. by Jane Jenson – Elizabeth Hagen – Ceallaigh Reddy. Polity Press: Oxford.

Hajba, Sirpa (1987a) Nainen yrittäjänä: yritysten uusperustantaa koskeva tutkimus. In: *Yrittäjyys ja aluetutkimus.* Oulussa 16.-17.5.1985 pidetyn tutkijaseminaarin raportti, ed. by E. Toiviainen. Oulun yliopisto: Oulu.

Hajba, Sirpa (1987b) *Female Entrepreneurship: Some Motivational and Psychological Aspects.* Turun kauppakorkeakoulu. Hallinnon ja markkinoinnin laitos. Raportti 18. Turku.

Hakim, Catherine (1979) *Occupational Segregation.* Research Paper No. 9. Department of Employment: London.

Hakim, Catherine (1984) Homework and Outwork. *Employment Gazette Supplement* 1984: 1, 7-12.

Hakim, Catherine (1987) Trends in the flexible workforce. *Employment Gazette Supplement* 1987: 5, 549-560.

Hakim, Catherine. (1988) Self-employment in Britain: recent trends and current issues. *Work, Employment and Society* 1988: 2, 421-450.

Hallberg, Margareta (1992) *Kunskap och kön. En studie av feministisk vetenskapsteori.* Daidalos: Göteborg.

Hamilton, R. T. (1989) Unemployment and business formation rates: reconciling time-series and cross-section evidence. *Enviroment and Planning,* 1989: 2, 249-255.

Harding, Sandra (1982) Is Gender a Variable in Conceptions of Rationality? A Survey of Issues. *Dialectica* 1982: 3, 225-242.

Harding, Sandra (1983) Why has the sex/gender system become visible only now? In: *Discovering Reality: Feminist Perspectives on Epistemology, Metaphysics, Methodology, and the Philosophy of Science,* ed. by Sandra Harding – Merill B. Hintikka. D. Reidel Publishing Company: New York.

Harding, Sandra (1986) *The Science Question in Feminism.* The Free Press: New York.

Harding, Sandra (1987a) *Feminism and Methodology.* Open University Press: Indiana.

Harding, Sandra (1987b) The Method Question. *Hypatia* 1987: 3, 19-34.

Hartikainen, Antero (1987) Yrittäjä ja hänen yrityksensä jälkiteollisessa Suomessa I. Vaasan korkeakoulu. Hallinnon ja markkinoinnin laitos.

Taloussosiologian lisensiaatin tutkimus. Vaasa.

Hartmann, Heidi (1981) Kapitalismen, patriarkatet och könssegregationen i arbetet. *Kvinnovetenskaplig tidskrift* 1981: 2, 7-30.

Hartmann, Heidi (1983) Capitalism, Patriarchy and Job Segregation by Sex. In: *Women, Gender and Scholarship*, ed. by E. Abel. The University of Chigago Press: London.

Hekman, Susan (1987) The Feminization of Epistemology: Gender and the Social Sciences. In: *Feminism and Epistemology*, ed. by Maria J. Falco. The Haworth Press: New York.

Hekman, Susan (1990) *Gender and Knowledge. Elements of a Postmodern Feminism.* Polity Press: Cambridge.

Helmreich, R. L. – Sawin, L. L. – Carsrud, A. L. (1986) The honeymoon effect in job performance: Temporal increases in the predicative power of achievement motivation. *Journal of Applied Psychology* 1986: 2, 185-188.

Hemmilä, Pirkko (1988) *Naisten palkkojen teoriaa ja käytäntöä.* Sosiaali- ja terveysministeriö. Tasa-arvojulkaisuja. Sarja A: 1 Tutkimuksia. Helsinki.

Hertzberg, Veronica (1989) Kvinnliga diplomingenjörers väg från studier till yrkesliv. In: *Kvinnor i mansdominerade yrken*, ed. by Harriet Silius. Publikationer från Institutet för kvinnoforskning vid Åbo Akademi. Nr. 5. Åbo.

Hiilamo, S. (1971) Suomen vaatetusteollisuuden rakennemuutokset vuosina 1954-167. Helsingin yliopisto. Kansantaloustieteen pro gradu. Helsinki.

Hirdman, Yvonne (1990) Genussystemet. In: *Demokrati och makt i Sverige*, Maktutredningens huvudrapport, 1990: 44. SOU: Stockholm.

Hisrich, R. D. – Brush, C. (1987) Woman Entrepreneurs: A Longitudinal Study. In: *Frontiers of Entrepreneurship Research*, ed. by K. H. Vesper. Babson College. Babson Centre for Entrepreneurial Studies: Wellesley, Mass.

Hisrich, R. D. – O'Brien, M. (1981) The Woman Entrepreneur. In: *Frontiers of Entrepreneurship Research*, ed. by K. H. Vesper. Babson College. Babson Centre for Entrepreneurial Studies: Wellesley, Mass.

Hjerppe, Riitta (1972) *Suomen teollisuuden toimipaikkojen jakauma suuruusluokkiin ja suhdanteet.* Helsingin yliopiston talous- ja sosiaalihistorian laitoksen tutkimuksia n:o 6. Helsinki.

Hjerppe, Riitta (1988) *Suomen talous 1860-1985. Kasvu ja rakennemuutos.* Suomen Pankki. Kasvututkimuksia: Helsinki.

Horner, Matina (1970) Toward an Understanding of Achievement Related Conflicts on Women. *Journal of Social Issues* 1982: 3, 373-385.

Hudson, J. (1984) Company births in Great Britain and the institutional enviroment. *International Business Journal* 1984: 1, 57-69.

Humphries, Jane – Rubery, Jill (1988) Recession and exploitation: Brorish women in a changing workplace 1979-1985. In: *Feminization of the Labour Force: Paradoxes and Promises*, ed. by Jane Jenson – Elizabeth Hagen – Ceallaigh Reddy. Polity Press: Oxford.

Ilmakunnas, Seija (1989) Naisten työvoiman tarjonnasta Suomessa: työvoimareservistä kokopäivätyöhön. *TTT katsaus*, No. 1: Naiset, työ ja talous, 1989. Helsinki.

Ingberg, M. – Lahdenperä, H. – Pulli, M. – Skurnik, S. (1986) PTT:n työvoiman tarjontatutkimus: Yhteenveto ja keskeiset johtopäätökset. *PTT Katsaus* 1986: 4, 23-32.

Jaggar, Alison – Bordo, Susan (1989) *Gender/Body/Knowledge. Feminist Reconstructions of Being and Knowing*. Rutgers University Press: New Brunswick.

Jallinoja, Riitta. (1984) Perhekäsityksistä perhettä koskeviin ratkaisuihin. In: *Perhe, työ ja tunteet*, ed. by E. Haavio-Mannila – R. Jallinoja – H. Strandell. WSOY: Juva.

Jallinoja, Riitta (1985) Miehet ja naiset. In: *Suomalaiset. Yhteiskunnan rakenne teollistumisen aikana*, ed. by Tapani Valkonen – Risto Alapuro – Matti Alestalo – Riitta Jallinoja – Tom Sandlund. WSOY: Helsinki.

Johnson, Peter (1981) Unemployment and self-employment: A survey. *Industrial Relations Journal*, 1981: (September-October), 5-15.

Johnson, Steve (1991) Small Firms and the UK Labour Market. In: *Paths of Enterprise. The Future of Small Business*, ed. by James Curran – Robert A. Blackburn. Routledge: London.

Jonasdottir, Anna G. (1988) Sex/Gender, Power and Politics: Towards a Theory of the Foundations of Male Authority in the Formally Equal Society. *Acta Sociologica* 1988: 2, 157-174.

Julkunen, Raija (1985) Tarvitseeko nainen palkkatyötä? *Työelämä* 1985: 1, 55-59.

Julkunen, Raija (1992) *Hyvinvointivaltio käännekohdassa*. Vastapaino: Tampere.

Julkunen, Raija – Rantalaiho, Liisa (1989) Hyvinvointivaltion sukupuolijärjestelmä. Jyväskylän yliopisto. Yhteiskuntapolitiikan laitoksen työpapereita 56. Jyväskylä.

Kallinen, T. (1986) *Työn tuottavuuden taso ja ansiotaso Pohjoismaiden tehdasteollisuudessa vuosina 1973, 1982, 1983*. ETLA C: 40. Helsinki.

Kandal, Terry (1988) *The Woman Question in Classical Sociological Theory*. Florida International Press: Miami.

Kandiyoti, Deniz (1991) Bargaining with Patriarchy. In: *The Socal Construction of Gender*, ed. by Judith Lorber – Susan A. Farrell. Sage:

Newbury Park.

Kankaanpää, Arto – Leimu, Heikki (1982) *Yrittäjien käsitykset yrityksensä perustamissyistä ja merkityksestä pienteollisuudessa.* Turun kauppakorkeakoulun julkaisuja. Sarja A 8: 1982. Turku.

Kanter, Rosemary M. (1977) *Men and women of the Corporation.* Basic Books: New York.

Kasvio, Antti (1985) *Naiset ja teollisuustyö.* Tampereen yliopisto. Yhteiskuntatieteiden tutkimuslaitos. Sarja D 78. Tampere.

Kasvio, Antti (1988) *Teollisuuden rakennemuutos ja naistyöntekijät.* Tampereen yliopisto. Työelämän tutkimuslaitos. Sarja T 1. Tampere.

Kasvio, Antti (1991) *Tulevaisuuden vaatetustehdas.* Tampereen yliopisto, yhteiskuntatieteiden tutkimuslaitos, työelämän tutkimuskeskus, sarja T8/1991. Tampere.

Kauppi, Taina (1982) Teollisuuden pienyritystoiminnan kehitys Suomessa toisen maailmansodan jälkeen. Sosiologian pro gradu. Helsingin yliopisto. Helsinki.

Kauppinen-Toropainen, Kaisa – Kandolin, Irja – Haavio-Mannila, Elina(1986) *Töiden jakautuminen sukupuolen mukaan ja naisten työn laatu.* Työterveyslaitoksen tutkimuksia, 4: 3. Helsinki

Kelly, Aidan (1991) The enterprise culture and the welfare state: restructuring the management of the health and personal social services. In: *Deciphering the Enterprise Culture,* ed. by Roger Burrows. Routledge: London.

Kelly, Rita Mae (1991) *The Gendered Economy. Work, Career and Success.* Sage: London.

Kendrick, Jane (1981) Politics and the construction of women as second class workers. In: *The Dynamics of Labour Market Segmentation,* ed. by Frank Wilkinson. Academic Press: New York.

Kerkelä, Heikki (1982) *Suomalaisen luokka- ja kerrostumarakenteen kehityspiirteitä 1900-luvulla.* Tampereen yliopisto. Sosiologian ja sosiaalipsykologian laitos. Tutkimuksia 47. Tampere.

Kets de Vries, M. F. R. (1977) The Entrepreneurial Personality: A Person at the Crossroads. *Journal of Management Studies* 1977: 2, 34-57.

Kettunen, Pertti (1980) *Pienen teollisen yrityksen kasvun ja kehityksen edellytykset.* Jyväskylän yliopiston taloustieteen laitos. Julkaisuja 51. Jyväskylä.

Kinnunen, Merja (1989) *Työt, toimet ja luokittelut.* Tampereen yliopisto. Työelämän tutkimuskeskus. Sarja T 2/1989. Tampere.

Kivinen, Markku (1989) *The New Middle Classes and The Labour Process. Class Criteria Revisited.* Helsingin yliopiston sosiologian laitoksen tutkimuksia no. 223. Yliopistopaino: Helsinki.

255

Knight, R. M. (1984) The Independence of the Franchisee Entrepreneur. *Journal of Small Business Management* 1984: 4, 53-61.

Koch, Ulla (1989) Kvindeforskning i økonomisk forskning - en metodediskussion. Institut for økonomi, politik og forvaltning. Aalborg universitetscenter. Presented paper in Bergen University.

Koistinen, Pertti (1984) *Teknologiset uudistukset ja työvoiman käyttö.* Työvoimaministeriö. Suunnitteluosasto. Työvoimapoliittisia tutkimuksia 47. Helsinki.

Kolehmainen, Sirpa (1991) Naisten työmarkkinat ja työttömyys. Tampereen yliopisto. Sosiaalipolitiikan laitos. Tutkimuksia B 8. Tampere.

Kovalainen, Anne (1988) Yrittäjyyden käsite naistutkimuksen näkökulmasta. Alustus tutkijaseminaaarissa. Turku.

Kovalainen, Anne (1989a) Vilka aktiviterer finns det för kvinnliga företagare i Finland? Presentation 19.5.1989 in Helsingør, "Kvindelige iværksættere i Norden".

Kovalainen, Anne (1989b) The concept of entrepreneur in business economics. *Liiketaloudellinen Aikakauskirja* 1989: 2, 82-93.

Kovalainen, Anne (1989c) Women Entrepreneurs - a Future Resource for Declining Economies? In: *Doctoral Thesis in Management Studies. A Visit to London.* Liikkeenjohtotieteen kerho KVANTTI: Turku.

Kovalainen, Anne (1990) Palkkatyökokemusten merkitys naisten yrittäjäksi ryhtymiselle - Vammalan naisyrittäjäkurssille osallistuneiden kokemuksia. In: *Vammalan naisyrittäjäkurssi,* ed. by L. Räsänen. Työministeriön julkaisuja. Työvoimapoliittisia selvityksiä. Työministeriö: Helsinki.

Kovalainen, Anne (1992) The Changing Position of Women Entrepreneurs in Finland 1960-1990. Unpublished working paper.

Labour Studies Group (1985) Economic, social and political factors in the operation of the labour market. In: *New Approaches to Economic Life,* ed. by B. Roberts – R. Finnegan – D. Gallie. Polity Press: Cambridge.

Lahti, Arto (1988) Yrittäjyys käytännön ja tutkimuksen haasteena. *Hallinnon tutkimus* 1988: 2, 85-96.

Lane, J. E. (1985) Introduction: public or policy markets? The demarcation problem. In: *State and Market,* ed. by J. E. Lane. Sage: London.

Lastikka, P. (1984) *Suomen palvelusektorin rakenne ja kehitys vuosina 1948-88.* Elinkeinoelämän tutkimuslaitos C: 33. Helsinki.

Lazarus, Richard S. (1977) *Persoonallisuus.* Weilin+Göös: Espoo.

Leiulfsrud, Håkon – Woodward, Alison (1985) Women at Class Crossroads. Paper presented at the 13th bi-annual Nordic Sociology Conference. 14.-16.6.1985. Gothenburg.

Lilja, Reija – Santamäki, Tuire (1988) Työllisyyden rakennemuutokset -

muutosten voima ja kipeys. *TTT katsaus* 1988: 4, 51-68.

Lillydahl, J. H. (1986) Women and Traditionally Male Blue-Collar Jobs. *Work and Occupations* 1986: 3, 307-323.

Linder, Mark (1983) Self-Employment as a Cyclical Escape from Unemployment. *Research in Sociology of Work* 1983: 4, 261-274.

Lindmark, L. (1982) *Small firms in a new context - the case of Sweden.* Umeå Universitetet. Institut för företagsekonomi. FE-publ. 42. Umeå.

Lipman-Blumen, J. - Handley-Isaksen, A. - Leavitt, H. J. (1983) Achieving Styles in Men and Women: A Model, an Instrument, and Some Findings. In: *Achievement and Achievement Motives*, ed. by J. T. Spence. Freeman and Comp: San Francisco.

Lockwood, D. (1986) Class, status and gender. In: *Gender and Stratification*, ed. by Rosemary Crompton - Michael Mann. Polity Press: Cambridge.

Lundin, R.A. (1986) *Teori och metod i småföretagsforskningen - en kritisk granskning.* Umeå Universitet. Institut för företagsekonomi: Umeå.

Lyytikäinen, I. (1984) *Suomen työvoimamarkkinoiden ekonometrinen malli.* Suomen Pankki D: 58. Helsinki.

Macdonald, R. (1965) Schumpeter and Max Weber: Central Visions and Social Theories. *Quarterly Journal of Economics* 1965: 3, 373-396.

Manicas, Peter T. (1987) *A History & Philosophy of the Social Sciences.* Basil Blackwell: Oxford.

Marchesnay, M. (1990) The Small Business: As A Transaction Space. Entrepreneurship & Regional Development. Manuscript. Forthcoming.

Marini, M. M. - Brinton, M. C. (1984) Sex typing in occupational socialization. In: *Sex Segregation in the Workplace: Trends, Explanations, Remedies*, ed. by. B. R. Reskin. National Academy Press: Washington D. C.

Marjosola, Iiris (1979) *Yrittäjyys tahtona ja mahdollisuutena.* Jyväskylän yliopisto. Yrityksen taloustieteen laitos. Jyväskylä.

Markkola, Pirjo (1989) Maaseudun työläisvaimot. In: *Tuntematon työläisnainen*, ed. by Leena Laine - Pirjo Markkola. Vastapaino: Tampere.

Martin, J. - Roberts, C. (1984) *Women and Employment. A Lifetime Perspective.* The Report of the 1980 DE /OPCS Women and Employment Survey: London.

Maslow, A. H. (1943) A theory of human motivation. *Psychological Review* 1943: 4, 370-396.

Maynard, Mary (1990) The Re-shaping of Sociology? Trends in the study of gender. *Sociology* 1990: 2, 269-290.

McClelland, David C. (1961) *The Achieving Society.* Princeton. Van Nostrand: New Jersey.

McClelland, David C. (1961/1971) The Achievement Motive in Economic Growth. In: *Entrepreneurship and Economic Development*, ed. by P. Kilby. The Free Press: New York.

McClelland. David C. (1987) Characteristics of Successful Entrepreneurs. *Journal of Creative Behavior* 1987: 3, 219-233.

McGee, J. (1989) Barriers to Growth: The Effects of Market Structure. In: *Barriers to Growth in Small Firms*, ed. by J. Barber – J.-S. Metcalfe – M. Porteous. Routledge: London.

Meulders, D. – Plasman, R. (1989) Women in work. Department of Applied Economics of the Free University of Brussels. Unpublished Research Paper. Bryssel.

Mincer, Jacob (1962/1980) Labor Force Participation of Married Women: A Study of Labor Supply. In: *The Economics of Women and Work*, ed. by Alice H. Amsden. St. Martins Press: New York.

Mincer, Jacob – Polachek, Solomon (1974/1980) Family Investments in Human Capital: Earnings of Women. In: *The Economics of Women and Work*, ed. by Alice H. Amsden. St. Martins Press: New York.

Mitter, Swasti (1986) Industrial Restructuring and Manufacturing Homework: Immigrant Women in the UK Clothing Industry. *Capital and Class* 1986: 27, 37-80.

Murgatroyd, Linda (1986) Occupational stratification and gender. In: *Localities, Class and Gender*. The Lancaster Regionalism Group. Pion Ltd: London.

Mønsted, Mette. (1982) *Familiearbejdskraft i små virkomheder*. Nyt fra samfundsvidenskaberne: København.

Nicholson, Linda J. (1990) Introduction. In: *Feminism/Postmodernism*, ed. by Linda J. Nicholson. Routledge: London.

Nicholson, N. – West, M. (1988) *Managerial job change: men and women in transition*. Cambridge University Press: Cambridge.

Niemi, Beth (1974/1980) The Female-Male Differential in Unemployment Rates. In: *The Economics of Women and Work*, ed. by Alice H. Amsden. St. Martins Press: New York.

Nooteboom, B. (1988) The Facts About Small Business and the Real Values of Its 'Life World'. *American Journal of Economics and Sociology* 1988: 3, 299-315.

Nordic Council of Ministers and the Nordic Secreteriat (1989) Yearbook of Nordic Statistics 1988, Vol. 27. Stockholm.

NSF (1979) National Science Foundation. NSF Small Business Research Program: Washington DC. April.

Näre, Sari (1987) Tiede logoskulttina. In: *Naistutkimuksen tieteidenvälisiä ongelmia*, ed. by. Liisa Rantalaiho – Aino Saarinen. Tampereen yliopisto. Sosiologian ja sosiaalipsykologian laitos. Sarja B-22. Tampere.

Nätti, Jouko (1985) *Katsaus työmarkkinoiden segmentaatioteorioihin.* Työvoimaministeriö. Työvoimapoliittisia tutkimuksia 56. Helsinki.

Nätti, Jouko (1989) *Työmarkkinoiden lohkoutuminen. Segmentaatioteoriat, Suomen työmarkkinat ja yritysten työvoimastrategiat.* Jyväskylän yliopisto. Tutkimuksia, 68. Jyväskylä.

Nätti, Jouko (1990) Ei-tyypillisistä työsuhdemalleista. Presentation at the national meeting of the Westermarck Society, 24.3.1990. Tampere.

OECD (1986a) Employment Outlook September. Organization for economic co-operation and development. Paris.

OECD (1986b) Women - Local Initiatives - Job Creation ILE Secreteriat Conference Paper, no. 6. OECD. Paris.

OECD (1986c) Personal Income Tax Systems Organization for economic co-operation and development. Paris.

OECD (1987a) Employment Outlook September. Organization for economic co-operation and development. Paris.

OECD (1987b) Labour Force Statistics 1965-1985. Organization for economic co-operation and development. Paris.

OECD (1987c) Employment prospects. Organization for economic co-operation and development. Paris.

OECD (1988a) Employment Outlook September. Organization for economic co-operation and development. Paris.

OECD (1988b) Economic Outlook December. Organization for economic co-operation and development. Paris.

OECD (1992) Employment Outlook. Organization for economic co-operation and development. Paris.

Okko, Paavo (1985) *Metalliteollisuus ja sen sopeutumishaaste.* ETLA B: 41. Helsinki.

Owen, S. J. – Joshi, H. E. (1987) Does Elastic Retract: The Effect of Recession on Women's Labour Force Participation. *British Journal of Industrial Relations* 1987: 1, 125-143.

Pateman, Carole (1988) *The sexual contract.* Polity Press: Cambridge.

Phizacklea, Annie (1989) Entrepreneurship, ethnicity, and gender. In: *Enterprising Women. Ethnicity, Economy and Gender Relations*, ed. by Sallie Westwood – Parminder Bhachu. Routledge: London.

Pipping, H. E. – Bärlund, R. (1966) *Suomen talouselämä.* Söderström & Co: Helsinki.

Pollert, Anna (1988) Dismantling Flexibility. *Capital and Class*, 1988: 34, 42-75.

259

Prandy, K. (1986) Similarities of Life-style and Occupations of Women. In: *Gender and Stratification*, ed. by Rosemary Crompton – Michael Mann. Polity Press: Cambridge.

Pusila, Juha (1992) *Ammatillinen segregaatio sukupuolen mukaan.* Turun kauppakorkeakoulun julkaisuja. Sarja keskusteluja ja raportteja 4. Turku.

Quinn, Joseph F. (1980) Labour force participation of older self-employed workers. *Social Security Bulletin*, 1980: (April), 17-28.

Rainbird, H. (1991) Self-employment: a form of disguised waged labour? In: *Farewell to Flexibility? Questions of Restructuring Work and Employment*, ed. by A. Pollert. Basil Blackwell: Oxford.

Rainnie, A. (1989) *Industrial Relations in Small Firms. Small isn't beautiful.* Routledge: London.

Rainnie, A. – Scott, M. (1986) Industrial Relations in the Small Firm. In: *The Survival of the Small Firm. Vol. 2. Employment, Growth, Technology and Politics*, ed. by J. Curran – J. Stanworth – D. Watkins. Gower: Aldershot.

Rantalaiho, Liisa (1986a) A discussion comment. In: *Naistutkimuksen tieteidenvälisiä ongemia*, ed. by Liisa Rantalaiho – Aino Saarinen. Tampereen yliopisto. Sosiologian ja sosiaalipsykologian laitos. Sarja B-22. Tampere.

Rantalaiho, Liisa (1986b) Miesten tiede, naisten puuhat. In: *Miesten tiede, naisten puuhat*, ed. by Liisa Rantalaiho. Vastapaino: Tampere.

Rantalaiho, Liisa (1986c) *Toimistotyö, toimistotyöntekijät ja toimistoautomaatio.* Tampereen yliopisto. Sosiologian ja sosiaalipsykologian laitos. Sarja B-45. Tampere.

Rantalaiho, Liisa (1988) Naistutkimuksen metodologiasta. In: *Akanvirtaan*, ed. by P. Setälä – H. Kurki. Gaudeamus: Helsinki.

Rantalaiho, Liisa (1993) The gender contract. In: *Shaping Structural Change in Finland. The Role of Women*, ed by Hannele Varsa. Ministry of Social Affairs and Health. Equality Publications. Series B: 2/1993. Helsinki 1993.

Reinharz, Shulamit (1992) Feminist Methods in Social research. Oxford University Press: Oxford.

Ripatti, Antti – Vartia, Pentti – Ylä-Anttila, Pekka (1989) *Suomen talouden ja yritysrakenteen muutokset 1938-1988.* ETLA. The Research Institute of the Finnish Economy. Discussion papers 297. Helsinki.

Riska, Elianne (1981) Itsehoidon yhteiskunnalliset funktiot. *Sosiaalilääketieteellinen Aikakauslehti* 1981: 2, 148-154.

Riska, Elianne – Wegar, Katarina (1989) Kvinnliga läkares ställning i läkarkåren - integration eller separatism? In: *Kvinnor i mansdominerade yrken*, ed. by H. Silius. Publikationer från Institutet för kvinnoforskning vid Åbo Akademi, nr. 5. Åbo.

Roos, Patricia A. (1985) *Gender and Work: A Comparative Analysis of*

Industrial Societies. State University of New York Press: New York.

Rothwell, Roy (1986) The Role of Small Firms in Technological Innovation. In: *The Survival of the Small Firm. Vol. 2. Employment, Growth, Technology and Politics*, ed. by J. Curran – J. Stanworth – D. Watkins. Gower: Aldershot.

Rothwell, Roy (1989) Small Firms, Innovation and Industrial Change. *Small Business Economics* 1989: 1, 51-64.

Rothwell, Roy – Zegveld, William (1982) *Innovation and the Small and Medium Sized Firms.* Francis Pinter: London.

Rubery, Jill – Tarling, Roger (1984) *Women in Recession.* University of Cambridge. Department of Applied Economics, economic reprint 68. Cambridge.

Ruoho, Iiris (1990) *"Naisnäkökulman" ongelmia. Yhdysvaltalaisista standpoint-teorioista ja postmodernista feminismistä.* Tampereen yliopisto, yhteiskuntatieteiden tutkimuslaitos, naistutkimusyksikkö, sarja N julkaisuja nro 3/1990. Tampere.

Ruotsalainen, Ritva (1992) Keisarinnan uudet vaatteet. Naistutkimuksen tieto-oppia. *Tiede&Edistys* 1992: 1, 28-36.

Saarinen, Aino (1986) Naistutkimus – paradigmahaaste yhteiskuntatieteille? In: *Miesten tiede, naisten puuhat*, ed. by Liisa Rantalaiho. Vastapaino: Tampere.

Saarinen, Aino (1992) *Feminist Research – An Intellectual Adventure?* University of Tampere. Research Institute for Social Sciences, publications 1992: 4. Tampere.

Salmi, Minna (1991) *Ansiotyö kotona – toiveuni vai painajainen?* Helsingin yliopisto. Sosiologian laitoksen tutkimuksia 225. Helsinki.

Santamäki, Tuire (1986) *Työmarkkinoiden tutkiminen – katsaus työn talous-tieteeseen.* Työväen taloudellinen tutkimuslaitos, tutkimusselosteita 54. Helsinki.

SBA (1980) Small Business Administration: Annual Report to the President – Interagency Committee on Women's Business Enterprise. U.S. Washington D. C.

SBA (1986) Small Business Administration: The State of Small Business: A Report of the President. Washington.

Scase, Richard (1982) The petty bourgeoisie and modern capitalism: a consideration of recent theories. In: *Social Class and the Division of Labour: Essays in hounour of Ilya Neustadt*, ed. by A. Giddens – G. Mackenzie. University Press: Cambridge.

Scase, Richard – Goffee, Robert. (1980) *The Real World of the Small Business Owner.* Croom Helm: London.

Schatz, S. P. (1971) An Achievement and economic growth: a critical appraisal. In: *Entrepreneurship and Economic Development*, ed. by P. Kilby. The Free Press: New York.

Schumpeter, J. A. (1934) *The Theory of Economic Development*. Harward University Press: Cambridge.

Schumpeter, J. A. (1951/1989) *Essays on Entrepreneurs, Innovations, Business Cycles, and the Evolution of Capitalism*, ed. by R. V. Clemence – R. Swedberg. Transaction: New York.

Schwartz, E. G. (1976) Entrepreneurship: A New Female Frontier. *Journal of Contemporary Business* 1976: 1, 47-76.

Scott, Joan (1986) Gender: A Useful category of Historical Analysis. *American Historical Review* 1986: 10, 53-75.

Scott, Joan (1988) Deconstructing equality - versus - difference: or the uses of poststructuralistist theory for feminism. *Feminist Studies* 1988: 1, 33-50.

Sexton, D. – Kent, C. (1981) Female Executives versus Female Entrepreneurs. In: *Frontiers of Entrepreneurship Research*, ed. by K. H. Vesper. Babson Centre for Entrepreneurial Studies: Wellesley, Mass.

Shutt, J. – Whittington, R. (1987) Large Firm Strategies and the Rise of Small Units. In: *Readings in Small Business*, ed. by T. Faulkner – G. Beaver – J. Lewis – A. Gibb. Gower: Aldershot.

Silius, Harriet (1989) Könssegregeringen i ingenjörs-, jurist- och läkarkårerna. In: *Kvinnor i mansdominerade yrken*, ed. by H. Silius. Publikationer från Institutet för kvinnoforskning vid Åbo Akademi, nr. 5. Åbo.

Silius, Harriet (1992) *Den kringgärdade kvinnligheten. att vara kvinnlig jurist i Finland*. Åbo Academy Press: Åbo.

Siltanen, Jane (1986) Domestic Responsibilities and the Structuring of Employment. In: *Gender and Stratification*, ed. by Rosemary Crompton. – Michael Mann. Polity Press: Cambridge.

Simonen, Leila (1990) *Contradictions of the Welfare State, Women and Caring*. Acta Universitatis Tamperensis A: 295. University of Tampere: Tampere.

Simonen, Leila (1993) A woman´s place is home? The transformations of the welfare state in the 1990s Finland. In: *Shaping Structural Change in Finland. The Role of Women*, ed by Hannele Varsa. Ministry of Social Affairs and Health. Equality Publications. Series B: 2/1993. Helsinki 1993.

Simpanen, Matti (1986) *Ruotsinsuomalaiset paluumuuttajat yrittäjinä*. Työvoimaministeriö. Siirtolaisuustutkimuksia 19. Valtion painatuskeskus: Helsinki.

Smeltzer, L. R. – Fann, G. L. (1989) Gender Differences in External Networks of Small Business Owners/Managers. *Journal of Small Business Management* 1989: 2, 25-32.

Smith, Adam (1776/1982) *The Wealth of Nations.* Books I - III. With an introduction by A. Skinner. Penguin Books: Middlesex.

Smith, Dorothy, E. (1990) *The Conceptual Practices of Power. A Feminist Sociology of Knowledge.* Northeastern University Press: Boston.

Smith, Nina (1989) *Kan økonomiske teorier forklare kvinders placering på arbejdsmarkedet?* Institut for Statskundskab. Aarhus Universitet: Aarhus.

Smith, N. R. (1967) *The entrepreneur and his firm: the relationship between type of man and type of company.* East Lancing: Michigan.

Stanley, Liz – Wise, Sue (1983) *Breaking Out: feminist consciousness and feminist research.* Routledge: London.

Stanworth John – Curran, James (1973) *Management motivation in the smaller business.* Gower: Aldershot.

Stanworth John – Curran, James (1986) Small Firms, Industrial Relations and Economic Restructuring. In: *Readings in Small Business,* ed. by T. Faulkner, G. – Beaver – J. Lewis – A. Gibb. Gower: Aldershot.

Stanworth J. – Stanworth, C. – Granger, B. – Blyth, S. (1989) Who becomes an Entrepreneur? *International Small Business Journal* 1989: 1, 11-50.

Statens offentliga utredningar 1987: 17. Franchising: betänkande av franchiseutredningen (1987). Stockholm.

Steinmetz, G.– Wright, E. O. (1989) The Fall and Rise of the Petty Bourgeoisie: Changing Patterns of Self-Employment in the Postwar United States. *American Journal of Sociology* 1989: 5, 973-1018.

Stigler, G. J. – Becker, G. S. (1977) De Gustibus Non Est Disputandum. *American Economic Review* 1977: 2, 76-90.

Strandell, Harriet (1983) Kvinnosocialisation och lönearbetets betydelse. Kvinnor i fabriks-, kontors- coh omsorgsyrken. Helsingfors Universitet. Licentiatavhandling i sociologi. Unpublished licenciate thesis.

Sundin, Elisabet – Holmqvist, Carin (1989) *Kvinnor som företagare.* Liber: Malmö.

Swedberg, Richard (1987) Economic Sociology. Past and Present. Part I and Part II. *Current Sociology* 1987: 1, 1-221.

Swedberg, Richard (1989) Introduction to the Transaction Edition. Introduction in: Schumpeter, J. (1951/1989) *Essays on Entrepreneurs, Innovations, Business Cycles, and the Evolution of Capitalism.*

Szymanski, A. (1983) *Class Structure: A Critical Perspective.* Praeger: New York.

Söderling, Ismo (1988) *Maassamuuton ulottuvuudet. Yksilö-, alue- ja yhteiskuntatason tarkastelu Suomessa vuosina 1977-1978 maassamuuttaneista.* Turun yliopiston julkaisuja C: 65. Turku.

Tamminen, Rauno (1981) *Yrityksen persoonallisuus ja kannattavuus.* Jyväskylän yliopisto. Taloustieteen laitos. Työpaperi 9/81. Jyväskylä.

Tamminen, Rauno (1983) Positiivisesti korreloivien indeksien ongelma eli selittääkö yrittäjän persoonallisuus yrityksen menestymisen. *Liiketaloudellinen aikakauskirja* 1983: 2, 193-205.

Tervo, Hannu (1985) *Aluepolitiikan vaikutukset teollisuuden kasvuun ja kehitykseen.* Jyväskylän yliopisto. Keski-Suomen taloudellisen tutkimuskeskuksen julkaisuja 65/1985. Jyväskylä.

Tervo, Hannu – Okko, Paavo (1983) A Note on Shift-Share Analysis as a Method of Estimating the Employment Effects of Regional Economic Policy. *Journal of Regional Science* 1983: 1, 115-121.

Timmons, J. A. (1978) Characteristics and Role Demands of Entrepreneurship. *American Journal of Small Busines* 1978

Toivonen, Timo (1984) Yrittäjien uusi nousu? *Tiede ja Edistys* 1984: 3, 193-202.

Toivonen, Timo (1987) The New Rise of Self-employment and Industrial Structure. Presentation 22.-24.7.1987. In the Egos-Kollokvium. University of Antwerpen.

Toivonen, Timo (1988) *Rakennemuutos 1930-1985.* Turun kauppakorkeakoulun julkaisuja. Sarja A-1:1988. Turku.

Toivonen, Timo (1989) Social Class and Consumption. Employers as a Special Case. Paper presented at the Second Conference on the Sociology of Consumption. Helsinki. 18.-22.9.1989.

Toivonen, Timo (1990) The New Rise of Self-Employment and Industrial Structure. In: *Organization Theory and Class Analysis*, ed. by S. R. Clegg. Gruyter: New York.

Työvoimaministeriö(1985) Työmarkkinoiden muutosten tutkiminen. Työvoimapoliittisia tutkimuksia No 56. Työvoimaministeriö, Suunnitteluosasto: Helsinki.

Uimonen, Marja-Terttu (1987) Naisyrittäjätutkimuksesta. Hahmotelma psykologian lisensiaattityöksi. Presentation at the seminar of the female research network of Finnish Academy. Tampere 1987.

Valkonen, Tapani (1985) Alueelliset erot. In: *Suomalaiset. Yhteiskunnan rakenne teollistumisen aikana*, ed. by Tapani Valkonen – Risto Alapuro – Matti Alestalo – Riitta Jallinoja – Tom Sandlund. WSOY: Helsinki.

Vartia, Pentti (1990) *New technologies and structural changes in a small country.* The Research Institute of the Finnish Economy. Discussion papers 317. Helsinki.

Vattula, Kaarina (1989) Lähtöviivallako? Naisten ammatissatoimivuudesta, tilastoista ja kotitaloudesta. In: *Tuntematon työläisnainen*, ed. by Leena Laine – Pirjo Markkola. Vastapaino: Tampere.

Vuori, Synnöve – Ylä-Anttila, Pekka (1989) *Vaatetusteollisuus tienhaarassa. Joustavan teknologian mahdollisuudet perinnäisellä toimialalla.* SITRA A:93. Helsinki.

Walby, Sylvia (1986) *Patriarchy at Work.* Polity Press: Worchester.

Walby, Sylvia (1988) Gender politics and social theory. *Sociology* 1988:2, 215-222.

Walby, Sylvia (1989) Theorising patriarchy. *Sociology* 1989: 2, 213-234.

Walby, Sylvia (1990) *Theorising Patriarchy.* Blackwell: Oxford.

Walby, Sylvia (1992) Post-Post-Modernism? In: *Destablizing Theory. Contemporary Feminist Debates,* ed. by M. Barrett – A. Phillips. Polity Press: Cambridge.

Walby, Sylvia – Bagguley, Paul (1990) Sex segregation in local labour markets. *Work, Employment & Society* 1990: 1, 59-81.

Waters, Malcolm (1989) Patriarchy and viriarchy: an exploration and reconstruction of concepts of masculine domination. *Sociology* 1989: 2, 193-211.

Watkins, J. (1982) The Female Entrepreneur - American Experience and its Implications for the UK. In: *Perspectives on a Decade of Small Business Research. Bolton Ten Years On,* ed. by J. Stanworth – A. Westrip – D. Watkins – J. Lewis. Gower: Aldershot.

Watkins, D. – Watkins, J. (1986) The Female Entrepreneur in Britain: some results of a pilot survey with special emphasis on educational needs. In: *Small Business Growth and Development,* ed. by M. Scott – A, Gibb – J. Lewis – T. Faulkner. Gower: Aldershot.

Watkins, J. – Watkins, D. (1984) The Female Entrepreneur: Background and Determinants of Business Choice. *International Small Business Journal* 1984: 4, 21-31.

Webb, M. (1982) The Labour Market. In: *Sex Differences in Britain,* ed. by I. Reid – E. Wormald. McIntyre: London.

Weber, Max (1923/1961) *General Economic Theory.* (F. H. Knight, transl.). Collier-Macmillan: New York.

Weber, Max (1922/1964) The Household Community. Translated by F. Kolegar from Wirtschaft und Gesellschaft. In: *Theories of Society: Foundations of Modern Sociological Theory,* ed. by T. Parsons – E. Shields – K. D. Naegle – J. R. Pitts. Free Press: New York.

Weber, Max (1975) *Roscher And Kneis: The Logical Problems Of Historical Economics.* Free Press: New York.

Welsch, Harold – Young, Edvard (1984) Male and Female Entrepreneurial Characteristics and Behaviors: A Profile of Similarities and Differences. *International Small Business Journal* 1984: 4, 11-20.

Westwood, Sallie – Bhachu, Barminder (1989) Introduction. In: *Enterprising Women*, ed. by S. Westwood – P. Bhachu. Routledge: London.

Wickmann, Jane (1989a) Kvindelige iværksættere - et væsentligt element i erhvervsudviklingen. Presentation 19.5.1989 in Helsingør, "Kvindelige iværksættere i Norden" -seminar.

Wilken, P. (1971) *Entrepreneurship - A Comparative and Historical Study.* Ablex Publ. Corp: New Jersey.

Woodward, Alison E. – Leiulfrud, Håkon (1987) Masculine/Feminine Organization - Class versus Gender in Swedish Unions. Paper presented in EGOS 8th Colloquium, Antwerp, July 22.-24., 1987.

Wright, E. O. (1985) *Classes.* Verso: London.

Ylä-Anttila, Pekka – Heikkilä, Armo (1980) *Teollisuuden kannattavuuskehitys toimialoittain.* Elinkeinoelämän tutkimuslaitos B:24. Helsinki.

Yrittäjätyöryhmän raportti(1986) Yrittäjäkäsite tilastoissa. Tilastokeskus. Helsinki.

Zighera, J. A. (1989) Female Employment in E.C. Countries. Unpublished paper presented at the 9th World Congress of International Economic Association. 28.8.-1.9.1989 Athens.

Interviews:

Wickmann, Jane (1989b). Interview 19.5.1989. Teknologisk Institut. Helsingør. Danmark.

Name index

270

Subject index